LAS VEGAS

The BEST of GLITTER CITY

an impertinent insider's guide
By Don & Betty Martin

Pine Cone Press, Inc. • Henderson, Nevada

BOOKS BY DON AND BETTY MARTIN

Adventure Cruising • 1996
Arizona Discovery Guide • 1990, 1993, 1994, 1996
Arizona in Your Future • 1991, 1993, 1998
The Best of the Gold Country • 1987, 1990, 1992
The Best of San Francisco • 1986, 1990, 1994, 1997
The Best of the Wine Country • 1991, 1994, 1995, 1997
Inside San Francisco • 1991
Las Vegas: The Best of Glitter City • 1998
Nevada Discovery Guide • 1992, 1997
New Mexico Discovery Guide • 1998
Northern California Discovery Guide • 1993
Oregon Discovery Guide • 1993, 1995, 1996, 1998
San Francisco's Ultimate Dining Guide • 1988
The Toll-free Traveler • 1997
The Ultimate Wine Book • 1993, 1997
Utah Discovery Guide • 1995
Washington Discovery Guide • 1994, 1997

Library of Congress Cataloging-in-Publication Data
Martin, Don and Betty —
Las Vegas: The Best of Glitter City
Includes index.
1. Las Vegas—description and travel
2. Las Vegas—history
ISBN: 0-942053-24-9
Library of Congress catalog card number: 97-67633

COVER DESIGN BY DAVE BONNOT, Columbine Type and Design, Sonora, California

This book is dedicated to the memory of Winnemucca rancher Phil Tobin who, as a 29-year-old Nevada assemblyman, introduced a bill in 1931 to legalize gambling in the state. As far as we know, he never set foot in Las Vegas. However, without Phil's bill, Glitter City might still be nothing more than a dusty railroad town.

CONTENTS

WELCOME TO GLITTER CITY

Nearly thirty million people visit Las Vegas each year, filling most of its ninety thousand hotel rooms and leaving behind twenty billion dollars and change—which probably goes into the slot machines. This is the world's greatest party town, offering a myriad of choices to those multitudes—more than sixty casino resorts, dozens of shows, hundreds of restaurants and scores of attractions.

Of course, all of this can overwhelm a newcomer. Particularly since the average visitor stays only three or four days. Where to begin? What to do first? Where's the best place to eat, to party, to gamble? Dozens of guidebooks have been written about Glitter City, yet they tend to muddle the picture, for they stuff hundreds of choices between their covers. They are long on information and short on selections. Who has time to sort through all of this, to determine which casino resorts, restaurants and attractions are the best? Particularly in a city where everything is constantly changing?

Fortunately, we did. We've written a special kind of guidebook, patterned after our highly successful *Best of San Francisco*, now in its fourth edition. *The Best of Glitter City* is precisely that—a hit parade of the Ten Best places to eat, sleep, party, gamble and play tourist in Las Vegas. It tells you—at the flip of a page—where to find the best buffet or the cheapest, what casinos claim to offer the best odds and which resorts are the most dazzling. We aim you toward the best attractions, the liveliest bars, the glitziest gaming areas, the tastiest shrimp cocktails and even the best views and photo angles.

In addition, we've included "Quicklists" of facilities at every casino hotel in town. You can tell at a glance which resort has major shows, amusement arcades, buffets, swimming pools and such.

We've been patronizing Las Vegas for decades, initially out of curiosity and then to research our *Nevada Discovery Guide* and its forerunner, *The Best of Nevada*. Through the years, we've seen it grow from a midsize party town to a sprawling megalopolis of more than a million citizens. Las Vegas is raucous, outrageous, noisy, often overcrowded, definitely oversexed and frequently silly.

Further, it's an environmental disaster, placing heavy demands on neighboring Hoover Dam to keep it supplied with water and power as it spreads its glitter and asphalt over the fragile desert. It's a place where urban planning has run amuck—where a rollercoaster twists around a fake New York skyline; where a traffic-stopping volcano burps on command and a pretend pyramid crowds the horizon; where gaudiness is routine.

So one day we decided: "Gee, what a neat place to live!"

Our environmentally sensitive conscience would have none of that, so we moved to next-door Henderson, a perfectly sane community. Here, we can pose as proper citizens, while stealing frequently and furtively into Glitter City to sample the good life of the liveliest place on the planet.

Don W. Martin
Hanging out in Henderson

KEEPING UP WITH THE CHANGES

No city in the world changes more quickly than Las Vegas, which is currently America's fastest metropolitan area. Casinos are being replaced so briskly that the current fashion is to dynamite the old ones. Even those that survive this ritual are constantly being expanded and redesigned. Every time we go to Las Vegas, we find something new, and we live just fifteen miles away!

If you find something afresh on your next visit, or if you catch an error in this book, let us know. And drop us a note if you discover that a casino has become a parking lot, or the other way around.

We'd also like to invite you to submit your own nominations for future editions of *The Best of Glitter City*. We've provided a form in Chapter seventeen. Readers who participate in our poll with at least ten selections will be able to buy any of our other *Pine Cone Press* guidebooks at a thirty percent discount. A complete list of our publications appears in the back of this book.

Address your comments to:

Pine Cone Press, Inc.
631 N. Stephanie St., #138
Henderson, NV 89014

No attempt has been made to introduce pseudo-romantic architectural themes, or to give it artificial glamour and gaiety. Las Vegas is itself—natural and therefore very appealing...
— Nevada, a Guide to the Silver State, **1940** edition

Chapter one

VIVA LAS VEGAS!

IT'S A NICE PLACE TO VISIT, BUT...

In a recent issue of *Money Magazine*, Las Vegas was ranked only 114th on its list of "The 300 Best Places to Live in America." Madison, Wisconsin, and Rochester, Minnesota—where it gets colder than a well-digger's fanny in the Klondike—were ranked first and third. Punta Gorda, Florida, where at least it's warm, finished second.

However, we aren't suggesting that you *move* to Las Vegas, although we'd certainly choose it over Madison and Rochester, and even Punta Gorda because it has too many mosquitoes. We're merely proposing that this is the greatest place on the planet to have a good time. In the chapters that follow, we list about five hundred ways to do so.

Each year, Las Vegas area casinos report gaming profits of more than $5.5 billion. Most of that money is the endowment of the city's thirty million annual visitors, although many locals gamble as well. Many of these visitors lose significant sums of cash and go home happy, convinced that they had a great time. Most of them did, since this is the ultimate party town, with more lavish resorts and more places to play and more great shows than any other city on earth.

How did all of this happen? How did a dusty railroad division point miles from nowhere, a town that didn't exist until 1905, become Party

Central? How can the most geographically isolated major city in America also be the most visited city in America?

The completion of Hoover Dam in 1936 made it possible to build a city in the desert, with an ample supply of power and water. However, that didn't make it *happen*. Las Vegas happened because Nevada decided in 1931 to make gambling legal and because entrepreneurs, gamblers and crooks began building casinos in downtown Las Vegas and south on the Los Angeles Highway. Later, that highway was renamed Las Vegas Boulevard and it's now known to the entire world simply as The Strip. The casinos began as small gambling joints, and then the owners added restaurants and rooms. In 1946, mobster Benjamin Siegel decided to create a real resort hotel, the Fabulous Flamingo. Others then followed with even larger resorts, and Las Vegas—through depression, war, recession and occasional scandals—just kept on growing.

The mega-generation

In recent years, entrepreneurs and corporations decided to reverse the original formula. Instead of building a casino and adding hotel rooms and other facilities, why not build a destination resort and add a casino? It started with Jay Sarno's elaborate Caesars Palace in the Sixties. Other mega-resorts followed, such as the Excalibur and MGM Grand—each in turn claiming title as the world's largest hotel. Steve Wynn set the stage for destination resorts of the Nineties with his Mirage (erupting volcano and dolphin habitat) and Treasure Island (pirate ship battle). The mega-boom continues with the opening of New York New York in 1996, Wynn's luxury Italian-theme Bellagio in 1998 and Hilton's Paris Casino-Hotel soon after.

Toward the end of the century, a 6,000-room resort will rise on the site of the old Sands and claim title as the world's largest hotel—although only briefly. Circus Circus Enterprises has unveiled plans for a monster project totaling 13,800 rooms. It involves an 8,000-room hotel labeled "Project Z" south of its Luxor resort, a 2,000-room addition to the Luxor and the 3,800-room "Project Paradise" on the site of the old Hacienda. So many new high rise projects dominate the skyline, Wynn once commented, that the official Las Vegas bird is the construction crane.

A global tourist destination

With an anticipated 130,000 rooms by the millennium, Glitter City will remain a global tourist destination, drawing up to forty million annual visitors. Some folks will come for the mechanized volcano and rollercoasters wrapped around skyscrapers and observation towers. Others will come for the gambling and the big shows. High rollers will come to be pampered in luxury suites; low rollers will come for the $4.99 buffets and 99-cent shrimp cocktails.

No matter how many Indian casinos crop up from California to the Carolinas, no matter how many gambling ships are launched in the

Mississippi, and no matter how many other cities legalize gaming, Las Vegas will remain Party Central. Those other facilities merely whet peoples' appetites for the *real* mecca. Glitter City has too much of a head start; no Atlantic City or Deadwood, South Dakota, can ever catch it.

As the millions of visitors keep coming, investors build more mega-resorts that lure more millions, and the wheel of fortune just keeps spinning, spinning...and all at once, Las Vegas is the fastest growing city in the fastest growing state in America. That's right, students, not Madison or Rochester or even Punta Gorda, but Las Vegas. (Besides, why would anyone want to move to a place whose name in Spanish means Fat Point?)

One hundred and thirteen better places to live in America? Most likely. Are there any better places to party? Not that we know of.

It's for residents, too

Although this book isn't about moving to Las Vegas, it should prove useful for those who already live here, as well as for the millions of visitors. In a city with thousands of things to do, hundreds of places to play and—indeed—innumerable ways to spend your money, we offer simple selections. We give you a whimsical yet remarkably useful book of lists—the Ten Best of Glitter City in about fifty different categories.

Most Las Vegas casinos are on or near Fremont Street downtown and south along Las Vegas Boulevard. The majority of our selections are in these areas, although we've found many worthwhile choices out on the fringes. Some of the best low roller joints and cheapest food and lodging prices are in outlying casinos—places that cater mostly to locals and budget tour groups.

In each Ten Best list, we have chosen a Number One—our favorite—followed by the next nine in alphabetical order. Thus, we have no losers in *The Best of Glitter City*, only winners and runners-up.

From these lists, you can make your choices, spend your money and then go back to Madison or Punta Gorda or Rochester and tell everyone what a great time you had.

Welcome to Glitter City.

Before we begin...

One of the most useful insider guides to this town is the *Las Vegas Advisor*, a monthly newsletter published by Huntington Press, available by mail subscription for $50 a year. It offers tips on the best freebies and discounts on rooms, food and shows and it also contains reviews, gambling advice and discount coupons. To subscribe, contact Huntington Press, 3687 S. Procyon Ave., Las Vegas, NV 89103; (800) 244-2224.

Another useful publication is the *Las Vegas Review-Journal's* annual tabloid, *The Best of Las Vegas*, a compilation of favorite picks by the newspaper's readers and staff members. Issued each March, it covers everything from shrimp cocktails to favorite local casinos. It's generally available throughout the year at news racks around town for a dollar.

Neither of the above are solicited endorsements nor paid advertisements. Staff members of Huntington Press and the *Review-Journal* probably aren't even aware of this free plug. We just felt our readers should know of these two good insider information sources.

GETTING THERE & GETTING AROUND

Although Las Vegas is the most isolated major city in America, it is easy to reach. Served by fast freeways and highways, it's within a day's drive of most of the rest of the West, and a few hours by air from anywhere in the country.

McCarran International Airport is served by most major U.S. airlines, a few foreign ones and about twenty charter lines. The recently remodeled terminal is an attraction within itself—a pleasing study in palm tree landscaping, sculptures and leading-edge design. A ticket surcharge helped pay for all of this. And yes, you can feed your first slot or video poker machine even before you retrieve your luggage—but don't expect generous payouts here.

Amtrak and **Greyhound** both serve the city. The former Amtrak depot in Jackie Gaughan's Plaza was closed in 1997, which is a pity since this was the site of the original Union Station. This also was the spot where lots were auctioned off in 1905 to give birth to Las Vegas as a railroading center. Although the train no longer stops here, you can catch an Amtrak "Thruway" bus out front on Main Street near Fremont; it makes train connections in Los Angeles, Bakersfield and Barstow. Call (800) USA-RAIL for details. Greyhound (702-382-2640 or 800-231-2222) is next door to Gaughan's, at Main and Carson streets.

Taxis and rental cars

Las Vegas cabbies rival those in New York and Tokyo for their spirited driving as they hurl their sedans and minivans around town. However, they do get you where you're going quickly, and fares are reasonable. Don't try to flag one down along Las Vegas Boulevard, since the driver likely will be too busy dodging traffic to notice you. You'll find plenty of taxis at any hotel cab stand; just walk to the main entrance and get in the cab line.

If you arrive by plane or bus and you're going to be here a while, we'd recommend renting a car instead of fussing with public transit and cabs, because of the plenitude of free parking at Las Vegas casinos. Further, you may want to explore the surrounding area. And plan ahead! Nearly every rental car in town can vanish during big convention weekends and peak holiday periods. Even during quieter times, you may have to take a more expensive model because all of the little guys have been claimed by the time you arrive. Also, most rental car agencies have better rates for those who reserve in advance.

Transit: cheap but not rapid

CAT (Citizens Area Transit) operates out of the attractive Downtown Transportation Center at Stewart Avenue and Casino Center Boulevard, within two blocks of the Fremont Street casinos. The 301 line offers 24-hour service along Las Vegas Boulevard to Vacation Village, the southernmost casino resort on the Strip. Buses run every ten to fifteen minutes; less frequently late at night. They're often jammed in the daytime, particularly during morning and evening rush hours, causing delays in loading. With their frequent stops and the heavy Las Vegas Boulevard traffic, it can take an hour to get from downtown to the far end of the Strip. Service generally is faster at night.

A better bet is the 302 Strip Express, which makes fewer stops, although it runs only from 6 p.m. to midnight. Launching from the transit terminal, it stops at Las Vegas Boulevard and Fremont Street, the Stratosphere tower, Circus Circus, the Mirage, Excalibur and Vacation Village.

Fares for the Strip route—including the express—are $1.50 for adults and fifty cents for folks over 62 and kids five to 17. All other CAT routes are a dollar for adults and fifty cents for kids and seniors. You'll need exact change, although the money hoppers do take dollar bills. And you can buy a monthly pass at $20 for full fare passengers and $10 for seniors and teens. They're available at the Downtown Transportation Center. Call (702) 228-7433 for transit information.

The privately operated Las Vegas Strip Trolley (702-382-1404) starts at the Hilton and runs along Las Vegas Boulevard from the Sahara to the Luxor, dropping you at the front doors of twenty-five major hotels. Fare is $1.30 and the rigs run every fifteen minutes from 9:30 a.m. to 2 a.m. Look for old fashioned trolleys with tires. They're generally faster than the buses but not much, since they make two dozen stops.

OUR TEN FAVORITE LAS VEGAS MOMENTS

When you get to know a town as intimately as we know Las Vegas, you develop a mental list of those special things and hidden places that make it a favorite place. We decided to write our list down:

1 WATCHING THE SUNSET FROM STRATOSPHERE TOWER • *2000 Las Vegas Boulevard at Main; (702) 380-7777.*

Whenever we need to remind ourselves that the Las Vegas Strip is the most colorful place on earth, we take the elevator to the outdoor observation deck of the Stratosphere Tower just before sunset. Then we find a place along the rail, look south down the Strip and watch the nighttime city awaken.

2 WATCHING THE CITY GLITTER FROM THE MORMON
TEMPLE • *Upper Bonanza Road at Temple View Drive.*

While the Stratosphere tower provides a fine aerial vista of the Strip, the best overview of the city is from upper Bonanza Road at the foot of Sunrise Mountain, near the grand white-spired Las Vegas Mormon Temple. The night lights of Glitter City spread below like a vast carpet of scattered jewels, easily outshining and seemingly outnumbering the stars above.

3 HAVING CAFFÉ LATTE AT NEW YORK NEW YORK •
3790 S. Las Vegas Blvd. (Tropicana Avenue); (702) 740-6969.

It's a simple ritual, performed whenever we're along the Strip and need a caffeine fix. We step into New York New York Casino-Hotel, pick up a cup of caffé latte at the small Il Fornaio Café and carry it to the Village Eateries food court. There, in this pretend Greenwich Village environment, we find a table, sit and sip and watch the people parade.

4 EATING CASTLEBURGERS AT THE BOARDWALK •
Holiday Inn Boardwalk, 3750 S. Las Vegas Blvd. (near Harmon Avenue, between the Excalibur and the Bellagio); (702) 735-1167.

The cheerful Coney Island theme Boardwalk is our favorite small casino. For a quick and cheap lunch, we like to buy three "Castleburgers" and an iced tea at the Boardwalk's Deli. We carry our bounty outside to a bench on a small terrace facing Las Vegas Boulevard and enjoy an inexpensive snack while watching the world of Glitter City pass by. (For the uninitiated, Castleburgers are tiny hamburger patties with chopped onions, served on buns the size of dinner rolls. The Boardwalk sells them at three for $1.29.)

5 SNUGGLING IN THE FIRESIDE LOUNGE "PIT" • *At the*
Peppermill Inn, 2985 S. Las Vegas Blvd. (opposite the Stardust and beside Silver City); (702) 735-7635.

Although it's in an old 1950s style building with an ordinary looking restaurant up front, the Fireside Lounge is the most intimate bar in town. It's a sensual retreat with plush furniture and quiet music, bathed in soft blue and red light. Its centerpiece is a sunken seating pit with a gas flame rising from a burbling water fountain. This is a grand place to sit, sip and quietly contemplate.

6 PEOPLE-WATCHING ON FREMONT STREET • *"Fremont*
Street Experience" mall between Main and Fourth, downtown.

The "Fremont Street Experience" will crop up frequently in this book. Four blocks of the Downtown Casino Center have been converted into a pedestrian mall, with an overhead electronic canopy that presents impressive sound and light shows each evening. Day or night, it's our favorite spot for people-watching. The promenade is nicely landscaped, with benches and chairs that invite folks to linger awhile.

7 **SAMPLING CHOCOLATES AT ETHEL M's** • *Ethel M Chocolate Factory, Two Cactus Garden Drive, Henderson; (702) 433-2500. Open daily 8:30 to 7.*

Among the tiny sins permitted in Nevada that are forbidden in most other states is the making and selling of liquor-filled chocolates. Folks who tour the Ethel M production facility in next-door Henderson are rewarded with a free sample. Decisions, decisions! Do we want our chocolate filled with Amaretto, Irish cream or coffee liqueur? My wife and co-author Betty has been known to slip back into line for seconds.

8 **HAVING A SHRIMP COCKTAIL AT THE GOLDEN GATE CASINO** • *One Fremont St. (at Main); (702) 385-1906.*

The tradition of serving inexpensive shrimp cocktails to lure patrons into gaming areas began at this small San Francisco-style casino in 1959. It has spread to dozens of other places, although this is still our favorite. For a mere 99 cents, we get a generous shrimp cocktail with spicy sauce, served in a tulip glass. In the evening, we can listen to mellow piano music as we enjoy our budget repast. The Golden Gate is only place in town with a piano bar in its snack bar.

9 **OVEREATING AT A CASINO BUFFET** • *Take your pick; there are more than fifty.*

Whenever we feel like pigging out, we pick one of Glitter City's several dozen buffets and settle down for an evening of calorie abuse. Many of the buffets have special themes to match our appetites of the moment—seafood, Cajun/Creole, Mexican, Italian or barbecue. Boulder Station even has a midnight buffet for those nights when we just can't get to sleep. Only in Las Vegas can one get so much food for so little money. Our favorite buffets? See our selections in chapters four and five.

10 **SIPPING A PIÑA COLADA BESIDE THE MIRAGE RAINFOREST** • *Lagoon Saloon at the Mirage, 3400 S. Las Vegas Blvd. (adjacent to Caesars Palace); (702) 791-7111.*

Although Las Vegas has larger and flashier resorts, we still favor the Mirage and its imposing rainforest as one of the most appealing inner spaces in town. This lush indoor jungle is housed under a ninety-foot canopy and the Lagoon Saloon is adjacent. This is a fine place to sit and sip something tropical.

THE TEN BEST LAS VEGAS SUPERLATIVES

Glitter City might also be called Superlative City or perhaps Excess City, since it claims a number of American and world's records for the largest of this, the tallest of that and the most of those. To begin, it's the fastest growing city in America and the youngest large city, founded in 1905. It has more hotel rooms than any other city of its size, it's the most visited city in the country and it has most of the largest resort hotels in the world. However, those are rather broad-based statistics. Let's get to specifics, starting with—

1 AMERICA'S LARGEST HOTEL: MGM Grand ● 3799 Las Vegas Boulevard South (at Tropicana).

The Grand has 5,005 rooms, a dozen restaurants, a 33-acre amusement park and the world's largest casino, covering 171,500 square feet, with a total of 3,500 gaming machines. It's the world's second largest hotel, after the 5,100-room Ambassador City Jomtlen in Thailand. (However, expansion of the Luxor and the completion of a Circus Circus-owned 8,000-room resort may eclipse both records.) Currently, Las Vegas has nine of the ten largest hotels in the world, and fourteen out of twenty.

2 AMERICA'S TALLEST FREE-STANDING OBSERVATION TOWER: Stratosphere Tower ● 2000 S. Las Vegas Blvd. (Main Street).

Reaching 1,149 feet into the—well—the stratosphere, this is the tallest building of any kind west of the Mississippi. This observation tower also boasts America's and probably the world's highest revolving restaurant, casino, wedding chapel, rollercoaster and free-fall ride.

3 WORLD'S LARGEST INDOOR ATRIUM: Luxor Hotel and Casino ● 3900 Las Vegas Blvd. (near Tropicana).

From the second-story Attractions Level (actually the rooftop of the main casino), the Luxor pyramid is hollow, rising thirty stories above your head. Hotel rooms are situated along hanging balconies, served by elevators that travel at a 40-degree angle.

4 WORLD'S LARGEST BUFFET: Circus Circus Hotel and Casino ● 2880 S. Las Vegas Blvd. (upper Strip, south of the Sahara).

During peak periods, more than 1,200 people a day chow down at the largest buffet in town and in the world. It's also one of the cheapest. Is it one of the best? No.

5 WORLD'S LARGEST PRIVATE GOLD NUGGET DISPLAY: Golden Nugget Hotel & Casino ● 129 Fremont St.

The "Hand of Faith," weighing 857 troy ounces, is the world's largest nugget on public display; look for it in the left hand hallway leading from the Fremont Street casino entrance back to the hotel lobby. Surrounding it are several smaller nuggets.

6 WORLD'S LARGEST RACE AND SPORTS BOOK: Las Vegas Hilton ● 3000 Paradise Rd., east of Las Vegas Boulevard, next to Las Vegas Convention Center.

The massive sports and race book is larger than a good-sized department store. At one time, the Hilton was the world's largest resort hotel with the world's largest casino, although these two records have been eclipsed by newer mega-resorts.

7 WORLD'S LARGEST BLACKJACK TABLE AND SLOT MACHINE: Four Queens Hotel & Casino ● 202 Fremont St. (at the corner of Third Street).

The Queens' blackjack table can seat twelve players and it's covered by 6,408 square inches of felt. The "Queen Machine" measures ten by nineteen feet and can accommodate six coin-feeders at once.

8 WORLD'S LARGEST PRIVATE SPORTS MEMORABILIA COLLECTION: Las Vegas Club Hotel & Casino ● 18 Fremont St. (at Main Street).

Hundreds of sports collectibles are scattered throughout this downtown casino, from a collection of autographed World Series bats to Joe Montana's jersey and a basketball autographed by Scotty Pippin. Many of the items line a hallway between the main casino and John D's Grill and Sports Bar and others are in a closed kiosk between John D's and a sports logo place called the Pro Shop. You'll find more upstairs at the rear of the casino-hotel, lining the walls of the Upper Deck Restaurant and Dugout 24-hour coffee shop. Sports stars are sometimes invited to the Las Vegas Club to mingle with the public and sign autographs.

9 WORLD'S LARGEST SOUVENIR STORE: Bonanza Gift and Souvenir Shop ● 2460 S. Las Vegas Boulevard (near Sahara Boulevard).

This complex, the size of a small strip mall, is several souvenir shops in one, although they're all under one roof. It also includes a convenience mart and liquor store with some of the most reasonable booze prices on the Strip.

10 WORLD'S LARGEST ELECTRONIC CANOPY: Fremont Street Experience • Downtown, between Fourth and Main Streets.

Ready for a final stack of superlatives? This electronic barrel-arch canopy, where sound and light shows are presented nightly, cost $70 million, reaches ninety feet into the air, is 1,400 feet long and contains 2.1 million tiny colored light bulbs.

THE TEN MAJOR MOVERS AND SHAKERS

The world's largest resort and greatest party town didn't just evolve. Men with vision, the courage to gamble and in some cases—a little larceny in their souls—made it happen. These are the ten biggest names in town, listed in order of their appearance on the Las Vegas scene:

1 SENATOR WILLIAM CLARK

A Montana copper king, he took control of the defunct San Pedro, Los Angeles and Salt Lake Railroad and designated an oasis called "The Meadows" (*Las Vegas* in Spanish) as a major watering stop. His company formed the Las Vegas Land and Water Company and auctioned off lots for a townsite on May 15, 1905. Thus was born the youngest major city in America; Clark County is named in the senator's honor. The auction was held was at Main and Fremont streets, the present site of Jackie Gaughan's Plaza Casino. The railroad, now owned by the Union Pacific, still runs behind it.

2 PHIL TOBIN

This young state assemblyman and cowboy from Winnemucca probably never set foot in Las Vegas. However, at the age of 29, he introduced a bill in 1931 to legalize gambling to help Nevada recover from the doldrums of the Depression. Governor Fred Balzar signed his bill into law. Las Vegas, then just a dusty railroad town, was given a reason to amount to something.

3 HERBERT HOOVER

Our thirty-first President probably never set foot in Las Vegas, either. However, as secretary of commerce before his presidency, he successfully negotiated Colorado River water rights between Nevada, California and Arizona during the 1920s. This overcame a political stalemate and led to the construction of the dam now named in his honor. It is Hoover Dam that supplies the power and much of the water that makes it possible for a city of a million people to survive in the desert.

4 THOMAS HULL

In 1941, this southern California entrepreneur built El Rancho Vegas, the first casino south of town, way out on the Los Angeles Highway. Another transplanted southern Californian, casino owner Guy McAfee, later called this area "The Strip" in honor of the Sunset Strip of Los Angeles. Interestingly, he once served as head of the Los Angeles vice squad while operating several illegal casinos there!

5 BENJAMIN SIEGEL

A Brooklyn street punk and boyhood friend of Jewish Mafia leader Meyer Lansky was sent to Los Angeles in 1938 to consolidate gang activities. He later came to Las Vegas to muscle in on that newly emerging gaming center's race book action. The idea of legal gambling fascinated Bugsy. He saw the potential of a fancy casino resort on the Strip and convinced his gang bosses to finance the venture. His Fabulous Flamingo was indeed the first opulent "carpet joint" in Las Vegas. However, when the price tag ballooned from $1 million to $6 million, Bugsy was suspected of skimming construction funds and he fell from favor. Six months after his dream casino opened, someone emptied a thirty caliber Army carbine into him as he sat reading a newspaper at his girlfriend Virginia Hill's mansion in Beverly Hills. It was probably Virginia who did most of the skimming and she survived the hit.

The mob ran most of the major Las Vegas casinos for years until Tennessee Senator Estes Kevauver's Committee to Investigate Organized Crime started turning up the heat of public scrutiny. Ironically, many illegal gamblers from around the country fled to Las Vegas, where gaming was still legal. However, the negative publicity eventually spurred Nevada state officials to take command of gaming and push the mobsters out.

6 SAM BOYD

When young Sam Boyd came to Las Vegas in 1941, mob bosses were still running the town, although he steered clear of them. He represented a new generation of gambling boss—skilled in his profession yet basically honest. A Las Vegan for more than half a century, he became one its most respected citizens and one of its greatest philanthropists. Sam had been involved in gambling since he was seventeen, when he ran bingo games at the Pike Boardwalk in Long Beach, California, in 1927. Later, he worked on gambling ships off the California coast and in gaming parlors in Hawaii before coming to Las Vegas. He found a job in the Jackpot Club downtown and worked his way up to pit boss of several clubs, including the Fabulous Flamingo.

Boyd eventually became a casino executive and began investing in gaming properties. His Boyd Group of selected friends and family members is one of Nevada's more successful locally-based gaming corporations. It owns the Fremont, Stardust and Sam's Town, plus 12 other gaming properties in the U.S. The patriarch of the Boyd Group—indeed, a patriarch of honest gaming in Las Vegas—died in 1993.

7 JAY SARNO

Caesars Palace, the city's first true destination resort in Las Vegas, and Circus Circus, the first casino with a strong entertainment focus, were the work of the same man. Jay Sarno of Atlanta, Georgia, had no gambling background; he was a hotel builder and the owner of the Cabaña Motor Inn chain. However, he saw the potential of drawing customers with the opulent glitter of Caesars, opened in 1966, and the carnival lures of Circus Circus, opened two years later. Historians say it was Teamsters money that built Caesars Palace, although Sarno certainly was the concept man.

8 WILLIAM BENNETT

Circus Circus was a good idea, although Sarno never quite made it work. For one thing, it was an adults-only place with topless circus ladies. Further, only locals could get in free; outsiders had to pay admission for the privilege of gambling. In 1974, he sold to William Bennett, an Arizona furniture baron and executive with Del Webb's casino operations.

Bennett saw the potential of luring families to Las Vegas, setting a trend that continues to this day. He put tops on the circus ladies, added a carnival midway for kids, an RV park and clusters of hotel towers. Now a publicly-traded corporation, Circus Circus is one of the world's most successful gambling enterprises. In addition its original pink striped cement circus tent, the corporation owns another Circus Circus in Reno, two resorts in Laughlin, the Las Vegas Luxor, Excalibur and half the Monte Carlo. It has another 13,800 rooms in the works in three separate projects.

9 HOWARD HUGHES

The eccentric billionaire, while unstable himself, brought corporate stability to the Las Vegas gaming industry. A germaphobic recluse, he arrived in 1966 in a curtained ambulance and took over the penthouse of the Desert Inn. Months later, owner Moe Dalitz, one of the few surviving crime bosses still in town, asked him to leave because he needed the suites for his high rollers. Hughes solved the problem by buying the aging mobster out. He then spent more than $300 million buying up every Las Vegas casino on the market, plus thousands of acres of raw land and Harold's Club in Reno.

Never appearing in public, he did business via telephone and intermediaries. His coterie of Mormon guards so effectively kept the rest of the world at bay that no photograph exists of Hughes in Las Vegas. In 1970, exactly four years to the day after he'd arrived, he was spirited away in another curtained ambulance and flown to a refuge in the Caribbean. His mental and physical health continued deteriorating, probably from syphilis and an old head injury he's sustained in a flying accident. He died on April 5, 1976, aboard a plane returning him to his hometown of Houston, Texas.

10 STEVE WYNN

More than anyone else in town, Wynn represents a new entrepreneurial spirit that has led to the creation of the most opulent resorts on the globe. The son of a small-time Maryland bingo parlor operator, he came to town in 1967 and began speculating in real estate. He bought a piece of empty land beside Caesars Palace and spread word that he intended to build a competing casino. Caesars officials bought him out, giving him a substantial profit, which he used to gain controlling interest in a shaggy downtown club called the Golden Nugget. In 1973 at the tender age of 31, he began changing the Nugget into an opulent carpet joint. He later built and then sold a Golden Nugget in Atlantic City, then he purchased Del Webb's Nevada Club in nearby Laughlin and fashioned it into yet another Nugget.

Wynn was now ready to launch his most ambitious project. Raising $360 million—more than the combined prices of every other casino on the Las Vegas Strip, plus Hoover Dam—he built the Mirage. With a specially designed showroom, dolphin habitat, indoor rainforest and outdoor erupting volcano, Wynn brought casino resorts to a new level of showmanship. He followed with the family oriented Treasure Island with its pirate ship battle and, most recently, the lavish Italian theme billion-dollar Bellagio.

Las Vegas will be proud of the Flamingo. It will become one of the world's greatest playgrounds.

—Bugsy Siegel's comment to the press as his Fabulous Flamingo neared completion in 1946

Chapter two

EL CASINO REAL
THE BEST PLACES TO PLAY AND STAY

There is no other street like it on the planet. Mobster Benjamin Siegel first drew the world's attention to Las Vegas Boulevard with the 1946 opening of his Fabulous Flamingo. It was the boulevard's first opulent casino hotel, costing more than $6 million. Through the decades, more elaborate gaming resorts have followed and today, the Strip is lined with the world's largest and most famous palaces of pleasure. Some of their swimming pools cost more than Bugsy's Fabulous Flamingo! The MGM Grand and Bellagio price tags top one *billion* dollars and future projects will go even higher.

Of course, all of Glitter City's play palaces aren't on Las Vegas Boulevard. Several are in the downtown area on or near Fremont Street, which has been turned into a canopied mall. Local promoters call this area the Downtown Casino Center; writers call it Glitter Gulch. If you head southeast on Fremont Street it becomes the Boulder Highway. So many casinos have emerged along this stretch from Las Vegas through Henderson that it has earned the nickname of the Boulder Strip. Other casinos crop on freeways and highways leading into Las Vegas; several are on the west side of I-15, the main traffic artery.

By any measure, Las Vegas is the casino capital of the world and the resort hotel center of the universe. By the time you read this, the city and its suburbs will have more than a hundred thousand hotel rooms. On a good weekend or during a major convention, nearly every one of these rooms will be filled. More than thirty million people come to town each year.

Benny Siegel was more than right. Although the last shred of his Fabulous Flamingo has disappeared under Flamingo Hilton expansion, Glitter City has become one the world's greatest playgrounds.

THE TEN VERY BEST CASINO RESORTS

What's our criteria for selecting the Ten Best casinos out of more than fifty in Glitter City? They must be true destination resorts with comprehensive vacation facilities; complete worlds unto themselves. They must be so appealing that they would be worth a special trip even if they didn't have casinos. (Our Ten Best casino gaming areas are listed below.) They must be visually appealing and fun to explore.

Most of our selections are on the Las Vegas Strip, although three are elsewhere—the Las Vegas Hilton, a few long blocks away on Paradise Road; the Golden Nugget downtown; and the Rio, west of the Strip across I-10. We begin with our favorite choice, followed by the next nine in alphabetical order. This practice continues through the rest of the fifty or so lists in this book, unless indicated otherwise.

1 **THE MIRAGE** • *3400 S. Las Vegas Blvd. (adjacent to Caesars Palace); (800) 627-6667 or (702) 791-7111.*

We considered many other choices before selecting the Mirage as our favorite Las Vegas casino complex. Several others, both the newer ones and the remodeled older ones, offer all the amenities of major destination resorts. Many are larger than the Mirage with more extensive facilities. However, none quite match the flair and the style of this place. When Steve Wynn opened the Mirage in 1989, spending more than the combined cost of every previous resort on the Strip *plus* Hoover Dam, he set the tone for the next generation of Las Vegas mega-resorts. Even if the Mirage had been built in Mormon Promise, Utah, or Cornpone Center, Iowa—and had no gaming area—people would come. They would come in droves to see the multi-million dollar showroom designed specifically for the animal-magic act of Siegfried and Roy, to see the dolphin habitat out back, the erupting "volcano" up front and the canopied rainforest inside.

As Wynn intended, the Mirage is the complete resort. It lures the high rollers tucked into multi-million-dollar high roller suites, and the low and medium rollers who like to gamble in the lush tropical atmosphere of the casino. It attracts folks who stop to stare at that erupting

volcano outside and then come inside to be greeted by a rainforest under glass and a white tiger lair behind glass. It appeals to those who
want to catch the Siegfried and Roy Show and wonder how they make
an entire elephant disappear.

2 CAESARS PALACE • 3570 S. Las Vegas Blvd. (at Flamingo Road); (800) 634-6001 or (702) 731-7110.

The first true destination resort in Nevada, opulent and expansive
Caesars has been high roller country since it opened in 1966. In typical
Las Vegas fashion, it's an odd mix of grace and glitter, of marble statuary, cascading fountains, laser shows, Roman columns and a geodesic
dome. This thematic contradiction is best expressed in its two indoor
Roman style fountains in the Forum Shops. One is an accurate replica
with faithful reproductions of Roman marble; the other is a comic act
with a grinning Bacchus and assorted other animated Roman gods.

The best way to approach this *Circus Extremus* casino hotel is
aboard a moving walkway that takes you from the Strip's sidewalk
through the World of Caesar, where animated Romans invite you to
come inside and party. It's one of three people-movers leading into the
massive complex. Only one leads out; Caesar and Bacchus don't want
you to leave. And there's no need, really. It's all here—a score of restaurants, several casinos, an Omnimax theater, a major showroom and
several lesser lounges, an elaborate swimming complex, health spa
and more than a hundred shops. In the ever-changing world of Las
Vegas, the hotel is expanding even as we write this, with the addition
of a twenty-nine-story tower containing 1,200 rooms, shops and a
large health and fitness spa.

Caesars was built by Atlanta motel chain owner Jay Sarno, who
also built Circus Circus. It's now owned by the ITT Corporation, although it's being seriously courted by the Hilton chain.

3 FLAMINGO HILTON • 3555 S. Las Vegas Blvd. (near Fla- mingo Road); (800) 732-2111 or (702) 733-3111.

This is where the flamboyance of the Las Vegas Strip began, with
Benjamin "Bugsy" Siegel's Fabulous Flamingo in 1946. And here it continues, with the pink opulence of one of the Strip's flashiest and largest
casino resorts, with 3,640 rooms and expansive grounds covering dozens of acres. Bugsy's Fabulous Flamingo, with its 105 rooms, would
have fit inside the pool complex. Not a shred of his original resort remains. Siegel's old suite in the Oregon building vanished several years
ago with the expansion of the resort's huge pool lagoon. A plaque near
the wedding chapel commemorates his presence, and one could say
that his spirit lives in Bugsy's Celebrity Theatre and Bugsy's Deli—although he hated that nickname.

The Fabulous Flamingo passed through several hands until Hilton purchased the property in 1970, becoming the first hotel chain to own a Nevada casino. The corporation dropped the name "Fabulous" even while making it more so. With its bronze-windowed towers, monumental neon blossoms and glittering casino, it's one of the flashiest resorts on the Strip. And it's certainly among the most complete, with a huge and rambling gaming area, multiple restaurants, major showroom (New York's Rockettes were there when we last checked), that giant pool complex with tennis courts, and those bronze-windowed rooms rising above it all.

4 GOLDEN NUGGET HOTEL & CASINO • *129 Fremont St. (at Casino Center Boulevard); (800) 634-3454 or (702) 385-7111.*

The Golden Nugget is our refuge when we need a respite from the friendly chaos of downtown Las Vegas. Although most of the elaborate casino resorts are on the boulevard, the studied elegance of Steve Wynn's Golden Nugget matches anything on the Strip. Cloaked in white Grecian marble, with white and gold-leaf canopies, it's a vision of French New Orleans chic. The interior is richly done in polished marble, beaded golden lights, beveled mirrors and Tiffany style glass, with brass-on-white accents. Gold-leaf elevator walls and gold plated pay phones add nicely ostentatious touches.

Occupying two city blocks and marked by scalloped canopies, the Nugget is an island of elegance amidst the bright lights of downtown. A show room, pool, spa, sauna and complete health club are among its amenities. The hotel rooms are spacious and rather elegant, recently remodeled with contemporary color schemes and four-poster beds.

5 LAS VEGAS HILTON • *3000 Paradise Rd. (Riviera Boulevard); (800) 732-7117 or (702) 732-5111.*

This massive complex just off the Strip is one of the area's largest and most complete casino resorts. Offerings include the world's largest race and sports book, a dozen dining areas, a health club, large show lounge and a 220,000 square foot convention facility. It took its turn as the world's largest resort hotel when it was opened in 1969 as the International, built by entrepreneur Kirk Kerkorian. Hilton bought it in the early 1970s and expansions kept it in the lead as the world's biggest hotel until the Excalibur and MGM Grand opened.

There is much to explore here. The football field-sized casino is particularly impressive, with monumental beaded chandeliers, marble and polished woods. A new SpaceQuest Casino was added during the summer of 1997, a futuristic gaming area with special effects "space windows." Also check out the double hotel lobby, rows of shops and the distinctive rooftop recreation area with a pool, tennis courts and a putting green. Andrew Lloyd Weber's fantasy about a humanoid trains,

"Starlight Express," is currently dashing through the main showroom. It's based on a little boy's dream in which his toy trains come to life, portrayed by cleverly costumed rollerskating singers and dancers. It's a fast-paced, cute show if you can handle the rather silly concept.

A space age attraction, "Star Trek, the Experience," opened in the summer of 1997. It's a joint Hilton-Paramount venture featuring a space station dining and shopping area and a shuttlecraft voyage through space. Participants even get beamed aboard the Starship *Enterprise*. Say hello to Scotty.

Rooms at the Las Vegas Hilton are quite posh and start around $95.

6 MGM GRAND • *3799 S. Las Vegas Blvd. (at Tropicana); (800) 929-1111 or (702) 891-7777.*

In the Arizona desert north of Phoenix, a visionary named Paolo Soleri wants to build a self-contained city, sheltered from the distractions of the outside world. Someone should tell him that it's been done already. Sprawling over 113 acres, the emerald-green MGM Grand was opened in 1993 as the world's largest hotel, with 5,005 rooms. (It's now the second largest, after the 5,100-room Ambassador City Jomtlen in Thailand.)

Facilities include a dozen dining venues, more than a score of shops, plenty of pubs, two major showrooms, and a casino complex the size of quadruple football fields. One could easily live indefinitely within this giant complex. One might have to; the only thing that's difficult to find here is an exit. If you do manage to break into blue sky, you might be in the large swimming pool complex or the thirty-three-acre Grand Adventure theme park, instead of the *real* world outside. Film-reel paths in the carpet simplify navigation somewhat, since they lead to several kiosks with maps of the massive MGM Grand layout. However, we still get lost; it's difficult to figure out where to go if you can't figure out where you've been. But, never mind all that. With its complete facilities and great variety of lures, who needs to leave?

The Grand is one the few casino resorts large enough to have two "big rooms." At this writing, the $30 million Grand Theatre featured David Cassidy in "EFX," a high tech fantasy trip through time, which is supposed to be pronounced "Effects." Major personalities and occasional world champion boxing matches appear in the Grand Garden Arena. A third room, the Hollywood Theatre, features the likes of Gladys Knight, Randy Travis and the Righteous Brothers.

7 MONTE CARLO • *3770 Las Vegas Blvd. (north of Tropicana Avenue); (800) 311-8999 or (702) 730-7777.*

This new facility, styled after the refined Monte Carlo Casino in Monaco, is at once elegant and flashy—a perfectly appropriate condition in Glitter City. Pause to admire the bronze fountain and four marble statues out front and then let the cool marble floors convey you inside. The Hyper Market just to your left, offering fresh fruits, drinks and souvenirs, may melt your Grace Kelly-Prince Rainier vision somewhat. And as you continue inside, past the Lance Burton Theatre and through the casino, you'll find another architectural contradiction—a large brewpub with industrial strength décor. Overall, however, it's one of the most opulent resorts in town.

While a bit flashy for a Monaco clone, this Monte Carlo is indeed stylish, with Italian marble arched windows, crystal beaded chandeliers over the gaming area and lots of mirror glass. The casino is set with comfortable burgundy chairs before each video and slot machine. Of course, it has the full range of table games including baccarat, and a posh high roller room. In the hotel lobby, well removed from the casino, you can recover your melted vision of old Monaco, with beaded chandeliers, marble floors and carved wood paneling. This is a full service resort, with a pool and health spa, tennis courts, shopping arcade, food court, half a dozen restaurants and other essentials.

The Monte Carlo opened in 1996, built by Circus Circus Enterprises, with Mirage Resorts, Inc., as a managing partner. Rooms are in the upper price range and quite attractive.

8 NEW YORK NEW YORK HOTEL & CASINO ● 3790 S. Las Vegas Blvd. (Tropicana Avenue); (800) NY-FORME or (702) 740-6969.

Rising from Las Vegas Boulevard as a collection of fused-together Manhattan skyscrapers, New York New York opened in late 1996, with 2,034 rooms, an 80,000 square foot casino and a price tag approaching half a billion dollars. This is a delightful example of the heights that designers and architects can achieve if given free rein. A rollercoaster called Manhattan Express winds in and out of the skyline; the Statue of Liberty rises from New York Harbor, flanked by two fireboats that squirt water from their hoses—except when it's too windy. A 300-foot section of sidewalk has become the Brooklyn Bridge. Inside, you're on the streets of Manhattan, with a high, darkened ceiling creating the illusion that you're still outside, strolling through Central Park or along Wall Street. Except of course for the ranks of slot and video machines and gaming tables and the sexy looking drink girls in abbreviated tuxedos.

Although it's listed as number eight in our alphabetical order, it's a close second to the Mirage as our favorite Las Vegas place to play. We like the consistency of theme here, with its fun New York façades, change carts with black and yellow taxicab designs and gaming areas such as Brooklyn Dollars, Queens Dollars and the New York Slot Exchange. Other worthy features: A high casino ceiling that carries away the cigarette smoke; a good mix of cafés, food courts and bars; an elaborate fun zone with a Coney Island theme and that wild rollercoaster ride. It's a great people-watching place, from the balcony above the casino, or from chairs and tables along the Village Eatery. Finally, it's as upbeat as the real New York, with a great piano player in Bar at Times Square, lively performers in the Empire Lounge just off the casino and Motown sounds issuing from the Motown Café. Visitors can capture a glamorized version of New York Street entertainers in a show called Mad Hattan, Friday-Wednesday at 7:30 and 10.

This place is so lively that it makes you wanna go to the real New York, although the original probably isn't as much fun.

9 **RIO SUITE HOTEL & CASINO** ● *3700 W. Flamingo Rd. (at Valley View Boulevard, opposite the Gold Coast); (800) 888-1808 or (702) 252-7777.*

If we had a category for the ten most glamorous looking casino resorts, the Rio would top the list. From its stunning new oval hotel tower dressed in red and blue neon piping to its Copacabaña cocktail waitresses in their brief costumes, this place is sensuous. It's also one of the flashiest resorts in town, with party confetti carpeting, floral prints and other color splashes conveying its Rio de Janeiro carnival theme. The Zagat survey voted it the best casino hotel in town. Other surveys have picked its Carnival World Buffet as one of the best, and featured performer Danny Gans as one of the town's top entertainers.

The Rio is a full-service resort, with a pool complex and real sand beach, two large casinos, a dozen restaurants and twenty-six shops. Many of these are located along a balcony above the Masquerade Village Casino. This atrium-style gaming area is the venue for the periodic "Masquerade Show in the Sky," a glittering parade of floats suspended from ceiling tracks. It's daily except Wednesday at 1, 3, 5, 9 and 11 p.m.. For details, see Chapter five, page 87. The Rio even has a wine cellar offering designer wines by the taste, the glass or the bottle.

This flashy resort came to town in 1990 and was greatly expanded in 1997 with the addition of that sexy new tower. Rooms in the new tower has some of the best views in town. Although the resort is several blocks off the Strip, folks afoot can reach it by catching a shuttle at a Rio promotional office at Las Vegas Boulevard and Harmon Avenue, catty corner from Country Star American Music Grill.

10 **TROPICANA RESORT & CASINO** ● *3801 S. Las Vegas Blvd. (Tropicana Avenue, opposite the Excalibur); (800) 634-4000 or (702) 739-2222.*

The Trop is one of the Strip's older resorts, and a favorite of many longtime Glitter City fans. It continues reinventing itself to compete successfully with the new generation MGM Grand, Excalibur and New York New York. All three have risen in recent years at this intersection of Las Vegas Boulevard and Tropicana Avenue, and the new Monte Carlo is just up the way. This has become such a pivotal casino intersection that elaborate crosswalks have been built here, feeding folks directly from one resort into the next.

Appropriate to its name, the Trop has a tropical resort theme, with a five-acre garden and pool area out back that rivals that of the Flamingo Hilton (see below, on page 40). A recent addition is the "Wildlife Walk," a corridor lined with parrots, macaws, marmosets and other critters either in cages or on perches.

This is a medium to high-roller venue, with some impressive touches of elegance. Note the imposing 150-foot-long barrel-arch leaded glass canopy that extends over the main casino's table games area. The adjacent baccarat room is hung with Venetian crystal. The Tropicana has several dining areas, generally modestly priced, including a buffet and a deli. It also claims the longest running musical revue in Las Vegas. Shapely ladies of "Folies Bergere" have been strutting about topless in the Tiffany Theatre since 1959. A brand new edition, "The Best of Folies Bergere," was unveiled in 1997. Unveiled, indeed! We like to think of the show as Les Folies sans Brassiere.

The Trop is a survivor of Glitter City's gang era, opened in 1957 by a Frank Costello underling named "Dandy" Phil Kastel. It was far down the Strip at the time, although conveniently near the airport, allowing high rollers to get to the tables quickly. After several ownership changes, it was purchased by the Ramada Corporation in 1979.

THE TEN BEST OUTLYING CASINO RESORTS

Although most casinos are focused in downtown Las Vegas and along the Strip, visitors shouldn't ignore those in the surrounding areas. We aren't referring to small neighborhood sawdust joints. Our Ten Best selections are quite large, and many rival downtown and Strip casinos for their size and opulence. Most are geared to locals, so they offer such enticements as cheap food and loose slots to generate repeat business. They have hometown lures such as bowling alleys and movie theaters and one even has an ice rink.

These outer area casino resorts seek tourist dollars as well, tempting visitors with elaborate facilities and moderately priced lodging. Many of them market heavily to tour groups, giving them a captive audience away from the Strip and downtown. (They're hardly captive, however, since several of these outland casinos provide free shuttle service.)

If you've come to town on a busy weekend, a peak holiday period or during a major convention, outlying casinos offer escape from crowds and traffic. You can get into a lunch buffet without standing in line until it's dinner time, and you can find a place to park your car or RV in the large parking lots.

Like many of the Strip resorts, the outlying casinos often have specific themes, ranging from Western railroad and old New Orleans to Latino fiesta and Southwest modern. These casinos are easy to reach if you have wheels; we provide simple directions with each listing. The Showboat, Boulder Station and Sam's Town are along the Boulder Highway, a southeast extension of Fremont Street. If you don't mind a few traffic lights, you can hit them in succession, and you'll see several smaller casinos along the way.

1 SAM'S TOWN HOTEL & GAMBLING HALL • *5111 Boulder Highway (at Nellis Boulevard); (800) 634-6371 or (702) 456-7777. TO GET THERE: Follow Fremont Street (Boulder Highway) 4.5 miles from downtown. To get there faster, drive five miles southeast on I-515, take the Boulder Highway exit and continue another 2.5 miles.*

Sam's is the largest of the outlying casinos, with the most complete facilities, covering 136,000 square feet and employing 2,400 people. It rivals many of the Strip casinos in size. The marquee says this is "Where locals bring their friends," which may not be an exaggeration, since it draws both residents and visitors. A major expansion in 1992 created new hotel towers that surround "Mystic Falls." It's a climate-controlled 25,000-square-foot water park with a greenhouse roof, fake rocks, pretend bighorn sheep, real trees and flowers, and splashing streams. A "dancing waters" laser show is performed here periodically. (See Chapter five, page 88).

Gamblers will find it all here—low and high denomination slots, dozens of table games, a large race and sports book, a card room and bingo parlor. Diners will find it all as well—ten different restaurants including Willy and Jose's Cantina, Billy Bob's Steakhouse, Mary's Diner, Final Score Sport Bar, Diamond Lil's, Smokey Joe's and the Chuckwagon food court. Shoppers can get lost in the huge Western Emporium, larger than many department stores. It sells mostly Western wear, plus a large curio and souvenir section. Other facilities include stacks of hotel rooms, a swimming lagoon, bowling alley and a large RV park. Free 72-hour RV parking is permitted for rigs that don't fit in the RV facility.

2 ARIZONA CHARLIE'S HOTEL & CASINO • *740 S. Decatur Blvd.; (800) 342-2695 or (702) 258-5200. TO GET THERE: Take Charleston Boulevard about 2.5 miles west of downtown, turn right onto Decatur and you'll see it shortly on your left.*

Once a small sawdust joint, this mid-size neighborhood casino has been completely remodeled and dressed in cheerful Western attire. The low-ceiling but well ventilated casino has the full range of gaming devices and tables, from nickels to several dollars. Although it's in a commercial and retail neighborhood, Charlie's is a full service resort with rooms, swimming pool, a show lounge, a special events center, large sports and race book and bingo parlor. Its dining areas are particularly appealing. Chin's, a highly regarded Chinese restaurant at Fashion Show Mall, has a budget priced outlet here called Charlie Chins. The Sourdough Café has a clever mine shaft theme, and Yukon Charlie's has a clubby Alaska hunting lodge look. You'll find thrifty fare as well, particularly at the Sports Book Deli, with 99-cent shrimp cocktails and budget hot dogs and hamburgers. The Wild West Buffet is one of the least expensive in town; see Chapter five, page 98.

3 **BOOMTOWN HOTEL, CASINO & RV RESORT** • *3333 Blue Diamond Rd.; (800) 588-7711 or (702) 263-7777. TO GET THERE: Take I-15 exit 33 onto Blue Diamond Road, about five miles west of Las Vegas; you'll see it beside the freeway.*

Western historians will appreciate the clever décor of this busy casino complex on the southern edge of town. The interior is done up as an old mining camp, including a Chinatown section—perfectly appropriate since the Chinese were among the largest ethnic groups working mines in Nevada and California. *Fung Lum*, the traditional Chinese New Year, dragon hangs from the ceiling, twisting from "Chinatown" past a mock-up mine that houses the Rattlesnake Bar and show lounge. This is a low to medium roller establishment, with plenty of nickel machines and table limits starting at $2. It also has a sports and race book, poker room and modest high limit slot area—$5 to $25.

Live entertainment is presented in the Rattlesnake Saloon, almost always with a Western twang. Dining venues are the Abilene Steakhouse (American-continental) and Opera House (things barbecued), plus a café, snack bar and the Blue Diamond buffet. Winter snowbirds love to flock to this place, since it has one of the largest RV parks in Nevada. See the listing at the end of this chapter.

4 **BOULDER STATION HOTEL & CASINO** • *4111 Boulder Highway; (800) 683-7777 or (702) 432-7777. TO GET THERE: Follow Fremont Street (Boulder Highway) five miles southeast from downtown. Or follow I-515 for six miles, take the Boulder Highway exit and you'll see it almost immediately, on your right.*

You could be convinced—after a few 99-cent margaritas—that this is a turn-of-the-century Western railroad station, with its witch's hat clock tower, vaulted cupolas and wrought iron grillwork. Inside, plank floors mingle with carpets to carry on the railway waiting room theme. However, the ranks of slot and video machines and table games will convince you that you're waiting for Lady Luck, and not for a train. Folks like Boulder Station's low-end table limits and nickel and quarter machines that are said to be quite generous.

This is a near clone to Palace Station, just west of the I-15 freeway at Sahara and Rancho Drive. Both have large hotel towers, so they're geared as much to visitors as to locals. Of the two, we prefer Boulder

Station, with its more elaborate railroad décor. Note particularly the two leaded glass murals above the gaming area. There's also a pretend sky with puffy clouds, in case you're so busy feeding the machines that you've forgotten what daylight looks like. Dining spots include Guadalajara (serious Mexican, with eighteen salsas), the Broiler (steaks and seafood), Iron Horse Café (American), China Express take-out and Pasta and Pizza Palace, and a buffet called the Feast. If you have kids in tow, you can lose them at the Boulder Station Cinema movie complex or Station Arcade with video games. The resort even has a toddlers playground called Kids Quest, with child care.

5 FIESTA CASINO HOTEL • *2400 N. Rancho Dr. (at Lake Mead Boulevard); (702) 631-7000. TO GET THERE: Follow U.S. 95 freeway about 1.5 miles north of downtown, take Rancho Drive (exit 77) and continue north another two miles north to Lake Mead Boulevard.*

This cheery new mid-size casino is done up in brightly colored Latin fiesta attire. It's a low to medium roller place, with the usual slot and video machine range from a nickel and up, plus a bingo parlor, table games starting around $3 and something unique even for Las Vegas—a drive-up sports book. It also features rather tempting eating and drinking bargains, such as a weekend champagne brunch for $7.99, beer with chips and salsa for $1.50 and 99-cent margaritas. Farther up the dining scale, Garduño's Chili Packing Co. is the cutest Mexican restaurant in town; see Chapter four, page 65. Other food venues include the Old San Francisco Steak House and Dance Hall, Cactus Rose Café, a Chinese takeout and a deli. Among its resort facilities are a swimming pool, lounge entertainment, a showroom, meeting facilities and hotel rooms.

6 GOLD COAST HOTEL & CASINO • *4000 W. Flamingo Rd.; (800) 331-5334 or (702) 367-7111. TO GET THERE: It's just beyond the Rio; take Flamingo Road a miles west of the Strip to Valley View Boulevard.*

The look is colonial Spanish at this mid-sized casino next door to the Rio. Since it's near the freeway yet off the Strip, it's popular both with tourists and locals, who claim that the slots are rather generous. The casino is done in stucco and pink tile with brass chandeliers dangling over the gaming tables from vaulted ceilings. Lounges feature live amusements and several restaurants serve American, Latin, Chinese and Italian fare. Other facilities include a bowling alley, large bingo parlor, swimming pool, convention rooms, video arcade, swimming pool and modest priced hotel rooms. A free shuttle links the Gold Coast with its sister casinos, the Barbary Coast in the heart of the strip and the Orleans (below).

7 *ORLEANS HOTEL & CASINO* • *4500 W. Tropicana Ave. (Arville Avenue); (702) 365-7111. TO GET THERE: Take Tropicana Avenue west from the Strip, cross over the freeway and continue for a mile.*

Opened in the winter of 1996, the Orleans is one of the most appealing of Glitter City's outlying casinos. Start with its wonderful, brightly colored French Quarter façade, then step inside, where you're greeted by the monumental sculpture of an alligator band with trumpet, sax and bass viol. The gaming area behind them features a brilliant Mardi Gras décor, and it earned a spot above as one of the Ten Best gaming venues in town (see below).

Orleans is a complete destination resort, with a night club and lounge, pool complex, bowling alley, wedding chapel and a major show lounge featuring top name entertainers. Cinema buffs will be drawn to the large "12-Plex" movie theater, the only one in town with stadium seating. Appropriate to its New Orleans theme, it offers traditional Southern dining such as an oyster bar, gumbo house and a coffee and benet café. (For those not familiar with this New Orleans treat, benets are squared sugar covered doughnuts, great for coffee-dunking.) Other restaurants range from American steak and seafood to Mexican and Italian. The facility is owned by the creators of the Barbary Coast and Gold Coast, and a free shuttle connects all three.

8 *SANTA FE HOTEL & CASINO* • *4949 N. Rancho Dr.; (800) 872- 6823 or (702) 658-4900. TO GET THERE: Follow Freeway 95 about eight miles north to its the Rancho Drive exit.*

If you're in Las Vegas during the summer, you might want to head for the Santa Fe to cool off—not with an icy drink, but within an icy arena. In the world's only casino ice rink, you can rent a pair of skates and practice your pirouettes, or just sit in the cool stands and watch others play. You might catch the professional Las Vegas Thunder hockey team in action, for this is their practice arena. Beyond the rink, the Santa Fe has a cool Southwest look, with lots of beige, and salmon and turquoise accents. It has the usual gaming devices and—off to one side—a large bowling alley. The Santa Fe's most striking feature is its high ceiling main entry, styled after a turn-of-the-century Santa Fe railway station. An old fashioned bar occupies the center, and several restaurants and take-outs are on the fringes. Tables, chairs and library style newspaper racks invite lingering.

9 *SUNSET STATION HOTEL-CASINO* • *1301 W. Sunset Rd. (just west of I-515 interchange), Henderson, NV 89014; (888) SUNSET-9 or (702) 547-7777. TO GET THERE: Take I-515 about ten miles southeast of Las Vegas to the Sunset Road exit and go west (right under the freeway) less than a mile.*

A major destination resort in the Las Vegas suburb of Henderson? That's the goal of southern Nevada's newest outlying casino complex. Opened in the summer of 1997, Sunset Station is the largest and most elaborate of four facilities owned by Station Casinos, Inc. A busy, brightly colored façade has an appealing Spanish-Mediterranean look and the theme carries inside, with ceramic tiled columns, plazas and fountains. The interior is splashed with red, ocher and other flaming autumn colors. Particularly imposing is the table games area, done in a kind of grotto look with brilliant leaded glass insets in the ceiling. Spanish accents mark the Club Madrid show lounge, which features luminaries such as Dionne Warwick, Gladys Knight and a reincarnation of the Monkees. Rosalita's Cantina, the Seville Bar and Bullfighter's Bar continue the Latin theme, while the large Gordon Biersch microbrewery has a brick and stainless steel "industrial modern" look.

Built at a cost of nearly $200 million, Sunset Station is a full-facility resort, with a 448-room hotel, large gaming area, video arcade, thirteen-screen movie theater, swimming complex and a dozen restaurants, including the large Feast Around the World international buffet.

10 *TEXAS STATION GAMBLING HALL & HOTEL* •

North Rancho Drive at Lake Mead Boulevard; (702) 631-1000. TO GET THERE: Follow directions for the Fiesta; Texas Station is next door.

One of the area's larger outland casinos, this facility has a kind of cowboy-oilman theme, with branding irons and oil derricks. It's the kind of place J.R. from TV's *Dallas* might have built if he'd gone into the gaming business. The cute cocktail waitresses with their halter tops and fringed mini-skirts are the sort that J.R. would have hired.

Follow your feet as you explore this place, noting the Western theme carpet in the main casino and the interesting mix of tile and other floor treatments along the restaurant row. Texas Station is a medium roller venue, with lots of 25-cent slots and table minimums starting around $3. It also has live Western entertainment at the Armadillo Honky Tonk, a large bingo parlor and a multi-screen movie theater. Among its restaurants are the Yellow Rose Café with American fare tilted toward barbecue, Tex-Mex at the Laredo Cantina and Café, and steak and seafood at the cowboy-clubby Stockyard.

THE TEN MOST APPEALING CASINO GAMING AREAS

We enjoy hanging around casinos, even though we don't like the smoke and we don't gamble. We like the mixed cacophony of cocktail lounge entertainers, melodic sounds of machines, shouting craps shooters and the metallic clunk of coins falling to the lucky. This casino symphony sounds like a maniacal flute and percussion group tuning up before a concert. Most casinos have no clocks, windows or closing hours. Time is made to stand still, inviting folks to stay as long as they wish. There is food and drink and entertainment and clean bathrooms and thus no reason to leave.

Casinos are great places to people-watch. They attract the an intriguing cross-section of Americana—the wide-eyed mom and pop tourists from Kansas, the cool hand Luke gamblers, gorgeous women and dumpy ones, honeymooners still glowing from a night of love, senior citizens gleefully spending their children's' inheritance, and wheelchair-bound ex-smokers with their oxygen bottles, out for a final fling.

1 MONTE CARLO • *3770 Las Vegas Blvd. (north of Tropicana Avenue); (800) 311-8999 or (702) 730-7777.*

With its mix of Monacan elegance and Las Vegas glitter, this is the most attractive gaming area in town. Five beaded crystal chandeliers recessed in ceiling canopies shed their subtle light on the gaming areas. Plush carpets and mirrored columns complete this picture of casino elegance. This is as stylish as the original Monte Carlo casino, although it's much less conservative. In Monaco, slot and video machines are banished to a small side room called—with obvious European disdain—the "American Casino"; only table games occupy the opulent main gaming area.

In the Las Vegas version, more than 2,000 slots and videos share the large casino with the usual table games, adding their melodic din to the sound of rattling dice. This not to suggest that the casino is noisy; with its high ceiling to absorb the sound, it's one of the quieter ones in town. This is also an exceedingly comfortable place to play the machines; an upholstered burgundy chair is posted before each slot and video device. Not surprisingly, this is medium to high roller territory, with most machines starting at 25 cents and going as high as $100; table limits start at $5 and go to the thousands. Those who want even more action can step into the clubby high limit room with craps, blackjack, roulette and baccarat tables. This more resembles the casino in Monaco. There's also a "Top Hat" high denomination slot venue.

2 CAESARS PALACE • *3570 S. Las Vegas Blvd. (at Flamingo Road); (800) 634-6001 or (702) 731-7110.*

Casino? One must use the plural in this opulent resort. Caesars has several casinos, including one for high rollers tucked into an upper floor. Our favorite, back down to earth, is the Palace Casino, just off the hotel lobby. It's visually arresting, accented by three huge crystal canopies suspended over a block of table games, a gathering of slot machines and a high limit slot area. There is much to occupy the gambler and the browser in the Palace Casino—several bars, an elegant baccarat room attended by dealers in tuxedos, the high limit slot area, and a complete range of tables, slots and videos. Cleopatra's Barge, a late night dancing and entertainment lounge, and the smaller Bar by the Barge are just down the corridor.

3 HARD ROCK HOTEL AND CASINO • *4455 Paradise Road (at Harmon, just east of the Strip); (800) HRD-ROCK or (702) 693-5000.*

Stepping into this lively casino, listening to the raucous sounds of rock and admiring rock stars' regalia on the walls, you'll think you've entered a Hard Rock Café that's acquired a gaming license. You'll be right, in a sense. The Las Vegas Hard Rock Café opened at the corner of Paradise and Harmon in 1990, and the "world's first rock 'n' roll hotel-casino" followed five years later. Although it isn't as wonderfully cluttered with rock star memorabilia as the next-door café, the Hard Rock Casino still puts on a great visual show. Like, man, check out the roulette tables shaped like grand pianos, the gold lamé jacket of Elvis, the huge global Hard Rock logo hanging over the circular center bar, Bruce Springsteen's guitar and black and green performance outfit, and a delightfully outrageous Alice Cooper costume.

This is a medium to high roller venue, with table stakes starting around $3 to $5. It'll take a bit of searching to find nickel slots and videos. You can't get lost in this mid-sized casino. It's fashioned in a large circle, with restaurants, hotel desk and other auxiliary facilities on a raised landing around the fringes.

4 IMPERIAL PALACE • *3535 S. Las Vegas Blvd. (between Sands Avenue and Flamingo Road, opposite Caesars Palace); (800) 634-6441 or (702) 731-3311.*

Pardon my chauvinism, but gents who enjoy people-watching may find themselves mostly watching the cocktail waitresses at this venerable gaming establishment. Clad in low-cut, mini-skirted *cheongsams,* they're among the prettiest in town. Beyond these distractions, the Imperial Palace casino is appealing for its East-West look, with a curious mix of crystal chandeliers, curled-up pagoda style eves and Asian artifacts. The Asian theme carries throughout, from golden dragons to bright red lacquer temples (the Chinese color for good luck) to the Saké Bar, Ginza Bar and Geisha Bar.

Slots and table games are mostly in the moderate range, with some on the high-limit side, so the Imperial appeals to a wide range of gamblers. Pony players will find a TV set at every seat in the sports and race book. Those driven from the games by hunger can choose full service dining in an upstairs dining plaza or inexpensive snacks at

Betty's Diner. Car buffs will want to check out the Imperial Palace Automobile Collection (Chapter nine, page 152).

5 *MAIN STREET STATION* ● *200 Main Street (between Ogden and Stewart); (800) 713-8933 or (702) 387-1896.*

Recently acquired and reopened by the Boyd Group after a long sleep, the Main Street Station casino has been returned to its turn-of-the-century San Francisco-style elegance. Particularly striking are brilliant leaded glass and beveled glass windows along the Main Street side of the casino, and leaded glass skylights in coffered ceilings above the table games. Brass and crystal accents, polished woods, ornate pressed tin ceilings and dowel rail balconies above the main casino give this place the look of an opulent Gay Nineties gaming parlor. The theme carries into the adjacent Garden Court Buffet, with its ornate latticed ceiling arches, tulip chandeliers and potted ferns.

Pause for a drink at the main casino bar with its old style belt driven fans overhead and brass statuary along the marbled and mirrored backbar. Also worthy of a peek, between the casino and the adjacent Jackie Gaughan's Plaza, are two historic railroad passenger cars. They aren't open, although you can peek through the windows and admire their interior elegance. A pedestrian overcrossing links Main Street Station with the flagship of the Boyd casino fleet, the California Hotel and Casino.

6 *THE MIRAGE* ● *3400 S. Las Vegas Blvd. (adjacent to Caesars Palace); (800) 627-6667 or (702) 791-7111.*

The lush tropical theme, the imposing rainforest under glass and the open layout of the Mirage casino make it one of the most appealing in town. Although it's large, suspended Polynesian style roofs break it up into several smaller areas. This is medium to high roller turf, although one can find a few nickel slots here. Table stakes generally start around $5 and you can spend as much as $500 a pull on special token slot machines, or request an elegant private room where the smallest denomination chip is $1,000. Meanwhile, we mere mortals can spend hours in here, watching the action, enjoying the lush décor and investing an occasional quarter or dollar.

7 *ORLEANS HOTEL & CASINO* ● *4500 W. Tropicana Ave.; (702) 365-7111.*

This new casino is one of the most appealing in town, from its monumental and whimsical sculptures and wonderful Mardi Gras décor to its rather fetching cocktail waitress outfits. Visitors are greeted by a large, comical alligator combo at the main entrance. Inside, a four-story atrium courtyard with a French Quarter façade towers above the table games area. A cute touch here: Mannequins hang over the New Orleans style wrought iron balconies, looking down at the action.

The three main casino bars are particularly appealing and they're great venues for watching the action. A huge mock-up grand piano hangs upside down above the show lounge bar. Four grinning alligators hold up the ceiling of the Alligator Bar and busts of four masked Mardi Gras Queens hover above the sexy Mardi Gras Bar. The Orleans is a medium roller place, with table limits starting around $3, lots of 25 cent slots and videos and a few nickel ones. Drink prices are a bargain, starting at a dollar.

8 RIO SUITE HOTEL CASINO • 3700 W. Flamingo Rd. (at Valley View Boulevard, opposite the Gold Coast); (702) 252-7777.

The new Masquerade Village casino, added during a $200 million expansion of the highly successful the Rio, is appealing for two major reasons. It has a four-story atrium-style ceiling, carrying away the exhaust of smoking gamblers, and it has a mezzanine balcony where people-watchers can look down on the action. They also can look across at the distinctive "Masquerade Show in the Sky," a periodic parade of lavishly decorated and lighted floats suspended from the ceiling on tracks. The balcony also houses a row of shops and a couple of restaurants. The look of Masquerade Village, say its designers, is a blend of New Orleans, Rio and Venice Mardi Gras, and the balcony shopping area is fashioned as a 200-year-old Tuscan village. Somehow, all of this designer collision works well together.

Curiously, despite its bright and spacious appeal, Masquerade Village isn't as busy with gamblers as the original low-ceiling casino up front. Both gaming areas offer the full range of games, in the medium to high roller range. Table limits range from $2 to $5,000. Poker players have their own room off the main casino up front. People-watchers can sit in the large, circular Ipanema Bar, located on a transition route between the two casinos.

9 STARDUST HOTEL • 3000 S. Las Vegas Blvd. (Stardust Road); (800) 634-6757 or (702) 732-6111.

You could get lost in this place, although pleasantly so, for there is plenty to keep you occupied. The Stardust casino, about two blocks long, is a busy mix of machines, gaming tables, appealing little casino bars, a lounge with live entertainment and a six-pack of restaurants. Despite the intensity of action here, it's so spread out that it doesn't seem crowded, even on a good day. You can always find a semi-quiet corner where you can relax with a drink and feed a machine, or just sit and people-watch. Restaurants are conveniently arrayed along one side. The casino is one of the prettiest in town, done in mauve, pink and amber neon, trimmed with rows of golden glitter lights against black matte ceilings.

The large Stardust Race and Sports Book is mission control for serious bettors. It is here that the odds and point spreads are set for the entire Nevada gaming industry.

10 TREASURE ISLAND AT THE MIRAGE • 3300 S. Las Vegas Blvd. (Spring Mountain Road); (702) 894-7111.

This casino is appealing for its fun "Pirates of the Caribbean" theme. While serious gambling happens here, you can look up from your blackjack table or slot machine and admire bosomy figureheads sprouting from heavy beam ceilings, or pirates' booty tucked into niches. The Gold Bar near the center of casino, draped in more pretend plunder, is a good place to sit and watch the action. For action of a different kind, adjourn—well in advance—to the outdoor deck of the aptly-name Battle Bar to witness periodic clashes between British and pirate frigates. (See Chapter five, page 87.) The casino of course has all of the usual games of choice and chance; they're targeted toward the mid-rollers (neither high nor low), with lots of quarter machines and a few nickel ones, and table limits starting around $3.

THE TEN BEST CASINO SWIMMING AREAS

Nothing is more welcome in a desert than an oasis, and Las Vegas has more than any other arid city on the globe. By "oasis," we refer to those splendid landscaped swimming complexes, usually surrounded by the casino's hotel towers, where people can relax in relative isolation from the busy hum of traffic and gaming machines beyond.

1 FLAMINGO HILTON • 3555 S. Las Vegas Blvd. (near Flamingo Road); (800) 732-2111 or (702) 733-3111.

Bugsy Siegel would have loved it! When he built his oasis in the desert, he never dreamed it would become this lavish. The Flamingo Hilton's garden complex is expansive, with two large swimming pools and a lap pool, a multiple water slide, cascading waterfalls and acres of lush landscaping. Penguins and real flamingos waddle about in their own habitats. The entire complex is done in salmon and turquoise, with art deco accents. (Bugsy would have called it pink and blue.)

With a poolside bar and adjacent restaurant, one might be tempted to spend most of their vacation out here. Only the bronze-windowed towers rising above remind you that you're in Clark County, Nevada, and not a Caribbean retreat. Although pool use is for guests only, anyone is free to roam about the grounds. Many hotels limit swimming complex entry to their guests.

2 BALLY'S LAS VEGAS • *3645 S. Las Vegas Blvd., Las Vegas, NV 89109; (800) 634-3434 or (702) 739-4111.*

A huge outdoor whirlpool and even larger main pool are focal points of the Bally swimming complex. Green knolls and patches of palm trees break up the large expanses of concrete. Bathers can stroll over to an adjacent bar called On the Rocks for libations. Covered cabañas at one end of this extensive facility offer shady retreats. The adjacent Terrace Café provides pool-view dining.

3 CAESARS PALACE • *3570 S. Las Vegas Blvd. (at Flamingo Road); (702) 731-7110.*

Already opulent, the Garden of the Gods swimming complex at Caesars has been redone and expanded to more than four acres, with four pools and two whirlpool spas, accented by fountains and surrounded by Roman columns and statuary. Facilities include a snack bar, two cocktail bars and private cabañas that can be rented. This new Roman oasis, completed in early 1998, is part of a major hotel expansion that includes a new tower with 1,200 rooms, retail shops, and a 20,000-square-foot health and fitness center.

4 THE DESERT INN • *3145 S. Las Vegas Blvd. (at Desert Inn Road, opposite the Frontier); (702) 733-4444.*

A lush new tropic garden—truly an oasis in the desert—was opened in the fall of 1997 as part of a complete renovation of this longtime Las Vegas resort. It's a virtual water park, with a pool, outdoor spa and flowing streams. Guests can rent floats and run mini rapids beneath a palm tree canopy. With its acres of contoured landscaping, flower beds, bridges, rock gardens and waterfalls, this is one of the most appealing lagoon complexes in town.

5 HARD ROCK HOTEL AND CASINO • *4455 Paradise Road (at Harmon, just east of the Strip); (702) 693-5000.*

It would not be difficult to imagine the Hard Rock Café Beach Club as a setting for one of those Annette Funicello beach party movies. It has a sandy swatch of beach, free form pool with piped-in underwater music, a water slide, luxury cabañas and attractive landscaping. All of this basks under the curved *Miami moderne* sweep of the high rise Hard Rock Hotel. Since this casino resort appeals to young, upwardly mobile adults, you also may see some bikini-clad ladies who could have come for a beach bunny movie casting call. As you approach the Beach Club through a hotel corridor, you'll see Annette and others of her generation on a series of old beach party movie posters.

6 *MGM GRAND* • *3799 S. Las Vegas Blvd. (at Tropicana);* *(702) 891-7777.*

The Grand Oasis Pool requires a bit of a search, although you'll be pointed in the right direction if you ask. At the base of the Emerald Tower, it consists of one large pool with the requisite fake rock waterfalls, a whirlpool and a huge concrete sun deck, with a pool bar and delicatessen adjacent. Kids will like the walk-through fountain, where they can cavort beneath water jets. Although large like the rest of the Grand, the Oasis lacks the lush landscaping and contours of other Glitter City lagoons.

7 *THE MIRAGE* • *3400 S. Las Vegas Blvd. (adjacent to Caesars Palace); (800) 627-6667 or (702) 791-7111.*

Waterfalls splash from a rocky, palm-shaded island into the huge swimming lagoon; palms line meandering paths. It would be easy to be lulled into thinking you were in a South Seas hideaway, except for the surrounding hotel towers. The Dolphin Habitat and a gentle jungle with big cats and other critters, called the Secret Garden of Siegfried and Roy, are adjacent to the pool oasis. A $10 admission is charged to enter this lush domain, which is open weekdays 11 to 5:30 and weekends 10 to 5:30.

8 *RIO SUITE HOTEL & CASINO* • *3700 W. Flamingo Rd. (at Valley View Boulevard, opposite the Gold Coast); (702) 252-7777.*

Three large swimming pools with the requisite cascading waterfalls, a spa and a real sand beach are the lures at the Rio's swimming lagoon. One small negative—the large complex has too much concrete; it needs more landscaping with palm trees and a few grassy hummocks. However, it's nice to lie in the sand here, pretending you're on the beach at Ipanema. Should you need sustenance, a beach bar and café are near the main pool.

9 *SAM'S TOWN HOTEL & GAMBLING HALL* • *5111 Boulder Highway (Flamingo Road); (702) 456-7777.*

Sam's has two water attractions—a swimming lagoon and the new Mystic Falls Park. The palm-tree trimmed swimming oasis has a large free-form pool, spa and sandy volleyball court. Mystic Falls is a 25,000 square foot garden and water park under glass, in a courtyard formed by hotel towers. A free laser and "dancing waters" show is presented here daily at 2, 6, 8 and 10 p.m. This also is an inviting place to sit and listen to the soothing sounds of falling water.

10 TROPICANA RESORT & CASINO • *3801 S. Las Vegas Blvd. (Tropicana Avenue, opposite the Excalibur); (702) 739-2222.*

The Trop's huge garden and swimming complex rivals that of the Flamingo Hilton as the most elaborate in town. Covering five acres, it's lushly landscaped, with green knolls, palms and assorted other trees, bright floral gardens, *faux* stone mountains and even a pretend tunnel. It's a virtual aquatic park with two swimming pools and several cascading waterfalls, all connected by a wandering stream.

Flamingos stand one-legged in one enclosure and African crowned cranes strut about another, while multi-colored *koi* swim along the elaborate water course. The Tropicana swimming complex also boasts the only swim-up blackjack game in the world. (Keep your cards dry.)

THE TEN BEST CASINO RESORT WOWIES

A wowie, of course, is something that makes your eyes widen; that makes you stare and say: "Wow, look at that!" Of Glitter City's many casino wowies, here are the ten best:

1 THE BEST THEME RESORT: New York New York • *3790 S. Las Vegas Boulevard (Tropicana Avenue); (702) 740-6969.*

Many casino resorts start out with a primary theme and then clutter it up with inconsistencies. Witness the Monte Carlo with its elegant Monaco look, but with an industrial strength brewpub; and the Luxor pyramid with its New York-style Manhattan buffet. However, New York New York keeps its theme throughout, creating the best architectural-decorator vision in Glitter City. Outside are the Statue of Liberty, fireboats in New York Harbor, a mini-Brooklyn bridge, a compact New York skyline rising above, with a Coney Island style rollercoaster threaded through it.

Inside, you'll find New York style storefronts, a Stock Exchange façade (appropriately housing the main cashiers cage and casino counting house), an amusement arcade with a Coney Island theme, a Greenwich Village street scene encompassing both the food court and the shopping arcade. For *real* cute, the change carts have black and yellow New York taxicab themes. New York street entertainers perform in the Madhattan Theater Friday through Tuesday at 7:30 and 10. And of course you can get a Nathan's hot dog here. Not at the food court, silly; at the Coney Island snack bar.

2 THE MOST INTERESTING CASINO HOTEL LOBBY: The Mirage • *3400 S. Las Vegas Blvd. (adjacent to Caesars Palace); (702) 791-7111.*

Hotel lobbies in Las Vegas range from elegant (Golden Nugget, Monte Carlo and Hilton) to strange (Hard Rock Hotel). The one at the Mirage is the most interesting in town, with its lush tropic décor, marble floor and a 20,000-gallon saltwater aquarium behind the registration desks. It contains ninety kinds of fish, including an occasional shark.

3 THE MOST IMPOSING INNER SPACE: Luxor Hotel & Casino ● 3900 Las Vegas Blvd. (Tropicana); (702) 262-4000.

The main entrance to the Luxor pyramid, under the sphinx's tummy, is quite impressive with its matched monumental statues of Ramses II, flanked by rams head statues and a reflection pool. From here you can catch a glimpse of the interior of the pyramid. For a much better view of this inner space, catch an escalator or elevator to the Attractions Level and you'll have a clear view of the great hollow pyramid of the Luxor. It's the world's largest atrium, with hotel rooms stacked inversely above, off hanging balconies. The best place to see all of this space is near an obelisk in the center of the Attractions Level gaming area.

4 THE MOST ATTRACTIVE RESTROOMS: The Golden Nugget Hotel & Casino ● 129 Fremont St. (Casino Center Boulevard); (702) 385-7111.

The decorative elegance of the Golden Nugget carries into the restrooms on the right side of the main casino. Note the cross-hatched tile ceramic walls, mirror strips and little coffers in the ceilings set with fans. The counter tops are simulated black marble with white basins and of course the faucets are electronic.

5 THE BEST TIFFANY LOOK: Tropicana casino ● 3801 S. Las Vegas Blvd. (Tropicana Avenue); (702) 739-2222.

The Trop once was known as the "Tiffany of the Strip" because of a glittery urban Miami look. It has since changed its decorator theme to South Seas tropical, calling itself the "Island of Las Vegas." However, its most imposing "Tiffany" feature survives—a stunning 150-foot-long, 4,000-square-foot leaded glass canopy. It forms a glittering barrel-arch ceiling over the table games area in the main casino.

6 THE BEST INDOOR WOODLAND: Mirage rainforest ● 3400 S. Las Vegas Blvd. (adjacent to Caesars Palace); (800) 627-6667 or (702) 791-7111.

Step through the main entrance of the Mirage and you seemed to have stepped outside again—into a verdant rainforest. A lush canopy of vegetation—much of it real—thrives beneath a 90-foot glass dome. With its cascading waterfall, orchids and creepers entwining towering palms, it smells, looks and feels like a tropic forest. You almost expect to see macaws flitting about. A winding pathway and footbridge leads through the forest and into the casino. If you want to admire this indoor jungle while dining or sipping a drink, step into Kokomo's or the Lagoon Saloon, which are adjacent to the rainforest.

7 THE GLITTERIEST CASINO ENTRY: Circus Circus •
2880 S. Las Vegas Blvd. (upper Strip, south of the Sahara); (702) 734-0410.

In a town noted for its glitter, the Circus Circus out-glitters them all with its dazzling portico. Suspended over the main entrance, this huge canopy shimmers with thousands of red and yellow lights, enough to make new arrivals squint.

8 THE SEXIEST HOTEL TOWER: Rio Suite Hotel • 3700
W. Flamingo Rd. (at Valley View Boulevard, opposite the Gold Coast); (702) 252-7777.

This dramatic 41-story, $200 million hotel tower, completed in 1997, is the most impressive single piece of architecture in town. Note its distinctive oval shape, terraced rooftop and rainbow sweeps of red and mauve neon piping. A press release calls the high rise "one of the tallest inhabitable towers in the United States" although we aren't quite sure what that means. We'd certainly love to live there, particularly on the east side, where rooms feature absolutely splendid views of the nearby Strip.

9 THE WILDEST CASINO SCULPTURES: Orleans Hotel &
Casino • *4500 W. Tropicana Ave.; (702) 365-7111.*

August Rodin would've had a fit if he had seen the sculptures in this place, since he reportedly had no sense of humor. As you enter the main casino, you're greeted by larger-than-life figures of three grinning 'gators playing trumpet, sax and bass viol. Further inside, you'll find four more alligators holding up the roof of the Alligator Bar, and giant crawdads crawling over the roof of the Crawfish Bar. Nearby, formidable busts of four masked Mardi Gras Queens hover above the Mardi Gras Bar. After you've finished your sculpture lesson, check the mock-up grand piano hanging upside down above the show lounge bar, near the main entrance.

10 THE MOST IMPRESSIVE VIDEO DISPLAY: MGM
Grand hotel lobby • *3799 S. Las Vegas Blvd. (at Tropicana); (702) 891-7777.*

There is no shortage of video terminals in Las Vegas. Sports bars are hung with them and some race and sports books have a screen at every seating station. However, the MGM Grand's huge hotel lobby display tops them all. A computer-driven bank of eighty television monitors fills a wall behind the registration desk. It's fascinating to watch images change from full-screen to split-screen to eighty individual projections. It would be even more fascinating if the bank of screens transmitted something other than MGM Grand promotional videos. However, images of the super high tech show called "EFX" can become pretty wild.

CASINO RESORT RV PARKING

If you're traveling by recreational vehicle, you don't have to be deprived of easy casino access. Several Las Vegas resorts have their own RV parks, while others allow self-contained rigs to park free on their back lots. Further, most casinos with RV parks also permit free RV "dry camping" if their regular facilities are full. (Tent camping isn't allowed; the tent pegs raise havoc with the asphalt.)

Space is at a premium in these RV parks from November through April and sometimes beyond, so folks planning to roost their RVs in Glitter City should make reservations early. If you come to town without reservations, your best bet is to arrive at an RV park early in the morning and hope to catch someone leaving. At least one park—Circusland at Circus Circus—maintains a waiting list. It and most of the others accept advance phone reservations with a credit card.

Casino RV parks

These are listed in alphabetical order. The Circus Circus or Western Hotel rec vehicle parks would be our choices because the first is on the Strip and the other is just six blocks south of the canopied Fremont Street pedestrian mall.

1 BOOMTOWN GOLD RV PARK ● *3333 Blue Diamond Rd. (I-15 exit 33), Las Vegas, NV 89139; (800) 588-7711 or (702) 263-7777. RVs only; full hookups, $12 Sunday-Thursday, $16 weekends and holiday periods. Reservations accepted; major credit cards.*

This large park is adjacent to the Boomtown casino, seven miles west of Las Vegas. Facilities include showers, cable TV and phone outlets, pools and spas, a water slide, picnic and barbecue areas, a clubhouse, and mini-mart. A shuttle runs between the RV park and casino.

2 CIRCUSLAND RV PARK ● *At Circus Circus Casino, 500 Circus Circus Drive (just off Las Vegas Boulevard), Las Vegas, NV 89109; (800) 634-3450 or (702) 794-3757. RVs only; full hookups $12 Sun-*

day-Thursday and $16 Friday-Saturday and holiday weekends. Reservations advised well in advance; major credit cards. Waiting list available for those who arrive without reservations; check early in the morning.

This large park is the only surviving RV facility on the Strip, with the demise of the Hacienda Hotel and its rec vehicle area. Facilities include showers, pay phones, laundry, mini-mart, Propane, dump station, swimming pool, sauna and spa. Free shuttles and a nearby sky tram run between the park and main casino area.

3 **NEVADA PALACE RV PARK** • *5255 Boulder Hwy. (at Harmon Avenue, just beyond Sam's Town), Las Vegas, NV 89122; (800) 634-6283 or (702) 458-8810. RVs only, full hookups, $14. Reservations accepted; major credit cards.*

Located next door to Sam's Town on the Boulder Strip, this facility offers showers, pay phones, laundry and mini-mart. The full service Nevada Palace casino is adjacent.

4 **SAM'S TOWN RV PARK** • *5111 Boulder Highway (at Nellis Boulevard, eight miles southeast of downtown); (800) 634-6371 or (702) 456-7777. Las Vegas, NV 89122-6089; (800) 634-6371 or (702) 454-8055. RVs only, full hookups, $16. Reservations accepted; major credit cards.*

This large operation has showers, phones, laundry, recreation rooms, horseshoes, swimming pools and spas, and pet runs. The full facilities of Sam's Town are adjacent.

5 **SHOWBOAT RV RESORT** • *2800 Fremont St. (at Charleston, two miles east of downtown); (800) 826-2800 or (702) 385-9123. RVs only, full hookups, $14 Sunday-Thursday and $16 Friday-Saturday; ten-day stay limit. Reservations accepted; major credit cards.*

Opened in 1997, this attractive park is adjacent to the Showboat Hotel and Casino, located at the point where Fremont Street becomes the Boulder Strip. Facilities include full hookups, cable TV and phone hookups, laundry and showers.

6 **WESTERN HOTEL RV PARK** • *1023 Fremont Street (at Tenth, downtown), Las Vegas, NV 89125; (800) 634-6703 or (702) 384-1033. RVs only, full hookups $10. Major credit cards.*

This small, well maintained RV park is a block below the Western Hotel Casino, within a six-block walk of the Fremont Street Experience. Facilities include showers, coin laundry, arcade and snacks. It's the closest RV park to downtown Las Vegas.

Casinos that permit free RV parking

There may be others that we don't list here, and some of these may be gone by the time you arrive. Conditions change as parking lots are lost to expansion. Generally speaking, RVers who park out back in ground-level casino lots are rarely rousted by security. Our selections are listed in alphabetical order.

7 *GOLD COAST HOTEL & CASINO* ● *4000 W. Flamingo Rd. (about half a mile west across I-15, opposite the Rio).*

The Gold Coast's large outer lot is a popular rendezvous for RVers. A shuttle runs between here and its sister casinos, the Barbary Coast on the Strip at Las Vegas Boulevard and Flamingo Road, and Orleans Hotel and Casino at Tropicana and Arville Avenue.

8 *JACKIE OAUGHAN'S PLAZA* ● *Main and Bridger streets.*

Rec vehicles can stay free at the Plaza's large parking lot two blocks south of the casino. It's handy for downtown visitors, since it's only a three-block walk to the canopied Fremont Street. A sign at the parking lot calls this "validated parking" although the kiosk usually isn't manned.

9 *SAM'S TOWN HOTEL & GAMBLING HALL* ● *5111 Boulder Hwy. (at Nellis Boulevard east of downtown).*

In addition to its RV park (above), Sam's Town has a lot set aside for free no-hookup RV and trucker parking, with a 72-hour limit.

10 *STARDUST HOTEL* ● *3000 S. Las Vegas Blvd. (Stardust Road).*

Outer parking lots 52 through 54 on the hotel complex's north side have space for RVs. Coming from downtown, turn right opposite the Riviera's glittering mirrored tower and drive along the northern edge of the Stardust property until you reach the lots, which are beside the Westward Ho Apartment Suites. If you're coming from the south, find a place to do a U-turn and come back, since you can't turn left across the Boulevard into this entrance.

*"When the One Great Scorer comes to mark against your name,
He writes—not that you won or lost—but how you played the Game."*

—Grantland Rice

Chapter three

HOW TO LOSE MORE SLOWLY

THE RULE OF THE "HOUSE ADVANTAGE"

Before you even think of investing a nickel in a slot machine or placing a dollar chip on the cool green felt of a blackjack table, think of this phrase: "The house advantage."

Simply put, the house advantage means that in the long run, the house will win. It will win because a percentage of coins fed into slot and video poker machines drop into a galvanized bucket in the base, never to be paid out. It will win because in blackjack, despite near-even odds, the dealer takes the last hit, giving him or her the edge in most cases. It will win because wheels of fortune, keno and bingo games are heavily weighted in the house's favor. Even in roulette, where an odd/even bet should be 50-50, the house has an advantage because of the "zero-double zero."

Of course, the longer you stay at the machines or tables, the better the house's odds, unless you're on a hot streak. To keep you at your station, most casinos have created a pleasure vacuum. You're surrounded by glitter and pretty drink girls and jingling jackpot bells and the sound of money. There are no clocks, and most casinos have no windows to the outside world. Your every need is met—food, drinks, entertainment, clean restrooms. You need never go outside; just stay there and try to win!

Have you ever kept track of how much money you invest in your slot machine or table game while waiting for that leggy girl to return with your "free" drink? The philosophy is basic: keep the players happy and perhaps a little foggy and above all, *keep them!*

So what accounts for the great popularity of Nevada's casinos? Why do so many people travel so far to gamble? Simply put, the casinos play on human nature. To paraphrase a cliché, "to gamble is human." Anthropologists will lay you odds that some implements found in pre-historic digs were gaming devices. Crude dice have been discovered in Stone Age cultures of African bushmen, Australian aboriginals and Native Americans. Egyptian records show that dice were rolled in 3000 B.C. Chinese gambling has been traced to 2300 B.C., and they invented playing cards around 1000 A.D. There is historical evidence that an early form of keno helped finance construction of the Great Wall. Ancient Hebrews drew lots to determine God's will, which got Jonah thrown into the briny. With God as the pit boss, Moses used a lottery to divide up the nations of Israel. Roman soldiers gambled over Christ's robe.

Our daily gambles

We gamble every day of our lives—with the stock market, with business investments, with traffic, with our sanity in marriage. So what's so radical about investing a few dollars in the machines or tables in Las Vegas? There is something very tempting about putting a little money into a machine or onto a table and, with a bit of luck, getting a lot of money back. Out in the real world, we work forty hours a week to pay the bills and save up for a Las Vegas vacation. Once we get here, the idea of hitting a big jackpot or running a streak at the craps table, the idea of making money while having fun—that's seductive!

We personally do not gamble because we live here, and we know that even with lucky streaks, the odds eventually would catch up to us. Many residents do gamble; it's part of their recreation and most of them keep it in check. We aren't opposed to gambling; we have no moral stand on the issue one way or the other. If you choose to do so, invest only what you can afford to lose, have fun and good luck.

Incidentally, sixty to seventy percent of casino revenues come from slot and video poker machines—not necessarily because they have the worst odds, but because they're the most popular games in town. You don't need any gaming knowledge to drop a coin in a slot, pull a lever and watch the wheels spin.

"The good thing about slot machines is that they work twenty-four hours a day, seven days a week, including Jewish holidays," says hotel gaming consultant Burton M. Cohen. "They don't need uniforms, they don't belong to unions, and you don't have to feed them." They do get fed regularly, of course, by players.

Learn to play the game right

As Kenny Rogers sings in "The Gambler," the secret to gambling—and to life's choices—is knowing what to throw away and what to keep. Novice and nervous gamblers can learn by attending free gaming lessons, offered by many casinos. Among them are:

Aladdin—Baccarat, blackjack, craps and roulette; 736-0111.

Bally's—Baccarat, blackjack, craps, pai gow, pai gow poker, red dog and roulette; (702) 739-4111.

Caesars Palace—Blackjack, craps, pai gow poker, baccarat and roulette; (702) 731-7110.

Circus Circus—Blackjack, craps, pai gow and roulette; (702) 734-0410.

Flamingo Hilton—Baccarat, blackjack, craps, pai gow and roulette; (702) 733-3111.

Fitzgeralds—Blackjack, craps, red dog and roulette; 388-2400.

Four Queens—Blackjack, craps, keno, pai gow, poker, roulette and slots; (702) 385-4011.

Harrah's—Baccarat, blackjack, craps, pai gow, roulette and slots; (702) 369-5000.

Imperial Palace—Blackjack and craps; (702) 731-3311.

Lady Luck—Blackjack, craps, poker and roulette; 477-3000.

Las Vegas Hilton—Blackjack, craps, pai gow and roulette; (702) 732-5111.

MGM Grand—Blackjack, roulette and mini-baccarat; 891-7777.

New York New York—Blackjack, craps and roulette; 740-6969.

Palace Station—Blackjack, craps, pai gow, poker and roulette; (702) 367-2411.

Riviera—Baccarat, blackjack, craps, poker and roulette; (702) 734-5110.

Sahara—Blackjack, craps and roulette; (702) 737-2111.

Sam's Town—Poker; (702) 456-7777.

Stardust—Blackjack and craps; (702) 732-6111.

Stratosphere—Blackjack, craps and roulette; (702) 380-7777.

Slots A Fun—Blackjack, craps and pai gow; (702) 734-0410.

GAMES PEOPLE SHOULD & SHOULDN'T PLAY

If you've come to Las Vegas to gamble, or if you live here and you invest a certain amount of your paycheck in the casinos, you can reduce your losses and possibly even win occasionally by selecting the right game and playing it wisely. In our other book, *Nevada Discovery Guide*, we devote a lengthy chapter to "Beating the Odds." We consulted every available source on gambling and winning. We absorbed

Dr. Edwin O. Thorpe's now legendary *Beat the Dealer,* which started the blackjack card counting craze, and we read every other gaming book we could find.

From all of this emerged mathematical realities that are pretty well accepted by gaming experts. And from those realities we have created the Ten Best good bets and sucker bets. Incidentally, if you're new to gambling, you might want to read one of the many books written on the subject. You'll find a list of several recommended books and places where you can buy them at the end of this chapter. Also, we explain these games and card counting in our *Nevada Discovery Guide.*

The best gambling odds

1 **BLACKJACK** • This is the one game in which you can shift the odds slightly in your favor if you—literally—play your cards right. The key is to follow the flow of the cards to determine if high denomi nation or low denomination cards are likely to be dealt in the next hand, and adjust your bets accordingly. Blackjack is the most popular table game in Las Vegas and the eastest to learn. However, counting cards requires study and practice. The current trend is not to keep track of individual cards, but to note the *flow* of cards to determine which denominations likely will turn up in the next hand. This "rhythm counting" method works with multiple-deck blackjack, since you aren't trying to remember individual cards. Several books have been written on the subject, available at the outlets mentioned below.

2 **CRAPS** • This is a simple game with complicated betting pro-cedures. However, if you bet "pass or don't pass," combined with a free odds bet, the house advantage is less than one percent.

3 **BACCARAT** • High rollers love this glamorous game, which is very popular in Europe. Although the rules are complicated, betting is simple. You either bet with the bank (the house) or with the player, and the average house advantage is between one and two percent.

The worst gambling odds

4 **ROULETTE** • This is a simple game of betting on numbers, either individually or in combinations. Betting odd or even should mean that you win half the time but it doesn't, because of the "zero, double zero." Overall, the house advantage in roulette is 5.26 percent.

5 **SLOT MACHINES** • In a 1997 episode of ABC-TV's *Prime Time Live,* a fired employee of the State Gaming Control Board accused slot machine makers of rigging near misses to induce players to keep playing. The industry denied this, claiming that the individual in question had been caught rigging machines he was supposed to be inspecting in order to profit himself, and that he had copped a plea to get a lighter sentence. Whether or not, most slot machines aren't as user friendly as blackjack or baccarat. Overall, the one-armed bandits keep 16 to 20 percent of their take, although many casinos now claim 97 to 98 percent paybacks. These generally are on designed machines only, and only with maximum coin feed.

6 *VIDEO POKER MACHINES* • Video poker provides a little more flexibility than slot machines, since the player can control which cards to keep and which to throw away. A good poker player may be able to increase the odds slightly. Overall, however high payback slots probably yield more rewards than video poker machines.

7 *VIDEO BLACKJACK* • Similar to video poker, it allows you to take a hit or stand, just as in table blackjack. However, you can't count the flow or rhythm of cards since you're the only player, so the odds are probably worse than at regular blackjack.

8 *WHEEL OF FORTUNE* • Most gambling insiders say the wheel of fortune or "Big Six" is one of the industry's biggest sucker bets. The house edge ranges from 11 to 24 percent.

9 *BINGO* • The favorite game of Catholic charities and—in Las Vegas—of retired folks with time on their hands, bingo pays off big for the one winner in each round. Of course, it pays nothing to the losers, so it's an "all or nothing" game of chance. Gaming experts say the odds of winning at bingo are only slightly better than keno (see below).

10 *KENO* • Curiously, one of the most popular games in town offers the worst odds. Generally, the house keeps 20 to more than 40 percent of the money invested. The more "spots" you pick, the worse your odds.

THE ALLEGED TEN BEST PLACES TO GAMBLE

We say "alleged" because our selections are neither scientific nor proven in fact. Some casinos, like Binion's Horseshoe, have long-established reputations as places where serious gamblers like stack their chips. Others make this list because they claim to have extremely generous slot machine odds or loose gaming rules. This information was gathered from local sources and from advertised claims by the clubs.

We aren't gamblers; our expertise is limited, so don't blame us if you lose your lunch money.

A *caveat* **before we begin:** The Nevada State Gaming Commission does not set odds nor does it require casinos to report the odds they set on their machines. When a casino claims to have "the loosest slots in the world," you'll just have to take their word for it, along with a grain of salt. What you can accept as fact are claims by casinos that they use single decks in blackjack and employ liberal rules for their various table games, such as "crapless craps" (which sounds awful).

There is a presumption among many that downtown slot machines are more liberal than those on the Strip, although this has never been proven. (Insiders insist that small neighborhood casinos have the loosest machines, since this is where locals cash their paychecks. They won't keep coming back if they lose too fast.) It is a fact that blackjack rules generally are more liberal downtown than on the Strip.

We begin with the overall best gaming place, and then divide the rest into two categories—those with high limits that draw serious gamblers, and those with good odds that draw timid gamblers.

1 BINION'S HORSESHOE • *128 Fremont St. (at Casino Center Boulevard), (702) 382-1600.*

Founded by Texas gambler Benny Binion in 1951, the Horseshoe is considered by most high-stakes gamblers to be *the* place to parlay. "This is where the world comes to gamble," reads a sign and it certainly is. Binion's hosts the annual World Series of Poker each April. The globe's best poker players buy in for $10,000 and keep playing until someone has won the last chip.

Serious gamblers will find every legal parlaying device here, in high and low stakes—ranks of machines, blackjack, baccarat, a major poker room, large bingo hall, keno with a $200,000 pot and a race and sports book. The only music you'll hear at Benny's are the rattle of dice and the sound of coins clunking into hoppers. Binion's dominion catches them all—the serious high limit gamblers and mom and pop from Peoria with a few dollars, quarters or nickels to invest.

The best serious gambling venues

2 CAESARS PALACE • *3570 S. Las Vegas Blvd. (at Flamingo Road); (702) 731-7110.*

Caesars has been since its birth in 1966 a high-roller hangout and favorite party place of the rich, famous and sometimes infamous. Private jets bring stars and sheiks to high-roller suites. International zillionaires come to buy a stack of $10,000 denomination baccarat chips and sit down to a game attended by ladies and gentlemen in tuxedos.

They can drop $500 tokens into high-limit slot machines or play black-jack, craps and roulette with table limits ranging from $5 to $10,000. And the rest of you? There are great Roman ranks of quarter slot and video poker machines here, and if you search really hard, you'll find a few nickel ones.

3 **LAS VEGAS HILTON** • *3000 Paradise Rd. (east of Las Vegas Boulevard, next to Las Vegas Convention Center; (702) 732-5111.*

A great sea of blackjack, roulette and craps tables and ranks of slots and videos—all under crystal chandeliers—tells you this is a serious gaming place. Nickel machines are rare and table limits generally start at $5. At the far end is the Super Book, the world's largest sports and race book. Off to one side, in the Platinum Room, high rollers can drop $100-value tokens into slot machines. Unseen are posh high roller suites where those willing to invest substantial sums at the tables or machines are treated like royalty.

4 **THE MIRAGE** • *3400 S. Las Vegas Blvd. (adjacent to Caesars Palace); (702) 791-7111.*

The lushly decorated Mirage casino is a favorite venue for international high stakes gamblers, who are flown in and pampered in lavish high roller suites. One can play with $10,000 chips in a clubby baccarat room or feed slot machines with $100 tokens in another elegant side room. The rest of us, out in the main casino under a pretend South Seas canopy, will find the full range of gambling devices, with medium to high table limits, generally starting around $25. Slots and videos are in the 25-cent range and up. The huge race and sports book is divided into two sections, so bettors can choose between two simultaneous races. Dozens of video screens broadcast every race and sporting event within range of a TV camera.

5 **MGM GRAND** • *3799 S. Las Vegas Blvd. (at Tropicana); (800) 929-1111 or (702) 891-7777.*

If you're looking for action, you'll find several acres of it in the world's largest casino complex. Four theme gambling areas, equaling the size of four football fields, offer the full range of games of chance, and they tilt toward the high roller end. A few nickel slot machines are huddled near the entrance, although most of the machines start at a quarter and—in the high limit area—range up to $500 a pull. Table stakes vary from $5 to several thousand. Ladies and gents in tuxedos await high rollers in the clubby baccarat court, which is done up in marble and scalloped curtains. A gargantuan race and sports book and poker room complete this impressive gaming setup.

6 STARDUST HOTEL • *3000 S. Las Vegas Blvd. (Stardust Road); (702) 732-6111.*

If you like to play the ponies or bet for or against those darned Dallas Cowboys, this is your place. The Stardust has for decades been the "Home of the official Las Vegas line." It is here, in the cavernous race and sports book, that the odds are set on races and sports events for most of the rest of Nevada's gaming industry. At an adjacent sports handicappers' library, long computer printouts on the latest line, and even injury reports on players, dangle from the walls.

Gambling is a serious business throughout the huge casino. Table limits range from $5 to $3,000 and free gaming lessons are offered for the novices who want to play where the pros play. There are a few nickel slots; most begin at a quarter. In the clubby Carousel One high-limit area, you can drop $100 slugs into the machines. Serious gamblers will find a large poker room and a baccarat parlor.

Some casinos that claim the best odds

7 FIESTA CASINO HOTEL • *2400 N. Rancho Dr. (at Lake Mead Boulevard); (702) 631-7000.*

If you are to believe the annual *Las Vegas Review-Journal* readers' poll and claims by the hotel itself, the Fiesta is one of the best places in town for winners. In a recent readers poll, it was picked as the place with the best-paying slot machines and best video poker. The casino calls itself the "royal flush capital of the world" and it claims "up to" 99-percent payback on its dollar slots. It also has "can't lose blackjack," meaning that if you bust (as opposed to being beaten by the dealer), your bet carries over to the next hand.

8 LAS VEGAS CLUB SPORTS HOTEL & CASINO • *18 Fremont St. (at Main); (702) 385-1664.*

Billboards all over Las Vegas proclaim that the Las Vegas Club has the most liberal blackjack rules in town. Among the rules, which probably make sense to serious blackjack players, include doubling down on a 2, 3 or 4 card, splitting and re-splitting aces, and getting an automatic win with six cards under 21. The rules are posted on big signs above the blackjack pit. The Las Vegas Club offers all of the other games of chance, as well. The club also advertises 98 percent return on designated slot machines.

9 RIVIERA HOTEL • *2901 S. Las Vegas Blvd. (Riviera Avenue, opposite Circus Circus); (702) 794-9451.*

One of the oldest resort hotels on the Strip, the Riviera now claims to have the Strip's most generous slots. Banners inside and outside the casino proclaim that this has "The loosest slots at the loosest corner in the world." No payback percentages are given; the Riviera simply claims that its machines are set to the manufacturers' "highest paying program." The huge casino—third largest in the world—has something for every gambler, from medium and high limit tables to low limit slots and videos.

10 THE STRATOSPHERE ● 2000 S. Las Vegas Blvd. (upper end, at Main Street junction); (702) 380-7777.

It's easy for serious gamblers or anyone else to find the Stratosphere; just head for that high tower on the upper end of the Las Vegas Strip. While many come for the tower view, others are drawn by claims of generous returns on slots and video machines in the casino beneath it. The Stratosphere "certifies" 98 percent returns on most slots and more than 100 percent returns on designated 25-cent video poker machines, with maximum coins bet. (How do they do that? Wouldn't lucky gamblers eventually empty out all the cash?) The casino also claims a 99.5 percent return on all blackjack games. Signs state that this is the "best place to gamble on the planet." Is it? Does everyone come away a winner? Probably not, although it was busy with optimistic gamblers when we last passed through.

Gambling books and their sources

Dozens of books have been written about gambling, and you can find many of them at these outlets in Las Vegas:

Gamblers General Store, 800 S. Main St. (Gass), (800) 322-2447 or (702) 382-9903; **Gamblers Book Club**, 630 S. Eleventh, just off Charleston, (800) 522-1777 or (702) 382-7555; and **Gamblers Book Store** at 4460 W. Reno Ave., Suite J, (800) 816-6681 or (702) 365-1400.

Among the books we found to be most useful were these:

Beat the Dealer by Dr. Edward O. Thorp; Vintage Books. This is the book that started the blackjack card-counting rage a couple of decades ago. It has been updated, with some tear-out quick reference charts.

The Gambler's Playbook by Avery Cardoza; Cardoza Publishing. A slim book with not much depth, it's handy mostly as a quick reference guide to games and their terminology.

Win at the Casino by Dennis R. Harrison; Fell Publishers. Written with wit and humor, it explains card-counting in detail and discusses the odds of other gambling games.

The Winner's Guide to Casino Gambling by Edwin Silberstang; New American Library. This presents a good overall picture of the games people play and the odds of winning at them.

Part of the secret to success in life is to eat what you want and let the food fight it out inside.
— **Mark Twain**

Chapter four

OINK CITY
A DINING GUIDE

San Francisco claims to have more restaurants per capita than any other city it the world. This may be true, although it's a safe bet that Las Vegas residents and visitors consume more food than in any other place on the planet. It would appear that when folks aren't gambling, they're eating. Visitors and residents support dozens of buffets, scores of take-outs and specialty food stalls and hundreds of restaurants. With so many places to eat and so many people eating at them, you get the impression that no one who lives here ever cooks, except as a profession.

Many of the restaurants are excellent, rivaling those in any other major American city. The highly regarded Zagat survey added Las Vegas to its list of restaurant guides in 1996. "Fine and adventuresome dining has arrived in Las Vegas," writes Muriel Stevens, author of this Zagat guide. "Yet it wasn't so long ago that the local culinary landscape was as barren as the desert that surrounds the city."

The arrival of Wolfgang Puck's Spago from Los Angeles (Caesars Palace), Fog City Diner from San Francisco (Howard Hughes Center) and Emeril Lagasse's Fish House from New Orleans (MGM Grand) has encouraged other restaurateurs to look to Las Vegas. The theme restaurant scene is lively as well, with such places as the Hard Rock Café, Country Star American Music Grill and the All Star Café owned by six sports superstars.

Another distinctive feature of Las Vegas dining is that most of its restaurants are inside casino hotels. Every major resort has at least half a dozen dining venues, plus snack bars and buffets. Many of these are outstanding, such as Palace Court at Caesars, Hugo's Cellar at the Four Queens and, yes, the Steak House at Circus Circus. However, some of the town's finest restaurants are on the outside, like Chins in Fashion Show Mall, Andre's on Sixth Street near downtown and the Tillerman way out Flamingo Avenue.

Dining is relatively inexpensive in Las Vegas, and we aren't just talking about 99-cent shrimp cocktails and $1.49 casino breakfast specials. The average price of a typical restaurant meal is just over $20, according to the Zagat survey, compared with $25 in San Francisco, $24 in Los Angeles and nearly $30 in New York City. These figures refer to sit-down meals, of course. Nowhere else on the globe will one find greater extremes in food pricing. For instance, the Gold Spike snack bar offers shrimp cocktails for fifty cents. At the opulent Michael's in the Barbary Coast casino, a shrimp cocktail is $19. But of course, it's served flambée.

In the listings that follow, we use simple strings of dollar signs to indicate the price of a typical dinner with entrée, soup or salad and drink, not including wine or dessert: *$*=less than $10; *$$*=$10 to $19; *$$$*=$20 to $29; *$$$$*="Did you say you were buying?"

THE TEN VERY BEST RESTAURANTS

How can one possibly select the ten very best restaurants out of the thousands in Las Vegas? Obviously, these choices have to be quite arbitrary. The selections below represent our own dining experiences and recommendations of other non-commercial dining guides. We were *not* influenced by freebies, for we accepted not a single gratuitous nibble from any café in town.

1 EMERIL'S NEW ORLEANS FISH HOUSE ● MGM Grand, 3799 Las Vegas Blvd. (Tropicana); (702) 891-7374. Cajun/Creole; lunch and dinner daily. Reservations essential; major credit cards; $$$$.

So many people raved about Emeril Lagasse's *fishhaus* that we had to try it. We came away convinced that it is the finest restaurant in Las Vegas, beating out our longtime favorites such as the Tillerman, Chin's, Andre's and the Bootlegger. It's the premiere presence along the MGM Grand's newly designed Studio Walk—a pleasing study in

New Orleans French Quarter chic, clad in weathered brick. Diners can perch at a large raw bar open to the busy corridor, or adjourn to one of two inside dining rooms.

Wonderfully seasoned lobster and other seafood dishes are Lagasse's strong suite. If you're not in town long enough for repeat visits to sample such Cajun/Creole savories as lobster with onion marmalade, Cajun barbecued shrimp, steak with rémoulade and Cajun pork chops, try the multi-course sampler dinners. They're pricey, but just possibly worth it.

2 ANDRE'S • *401 S. Sixth St. (Lewis); (702) 385-5016. French; dinner nightly. Reservations essential; major credit cards; $$$$.*

Elegant and pricey, chef-owned Andre's occupies a California mission style cottage in a former residential area, with a pretty patio out front. Inside, it is pure Gaelic, fashioned as a genteel French country home. It's sought out by local power mongers and visitors seeking an exquisite French dining experience. Among its specialties are *chateaubriand*, stuffed pork tenderloin, marinated salmon *tartar* with cucumber salad, and rack of baby lamb. It has one of the finest wine cellars west of Bordeaux.

3 BATTISTA'S HOLE IN THE WALL • *4041 Audrie St. (Flamingo Road, behind the Flamingo Hilton); (702) 732-1424. Italian bistro fare; dinner nightly. Reservations accepted; major credit cards; $$.*

Never mind elegance; every Top Ten dining list must have a wonderfully funky local legend of a restaurant. To call the décor wildly eclectic would be gross understatement. Walls, ceilings and alcoves are busy with every imaginable kind of doodad from hanging baskets and buckets to personality photos to old vinyl records to boars heads to raffia bottles. It's a fun melee of singing servers, wandering accordion players and the sound of lively camaraderie. Meals, not fancy, are traditional Italian and ample, served with all the wine you can hold. Among the kitchen's better efforts are *al dente* pastas, veal *piccate*, chicken *cacciatore* and a lively chioppino. The restaurant was started in 1970 by Battista Localetti, a former opera singer turned truck driver turned restaurateur.

4 HUGO'S CELLAR • *Four Queens Hotel, 202 E. Fremont St. (Casino Center Boulevard); (702) 385-4011. American-continental; dinner nightly. Reservations recommended; major credit cards; $$$.*

Cellar indeed. Reached by a carpeted stairway from the main casino, Hugo's is more of an opulent sunken garden, dressed in brick, dark polished woods and brass. The look is clubby elegance and the cuisine is American-continental, with excellent steaks, medallions of beef tenderloin and seafood, plus European classics like lobster in white wine sauce with crushed red pepper and duck flambée. Nice touches: tiny cones of sorbet are served between courses, and chocolate dipped strawberries are served at the meal's end, whether or not you order dessert. Hugo's has one of the best wine lists in town.

5 **MICHAEL'S** • *Barbary Coast, 3595 S. Las Vegas Blvd. (Flamingo Road); (702) 737-7111. American-continental; dinner nightly. Scheduled seatings; reservations essential; major credit cards; $$$$.*

This is the most opulent and cozy dining space in town—an intimate arena of flocked wallpaper, crystal and high-backed burgundy chairs, accented by a striking leaded glass canopy. Downstairs off the main casino, it's completely isolated from the friendly chaos of Glitter City. The menu is traditional; don't look for sun dried tomatoes or air dried beef. Among the enticing and pricey entrées are beef sirloin in cognac sauce, fresh Main lobster with drawn butter and Florentine veal chops.

6 **MORTON'S OF CHICAGO** • *Fashion Show Mall, 3200 Las Vegas Blvd. (At the rear of the mall, off Spring Mountain Road); (702) 893-0703. American, mostly beef; dinner nightly. Reservations essential; major credit cards: $$$$.*

Probably more appealing to men than women, Morton's serves the finest steaks in town, in a dim, clubby atmosphere of old leather and polished oak. The Zagat survey described it as a "carnivore's paradise." Yet, with its subdued lighting and quiet corners, it's also one of the more romantic restaurants in Las Vegas, and we rate it so in Chapter eight, page 139. It features a fine wine list and personal wine lockers for residents. The menu is mostly Midwest corn-fed beef, although you can get excellent fresh seafood and well prepared lamb chops and chicken. Incidentally, don't go into the mall in search of Morton's; the entrance is on the outside, near the southeast corner, off Spring Mountain Road.

7 **PALACE COURT** • *Caesars Palace, 3570 S. Las Vegas Blvd. (Flamingo Road); (702) 731-7110. Continental; dinner nightly. Scheduled seatings; reservations required; major credit cards; $$$$.*

Far from the madding casino crowd, Palace Court offers both refuge and opulent continental dining. Unlike cozy, clubby Michael's (above), the Court is an elegance of space and light, with soft colors, brass and crystal accents, and a stained glass canopy overhead. Roman statuary, greenery and large murals complete this pleasing picture. While Michael's menu is more traditional, the Palace Court's is rather contemporary. The rack of lamb is spiced with sweet garlic, salmon is crust-roasted and accented with lemon vodka. If you're feeling particularly affluent, try one of the multiple course dinners, with wines matched to each serving.

8 **SPAGO** • *The Forum Shops at Caesars, 3500 S. Las Vegas Blvd. (Flamingo Road); (702) 369-6300. Italian nouveau, lunch and dinner nightly. Reservations for dinner only; major credit cards; $$$.*

From clubby Roman opulence, we adjourn to lighthearted Italian *nouveau*. Wolfgang Puck's Spago is informal, lively and definitely trendy. The casual café is open to the busy corridor of Caesars' Forum Shops promenade; the interior restaurant dining room is a mix of modern art and wrought iron. Puck's creations change daily. You might encounter smoked salmon pizza with dill cream, swordfish teriyaki, Sonoma lamb, or aged New York steak with goat cheese gratin. Some of Puck's delicious desserts never change; their names are painted on the café pillars as part of the decor. Try the white chocolate cheesecake or fresh peach cobbler with vanilla ice cream.

9 **STEFANO'S** • *Golden Nugget, 129 E. Fremont St. (Casino Center Boulevard); (702) 385-7111. Northern Italian; dinner nightly. Reservations recommended; major credit cards; $$$.*

While most gourmet rooms in Las Vegas casino resorts are subdued and clubby, Stefano's is bright and cheery. Murals enhance the walls and Venetian chandeliers add glitter to the ceilings. The waitstaff in this pleasant indoor slice of old Tuscany performs an occasional Italian aria, which is certainly appropriate, since the fare is of northern Italy. The *frutti di mare* mixed seafood dish is particularly excellent, as is the *osso bucco*. Also worthy of your gastronomic attention are the veal chops with porcine mushrooms and cheese, and veal scaloppini with prosciutto and asparagus. For dessert, the *crème brûlée* will have you singing along with your waiter.

10 **THE TILLERMAN** • *2245 E. Flamingo Rd. (Channel 10 Drive, just beyond Burnham); (702) 731-4036. American; mostly seafood; dinner nightly. Major credit cards; $$$.*

This locally popular seafood restaurant, housed in an oversized landscaped cottage, is several miles from the Strip, although locals and knowledgeable visitors have no trouble finding it. To get there, head east about four miles on Flamingo, and look for it on the right, just beyond a red Flamingo Business Park sign. Once inside, you'll find the best seafood in town, served in a pleasant garden setting. Ask your server what's just been flown in, since fresh fish arrives daily. Among its specialties are red snapper, Pacific salmon, sea bass and seafood pasta, plus steaks for landlubbers, and turf-n-surf for the undecided.

THE TEN BEST ETHNIC RESTAURANTS

Few people can agree on the authenticity of ethnic foods. What Americans consider Mexican cuisine has been altered by generations of Mexican-American cooks and by Southwest regional dishes. Although most Chinese restaurants in town are owned by Chinese, their cooking has been influenced by American tastes and the availability of native vegetables. And what's Italian these days? Certainly not smoked salmon pizza with dill cream, or air dried tomatoes and sun dried beef. (Or is it the other way around?) Yet, trendy "Italian" restaurants feature such items.

However, we're concerned more with variety than with authenticity. As more restaurants open in Las Vegas, they broaden the culinary landscape. It hardly rivals San Francisco or New York, but it has come a long way from the cowboy steak houses of the Fifties. We have no ethnic favorite; our selections are listed alphabetically by region.

1 CHINESE: Chin's • *Fashion Show Mall, 3200 Las Vegas Blvd. (Spring Mountain Road); (702) 733-8899. Also Charlie Chin's at Arizona Charlie's, 740 S. Decatur Blvd. (Charleston Boulevard); (702) 258-5200. Reservations accepted; major credit cards; $$$.*

Tola Chin serves the most creative Asian cooking in town at his fashionable Fashion Square Mall restaurant. Understated elegance best describes this place, with its soft colors, high-backed chairs and occasional touches of fine Asian art. Although the fare is essentially spicy Hong Kong style, he strays from tradition to offer American pepper steak and baby back ribs, with Oriental seasoning. Other specials are barbecued pork, steamed scallops, strawberry chicken and for dessert—lychee and cherries jubilee *flambée*, hardly a Chinese tradition. A branch at the neighborhood Arizona Charlie's casino hotel, called Charlie Chin's, is more mainstream Chinese and less expensive, with most dishes under $10.

2 FRENCH: Pamplemousse • *400 E. Sahara Ave. (between Paradise Road and Santa Rita Drive); (702) 733-2066. Dinner Tuesday-Sunday, closed Monday. Jacket and tie for gents. Reservations accepted, essential on weekends; major credit cards; $$$.*

Only in Las Vegas would the town's finest French restaurant be named for a grapefruit; that's what *Pamplemousse* means. Although the name is strange, the restaurant is country French cozy, housed in a cottage on the edge of an old residential district. Fabric walls are adorned with classic art. Patrons enter through a small wine cellar foyer, from where they are escorted to intimate, romantic dining areas with sheltering draperies. The cuisine is classic French with a few contemporary touches, such as salmon with orange sauce and curry, and roast duckling with green peppercorns and armagnac. Fresh seasonal fish is a specialty.

3 *GERMAN/SWISS: Alpine Village Inn* • *3003 Paradise Rd. (opposite Las Vegas Hilton); (702) 734-6888. Dinner nightly. Reservations accepted; major credit cards;* **$$**.

This charming restaurant, in business since 1950, is an architectural island in time. Housed in a Bavarian style cottage, it's surrounded by modern Las Vegas commercialism. The massive Las Vegas Hilton towers across Paradise Road and a *nouveau* cowboy store is next door. Inside, patrons will find Swiss-Bavarian murals on the walls and such standards as *wiener schnitzel, saurbraten*, barbecued pork chops and spiced stuffed duckling, plus a few American steaks. You expect someone in *liederhosen* to show up at any moment. The downstairs Rathskeller has a nightly piano player, and it serves lighter fare.

4 *INDIAN: Shalimar* • *3900 Paradise Rd. (in Citibank Park Plaza, opposite the First Interstate Tower); (702) 796-0302. Also at 2605 S. Decatur Blvd. (Sahara); (702) 252-8320. Lunch weekdays, dinner nightly. Reservations accepted; major credit cards;* **$$$**.

Shalimar is one of ten dining places here, making Citibank Park Plaza a virtual restaurant row. The list includes Hakase and Marrakech below. Shalimar's décor is rather spartan for an East Indian restaurant, although the spicy foods aren't. It features the traditional *tandoori* (Indian barbecue) lamb and chicken, seafood curries and nicely spiced vegetarian dinners. An inexpensive all-you-can eat luncheon is served on weekdays.

5 *ITALIAN: Il Fornaio* • *New York New York Hotel & Casino, 3790 S. Las Vegas Blvd. (Tropicana Avenue); (702) 740-6969. Lunch and dinner daily. Reservations accepted; major credit cards;* **$$** *to* **$$$**.

Las Vegas has several fine Italian restaurants where you can get properly *al dente* pasta and suitably spiced chicken *cacciatore*. However, none offers a more pleasing environment than Il Fornaio. This large restaurant sits under the lofty pretend sky of New York New York casino, with "outdoor" patio seating beside a moat. You can dine at water's edge while watching the lively casino action just beyond. Or you can sit inside the restaurant with its clean, modern Italian décor and busy open kitchen. Among Il Fornaio's specialties are *pollo Toscano* (chicken baked in a wood burning stove, spiced with rosemary, sage and wine), scaloppini with artichokes and lemon, and lightly done salmon marinated in olive oil and lemon. The menu also features a range of inexpensive pastas, pizzas and calzones—which explains our dual dollar sign listing. The adjacent Il Fornaio Caffe serves excellent espressos, lattes and Italian pastries.

6 *JAPANESE: Hakase* • *3900 Paradise Rd. (in Citibank Park Plaza, opposite the First Interstate Tower); (702) 796-1234. Lunch Tuesday-Friday, dinner Tuesday-Sunday, closed Monday. Reservations accepted; major credit cards; $$$.*

The look is spartan Japanese *moderne* with blond woods, *shoji* screens and deftly-placed folkware. Both table and tatami floor seating are available. The menu is typical *Nippon* and nicely presented. Offerings include *domburi* (lightly spiced meats and vegetables over rice), butterflied tempura shrimp and *shabu shabu* (a tasty broth of thin-sliced beef and vegetables). The sashimi is the freshest, tastiest and most nicely presented in town.

7 *JEWISH: Kosher Jerusalem Restaurant* • *1305 Vegas Valley Drive (just east of Maryland Parkway); (702) 696-1644. Lunch and dinner daily. Major credit cards; $$.*

This cheerful little storefront restaurant and deli serves assorted kosher schnitzels, stuffed bell peppers and kababs such as *shishlik*—spiced and marinated beef cubes on a skewer. It's bright and airy, with white walls accented by greenery and a little garden fountain in the center of the small dining room. The restaurant is located in a small strip mall called Plaza de Vegas.

8 *MEXICAN/SOUTHWESTERN: Mark Miller's Coyote Café and Grill Room* • *MGM Grand, 3799 Las Vegas Blvd. (Tropicana); (702) 891-7349. Café open daily from 9 a.m., Grill open for lunch and dinner. Reservations accepted; major credit cards; $$ to $$$.*

Celebrity chef Mark Miller has joined MGM Grand's "signature restaurants" with his distinctive Santa Fe *nouveau* style of Southwest cuisine. He blends such regional fare as blue corn, peppers and roasted yellow tomatoes with a variety of meats, wild game and seafoods to create delicious, spicy meals. They're served in an appealing setting of *faux* adobe, accented by *Southwest moderne* angular geometry, and trimmed with strings of bell peppers and dried corn clusters. The Grill Room is enclosed and cozy while the less-expensive Coyote Café is open to the newly designed Studio Walk.

9 *MIDEASTERN: Marrakech Moroccan* • *3900 Paradise Rd. (in Citibank Park Plaza, opposite the First Interstate Tower); (702) 737-5611. Dinner nightly. Reservations accepted; required on weekends; major credit cards; $$$.*

This is one of the most lushly attired restaurants in town, all done up in warm, mixed colors, with fabric walls, tented fabric ceiling and thick carpeting. You'll think you've stepped into a Mideastern carpet shop or a sheik's tent. Once inside, you sit Moroccan style on the floor before low tables, half-buried in soft cushions. Sexy belly dancers wriggle past the diners most evenings, starting at 7. When you aren't watch gyrating navels, you can dine on fare such as stuffed grape leaves, assorted spicy lamb dishes and spiced Moroccan lemon chicken, supported by pocket bread and dabs of *couscous*.

10 SOUTHEAST ASIAN: Thai Spice • *4433 W. Flamingo Rd. (in Arville Plaza at Arville Street); (702) 362-5308.*

The *Review-Journal's* "Best of Las Vegas" survey has twice voted this the best Thai restaurant in town. After several meals there, we agree. Spice indeed! Try the chicken curry, mint leaf chicken with chili, or the chili beef. Spiciness is rated on a scale of one to ten and you can ask your server to tone it down or bring it up. Of course, not all the dishes are spicy, nor all of them Southeast Asian. You'll find several familiar Chinese entrées such as Szechuan chicken, and sweet and sour pork, plus in-house specialties like pepper steak with oyster sauce and a pan fried rice noodle dish with great name—wet & wild noodles. This storefront restaurant is exceptionally cheery, done up in white and green, with live orchids in wall sconces

THE TEN BEST THEME RESTAURANTS

The theme is the thing with many restaurants in Las Vegas, from surfacing submarines to sunken Japanese villages. Some seem more preoccupied with gimmickry than gourmet cooking; others provide an abundance of both. None have really bad food, or we wouldn't list them.

1 PLANET HOLLYWOOD • *The Forum Shops at Caesars, 3500 S. Las Vegas Blvd.; (702) 791-7827. In the Forum Shops. Trendy American; lunch and dinner daily. Major credit cards; $$.*

Say, what planet is this, anyway? With its darkly wild décor and collection of Hollywood memorabilia, Planet Hollywood is the best theme restaurant in town and perhaps the best on—well—the planet. Decorator items aren't mere movie memorabilia; much of it is *strange* stuff. You can dine not far from the shriveled mummy of Norman Bates' mommy from the 1993 remake of *Psycho*, or sip a drink while admiring a badly mangled robotic Arnold Schwarzenegger from *Terminator II*. The menu, much lighter than the décor, ranges from typical American entrées to pizzas, burgers and pastas.

2 **ALL STAR CAFÉ** • *3785 S. Las Vegas Boulevard (near the MGM Grand at Tropicana); (702) 795-TEAM. American; lunch and dinner daily. Major credit cards; $$.*

Las Vegas resident Andre Agassi thought it would be fun to open a thematic sports bar and restaurant, so he invited a few friends to join him—Wayne Gretzky, Ken Griffey, Jr., Joe Montana, Shaquille O'Neal and Monica Seles. The All Star Café is more of a sports happening than a sports bar. Although current games are carried on a dozen or so monitors, they're almost overpowered by thudding rock music and a great oval ring of monitors along the upper walls that project non-stop "great moments in sports." These moments can be anything from Agassi slamming an ace and Montana hitting Rice with a bomb, to scenes of the America's Cup yachting race and cartoons of Goofy taking a header on the slopes. Think of all of this as sports MTV.

When you've finished your drink or basic American luncheon or dinner, stroll around to admire the sports memorabilia on the main floor and along stairways leading to a pair of upstairs dining rooms. Who knows? You might see Andre, Wayne, Ken, Shaquille, Joe and Monica seated at a corner booth, discussing their stock portfolios.

3 **BENIHANA VILLAGE** • *In the Las Vegas Hilton, 3000 Paradise Rd. (Riviera Boulevard); (702) 732-5111. Japanese-American; dinner nightly. Reservations accepted; major credit cards; $$$.*

This is not a gimmick theme but a handsomely done version of a Japanese temple garden, with a traditional *tori* arch, a trickling stream, tile-roofed temple structures, stones and stone lanterns. Two dining areas and the Kabuki Lounge bar are terraced above this sunken gardens, giving most patrons a view of the pleasing setting. The Japanese Steakhouse serves *hibachi* steak, shrimp and chicken dinners prepared at table side and the Seafood Grille offers grilled seafood, tempura (batter fried) seafood and *sashimi*. The restaurant is just off the south end of the main casino.

4 **COUNTRY STAR AMERICAN MUSIC GRILL** • *3720 S. Las Vegas Blvd. (Harmon); (702) 740-8400. American country; lunch and dinner daily. Major credit cards. $$.*

Well dang my britches if this ain't the best boot-stompin' country bar and grill this side of Nashville, and possibly even Branson. This Hard Rock Café for country fans brims with cowboy regalia and its distinctive circular ceiling is hung with TV monitors twanging out country videos. The waitstaff appears to be dressed for the next hoedown. The youthful, clean-scrubbed Country Star Dancers demonstrate their skill with the cowboy two-step for patrons, or they strut their boots on a patio out front for the benefit of the passing Las Vegas Boulevard crowds. All this and grub, too? Certainly. Country Star serves boat-sinking portions of excellent ribs, barbecued chicken and steaks. Try the pork ribs with Jack Daniels sauce; just ask for the Tracy Lawrence special.

5 *DIVE!* • *In Fashion Show Mall (South Las Vegas Boulevard at Spring Mountain Road); (702) 369-2270. American; the sub "Surfaces Daily," serving lunch and dinner. Major credit cards; $$.*

This thing looks rilly silly, poking its snout through the outer wall of the otherwise fashionable Fashion Show Mall. Its façade is a Tune Town version of a submarine, with portholes and a pretend hatch, through which customers enter. It's a Steven Spielberg creation with appropriate special effects. It hisses and gushes periodically at pass-ersby. Those inside dine to the sounds of periodic crash dives that almost makes one want to reach for a life jacket. Life jacket? Don't be silly, Willy, you're in a sub! The place appeals to kids and tourists, with a menu that should please them—pastas, oven-roasted entrées, pizzas, barbecued ribs and burgers.

6 *GARDUÑO'S CHILI PACKING CO.* • *In Fiesta Casino Hotel, 2400 N. Rancho Dr. (at Lake Mead Boulevard); (702) 631-7000. Mexican; lunch and dinner daily. Major credit cards; $$.*

South-of-the-border decorator schemes are common for Mexican restaurants, although Garduño's look is really quite exceptional. The entrance is fashioned as a Mexican courtyard done in proper tans and beiges. Once inside the restaurant, you appear to be outside, seated in a cheery Mexican village with brick-lined arches, garlands of chilies and pretend plants. Although it's part of the Fiesta Casino, it's oper-ated by the Garduño family of Albuquerque, where their original res-taurant is located.

Las Vegans like the place and voted it as the Best Mexican restau-rant in a recent *Review-Journal* poll. We like it as well, particularly for its salsa bar with twenty-four different varieties, and certainly for its ambiance and rather inexpensive fare. However, we favor the locally-owned Ricardo's for Mexican food; you'll find branches at Tropicana and Eastern (798-4515), in the Meadows Mall (870-1088) and at Decatur and Flamingo (871-7119).

7 *HARD ROCK CAFÉ* • *4475 Paradise Rd. (Harmon Avenue); (702) 733-8400. Light American; lunch and dinner daily. Major credit cards; $$.*

If you're a rock fan, you'll think you've gone to MTV heaven when you step into this wonderfully loud and raucous museum of rock 'n' roll. Check out the gold flake 1960 Cadillac Eldorado convertible parked above the bar, and the chaotic display of motorcycles, gold records, rock star costumes, instruments and other memorabilia. Most cafés Hard Rock were installed into existing buildings. This one was built from the ground up in 1990, with a free-standing 88-foot guitar as a marquee. The menu is rock 'n' roll American—burgers, barbecued chicken, chops and steaks, and Hard Rock's signature baby back ribs. The café was joined in 1995 by the Hard Rock Hotel and Casino, just across the parking lot.

8 ISIS ● *In the Luxor, 3900 S. Las Vegas Blvd. (Tropicana); (702) 262-4773. Continental; dinner nightly. Reservations advised. Major credit cards.*

Isis was the beautiful wife of the god Horus and this elegantly cozy café in the Luxor pyramid pays suitable homage to her, depicting the grand era of the Egyptian empire. One enters the restaurant through a stone honor guard of temple statuary; display cases along the dining room walls contain skillfully rendered copies of tomb artifacts. A small statue of Isis is a focal point, occupying an octagonal display case in the center of this circular restaurant. Despite the Egyptian theme, the menu is mostly continental. The only entrée that hints of North Africa is a sesame chicken dish. Otherwise, the land of the pharaohs is represented in culinary gimmickry—Ramses' Torch coffee and Baked Egypt (a baked Alaska in the shape of a pyramid).

An aside, having absolutely nothing to do with Las Vegas: When we were touring Egypt several years ago, our guide told us a great story about the gods. Seth wanted to get rid of his brother Horus, so he chopped him into fourteen pieces and buried thirteen of them in different places around Egypt. The fourteenth piece, his—uh—private part, was thrown into the Nile. Horus' faithful wife Isis managed to find all of the parts except that one item which, unfortunately, had been devoured by a catfish.

"So Isis, being a great goddess, was able to put heem back together and bring heem back to life," our guide said, then he added with an Egyptian shrug, "But the marriage, eet was never quite the same again."

9 MOTOWN CAFÉ ● *In New York New York Casino Hotel, 3790 S. Las Vegas Boulevard (Tropicana Avenue); (702) 740-6969. American; breakfast buffet from to 7 to 10:30; full table service for lunch and dinner. Recorded "Motown sounds" and live entertainment. Major credit cards; $$.*

This is a lively, fun theme restaurant, with golden statues of such performers as the Jackson Five, the Supremes and Boyz II Men. The Four Tops wave from their white Lincoln Continental convertible, and a stairway glitters with golden record insets. Photos and memorabilia of such stars as Marvin Gaye and Stevie Wonder are scattered about. While you dine or have a drink at the glossy bar, you can watch old black and white videos of the Jackson Five, Supremes and others in performance. The menu is "light American," from shrimp Creole and chicken pasta to assorted burgers and other sandwiches and salads.

10 **HIPPO & THE WILD BUNCH** • *4503 Paradise Road (near Harmon, opposite the Hard Rock Café); (702) 731-5446. Light fare; lunch and dinner daily. Major credit cards. $$.*

Georges la Forge, owner of the elegantly intimate Pamplemousse, also created this wild jungle-clad party place that's popular with the local college crowd and the current generation of yuppies. The look is Tune Town Wizard of Oz beach shack, with a battered corrugated tin roof, pretend bamboo walls, chubby cartoonish trees, animal footprints and random splashes of color. Two patios one on Harmon for traffic watchers and the other in the rear shaded by some real vegetation— invite *al fresco* dining and drinking. The fare is American beach party—pastas, 'burgers and pizza.

THE TEN BEST LOCAL FAVORITES

"So, where do the locals go?" It's a question often asked by tourists. In Las Vegas, they go where the tourists go, because it's impossible to get away from thirty million people a year. However, there are some local favorites, which may or may not have been discovered by tourists. If guidebook authors keep writing about them, they soon will be.

1 **THE GREEN SHACK** • *2504 E. Fremont St. (just southeast of Charleston Boulevard); (702) 383-0007. American; dinner Tuesday-Sunday, closed Monday. MC/VISA; $$.*

Looking more like a long and skinny mom and pop motel than a restaurant, the Green Shack is the oldest café in town, and an enduring favorite of Las Vegans. Opened in 1930, it fed Hoover Dam construction workers who came to town on the Boulder Highway to party. Western doodads hang from the walls inside and out and the pleasantly cluttered dining room walls are hung with historic photos. This is a basic American meat and potatoes place, noted for its fried chicken and giblets, batter fried shrimp and steak. Hefty dinners are served with biscuits and honey.

2 **BOB TAYLOR'S ORIGINAL RANCH HOUSE** • *6250 Rio Vista (eleven miles north; Ann Road exit from I-95); (702) 645-1399. Western American; dinner Tuesday-Sunday. Major credit cards; $$$.*

You must drive several miles north of town through former open desert to find this properly rustic ranch style restaurant. North Las Vegas subdivisions are surrounding the place like cattle rustlers after a herd, yet the "ranch" succeeds in keeping its country appearance, with peeled log fences and a tree-shaded yard and garden in front. Inside, the look and the menu are rustic American West, with a strong focus on mesquite broiled steaks, plus chops, chickens and seafood. The Ranch House has survived since 1955 and hopefully will survive the current subdivision attack. To get there, drive eleven miles north on the U.S. 95 freeway to the Ann Road exit, go right about half a mile to Rio Vista and then left one mile.

3 CHANG OF LAS VEGAS • *3055 S. Las Vegas Blvd. (in the rear of Gold Key mall, opposite the Stardust, at Cathedral Way); (702) 731-3388. Chinese; lunch and dinner daily; dim sum daily from 10 a.m. MC/VISA, AMEX; $$.*

Cool and stylish describes the look of this restaurant which, despite its Strip location, is frequented mostly by locals. Flower arrangements adorn tables laid with white nappery, and a few Asian *objets de art* grace the walls. The fare is mostly gently-spiced Cantonese, although a few lively Szechuan dishes are on the menu, such as hot and sour soup and kung pao chicken or shrimp. Dim sum aficionados, including local Chinese, come for those tasty "little heart" morsels, served daily from 10 a.m.

4 CROWN & ANCHOR PUB • *1350 E. Tropicana Blvd. (just beyond Maryland Parkway); (702) 739-8676. British "pub grub" and American; lunch and dinner daily. Major credit cards; $$.*

The "Anchor" is an authentic British pub occupying a white stucco cottage in the middle of growing eastside Las Vegas. Locals patronize the place for its more than eighty different international brews—thirty on tap and the balance in bottles. They come here to eat, as well. The Britts, Irish, Welsh and Scots go for familiar bangers and mash, shepherd's pie, fish and chips, and Cornish pasties. The rest of you tilt toward basic, hearty and inexpensive American fare. The Anchor has all the elements of a local hangout—lively bar, comfortable dining area, friendly staff and a couple of dart boards. The look is aquatic English.

5 O'ROSIE'S RESTAURANT • *5795 W. Tropicana Ave. (between Decatur and Jones, in the Galleria Plaza); (702) 253-1899. Traditional American; lunch weekdays, dinner Tuesday-Saturday. Major credit cards; $$.*

Well-prepared steaks, chickens, chops and seafood are served in this attractive café, which is little known beyond its westside neighborhood. Although it's a few miles from the Strip, finding it is no chore. Head west on Tropicana through the Decatur intersection and watch on your left for the Galleria Plaza; it's half a mile short of Jones. The restaurant occupies a corner cottage at the edge of the street. Despite its Irish name, the look is mostly early American, with exposed ceiling trusses, drop fans and lamps, wainscotting and café curtains.

6 **OUTBACK STEAKHOUSE** • *3685 W. Flamingo Road (opposite the Rio, just east of Valley View Boulevard); (702) 253-1020. Also locations at 4141 S. Pecos Rd. (Flamingo), (702) 898-3801; 1950 N. Rainbow Blvd. (Lake Mead Boulevard), (702) 647-1035; 8671 W. Sahara Ave. (Durango Drive), (702) 228-1088; and in Henderson at 4423 E. Sunset Rd. (between Mountain Vista Street and Green Valley Parkway); (702) 451-7808. Dinner nightly; major credit cards; $$.*

When local residents were asked by the *Las Vegas Review-Journal* to select their favorite steakhouse, this fast growing Australian theme franchise led the list. Most Outbacks are housed in prim cottages in or near shopping centers, with polished wood interiors accented by kangaroo-boomerang-shark jaw regalia. The menu is mostly steaks and chops with Aussie accents such as cheese-dipped fries and fried onions in batter. One respondent to a Zagat survey said the fare was "mostly grease," although that's unkind. To avoid anything greasy, ask the folks to put another shrimp on the barbie.

7 **PIERO'S** • *355 Convention Center Dr. (Paradise Road, adjacent to the Beach nightclub); (702) 369-2305. Italian; dinner nightly. Reservations recommended; major credit cards; $$$$.*

This clubby Italian restaurant dressed in dark woods and old world elegance is popular with local power brokers and well-heeled conventioneers, who cross the street from the nearby Las Vegas Convention Center. Some say the waiters can be rather haughty. Well-established locals may feel more comfortable here than visitors, although we were treated warmly. The fettuccine, calamari, *osso bucco* and cioppino rich with mussels, clams, lobster bits and scallops are among the best west of Naples. A few American dishes also emerge from the menu, including blue crab cakes, Maine lobster and other fresh seafood, plus steaks.

8 **POPPA GAR'S** • *1624 W. Oakey Blvd. (Western Avenue); (702) 384-4513. American regional; breakfast, lunch and dinner Monday-Saturday. No reservations or credit cards; $$.*

To find this folksy American diner, run by 90-year-old-plus Poppa Garland, take Wyoming Avenue west from the upper end of South Las Vegas Boulevard to its merger with Western and Oakey, just short of the I-15 freeway. Gar's is in a strip mall called Oakey Center, to your right. Once there, you'll find a wood-paneled diner busily decorated with game trophies and framed photos (animals heads on the wall; people in the photos). The menu wanders from spicy Cajun to game to Mexican to basic American steaks and 'burgers. You can perch at a counter or settle into a Naugahyde booth, if you don't mind a sad-faced elk watching you eat.

9 **SERGIO'S ITALIAN GARDENS** • *1955 E. Tropicana Ave. (just east of Spencer); (702) 739-1544. Italian; dinner nightly. Reservations accepted; major credit cards; $$$.*

Housed in a Colonial Spanish strip mall a block beyond the Liberace Museum, this large, open restaurant appeals to older generation Las Vegans who like a comfortable environment and hearty Italian fare. High ceilings, a garden-like setting, Roman columns and white lattice dividers dress up this long-established restaurant. The fare is predictable and hearty—assorted pastas, an excellent calamari, *osso bucco* and chicken cacciatore, plus a couple of good steaks.

10 **VIVA MERCADO'S** • *6182 W. Flamingo Rd. (just beyond Jones Boulevard, in an Albertson's mall on the right); (702) 871-8826. Also an outlet in Green Valley Town Center, 4500 E. Sunset Road at Green Valley Parkway, Henderson; (702) 425-6200. Mexican; lunch and dinner daily. Reservations accepted; MC/VISA, AMEX; $ to $$.*

South of the border, a *mercado* is a market. In Las Vegas, it's a cozy and lively Mexican restaurant and cantina. The café, draped with things *Latino* is divided into several sections, adding more coziness to an already small dining area. Drop lamps add dim intimacy to high-backed booths. The place may be intimate, but it isn't quiet; a lively bar occupies the rear of the dining room. Mercado serves the essential smashed beans and rice dishes, a few American entrées and several in-house specials. Try the *carne asada*, and pork loin marinated in garlic.

THE TEN BEST RESTAURANT ROWS AND FOOD COURTS

Is it restaurant rows or restaurants row? Some of the casino resorts focus their restaurants in one area instead of scattering them around, which we think is a great idea. Most post their menus outside, so you can compare selections and prices without wandering all over the property. Food courts also are becoming popular, with assorted ethnic takeouts and specialty food stalls surrounding a central eating area.

There aren't ten really good restaurants row or food courts in Las Vegas casinos, so they're going to have to share this category. We start with the best of each, and then continue with the rest.

1 THE BEST RESTAURANT ROW: MGM Grand • 3799 S. Las Vegas Blvd. (at Tropicana); (702) 891-7777.

Several renowned chefs have contributed their "signature" cafés to create the city's most impressive restaurant row, called Studio Walk. The list includes Mark Miller's Southwest style Grill Room (dinner) and adjacent Coyote Café (breakfast, lunch and dinner), a reincarnation of Hollywood's clubby Brown Derby (lunch and dinner), Emeril Lagasse's New Orleans Fish House (Cajun and Creole; lunch and dinner), the Dragon Court Restaurant (Chinese; dinner only); Franco Nuschese's Tre Visi and La Scala (upscale Italian; lunch and dinner). These trendy eateries share a broad hallway with several shops; see Chapter twelve, page 180. The newest "signature" edition of MGM Grand restaurants, Wolfgang Puck's Café, isn't on the restaurant row; it's out among the casinos, sitting back-to-back with the baccarat room.

1 THE BEST FOOD COURT: New York New York • 3790 S. Las Vegas Boulevard (Tropicana Avenue); (702) 740-6969.

We picked New York New York as the best theme casino resort in Chapter two, and that theme certainly carries into its large food court. Called Village Eateries, it's fashioned as a Greenwich Village street scene, complete with plastic trees and old storefront façades. Tables line the edges of these brick and cobblestone "streets." Food selections are New Yawkish as well, although they travel considerably beyond. Selections include Greenberg's Deli, Broadway Burgers, Gonzales Tex-Mex Grill, Tako's noodles and teriyaki, Broadway burgers, a Mango Hut that serves fruit slushes, Greenwich Village Coffee Company and a pizza and pasta venue.

The next best restaurants row

3 ALADDIN HOTEL & CASINO • 3667 S. Las Vegas Blvd. (opposite Bellagio); (702) 734-3583.

Most Aladdin dining venues are neatly arrayed along the northern end of the main casino—the left end as you face it from the street. Working right to left, you'll encounter the 24-hour Oasis Coffee Shop; Joe's Diner with a cute 1950s look (lunch and dinner); Sun Sun, serving Chinese, Vietnamese and Korean fare (dinner only); Wellington's Steakhouse with a dark, cross-timbered British look (dinner only); and Fisherman's Port (dinner only) with a cute little bar adjacent.

4 **EXCALIBUR** • *3850 S. Las Vegas Blvd. (Tropicana Avenue);* (702) 597-7777.

A nice feature of Excalibur's rather small restaurant row is its location on an upper level called the Medieval Village, away from the commotion of the casino and kiddie arcades. Among its offerings are Sir Galahad's prime rib and steaks (dinner only), Sherwood Forest Café (breakfast, lunch and dinner), Lance-a-Lotta Pasta (Italian, dinner only), Café Espresso, and Wild Bill's Saloon and Steak House with a Western theme and live country entertainment at night. The Roundtable buffet also occupies this floor.

5 **IMPERIAL PALACE** • *3535 S. Las Vegas Blvd. (between Sands Avenue and Flamingo Road, opposite Caesars Palace); 731-3311.*

The five palace restaurants are conveniently clustered the fifth floor Dining Plaza. Selections are the Seahouse (obviously seafood), Ming (Chinese), Pizza Palace (what else?), Embers (steak and lobster) and the Rib House (barbecue specialties). The five restaurants serve dinner only. The plaza itself has a small bar with cocktail tables and a grand piano, where you can sit and sip while waiting for your table.

6 **TEXAS STATION GAMBLING HALL & HOTEL** • *North Rancho Drive at Lake Mead Boulevard; (702) 631-1000.*

This suburban casino's restaurant row provides interesting visual appeal—if you look down. The restaurants are arrayed along one wall and the walkway patterns change to match each café's personality. Begin at the Market Street Buffet and walk past a waterfall (simulated plank floor), past the cashiers cage (simulated brick) to the Yellow Rose Café (Texas-American fare, open 24 hours; simulated paving blocks). Continue past a lobby bar and Spanish colonial fountain to the Laredo Cantina and Café (dinners only; beautiful patterned Mexican tile), and thence to the Stockyard Steak and Seafood House (dinner only; paving stones) and San Lorenzo Restaurant (dinner only) and pizza take-out (morning through evening; rough, glossy tile).

The next best food courts

7 **CHUCKWAGON FOOD COURT: Sam's Town Hotel & Gambling Hall** • *5111 Boulder Highway (at Nellis Boulevard); (702) 456-7777.*

This attractive Western theme food court off Mystic Falls Park has a Calamity Jane's Ice Cream parlor with a Coca-Cola museum, Sam's Barbecue Pit, Chinese Express, a pizza parlor and large drink station.

8 *LA PIAZZA: Caesars Palace* • *3570 S. Las Vegas Blvd. (at Flamingo Road); (702) 731-7110.*

The food court at Caesars is rather small, although it may be the prettiest of the casino take-outs, trimmed in red, blue and pink neon. Offerings include a French bake shop, New York style deli, Chinese and Japanese takeout, Mexican tacoria, Italian pasta and pizza place and an American takeout featuring rotisserie chicken.

9 *MONACO GARDEN: Monte Carlo* • *3770 Las Vegas Blvd. (north of Tropicana Avenue); (702) 730-7777.*

Small and attractively styled with Roman column façades, the Monte Carlo food court features Häagen-Daz ice cream, McDonald's, Nathans, Sbarro's Italian take-out and a bagel café. The food stations curve around a central eating area. For sugary dessert, you'll find a candy store at the far end.

10 *SAHARA CASINO FOOD COURT* • *2535 S. Las Vegas Blvd. (Sahara Avenue); (702) 737-2111.*

If you're traveling with kids, the odds are that they'll want to check out the food courts. With this in mind, the folks at the Sahara stationed their take-out venue just off the large video arcade. It's at the southwest corner of the casino, and some of the tables have views of Las Vegas Boulevard. Among its offerings are Subs and Spuds, Burger King, Weinerschnitchel, Panda Express (a Chinese takeout), a Pizza Hut, TCBY yogurt shop and an espresso booth.

THE BUFFET BUSINESS

When most people talk about food in Las Vegas, they don't talk about Spago or Emeril's Fish House. They talk about *buffets*, probably the best dining bargains in the land. Most are expansive yet inexpensive spreads, similar to midnight buffets on cruise ships, without the ice sculptures. However, in Las Vegas, you don't have to wait until midnight to pig out, and you have a choice of dozens of buffets.

At last count, there were about fifty in Las Vegas and surrounding Clark County communities. Most serve three meals a day, while some have a two meal policy on weekends—morning to noon brunch, followed by dinner. Most buffets include soft drinks and coffee but not alcohol, although a cocktail waitress usually works the area. (A few include one drink with the meal.)

Most buffet foods suffer the usual steam table trauma that you may recall from your dining days in military mess halls. We've found that most buffets seafoods and pastas are overcooked. However, some of the better operations now feature active food stations, where fresh fare is prepared as you watch. If wine with dinner is important, check with your hostess before you get too comfortable. Some buffets have drink service, while others require that you bring your drink from a nearby bar. (Who can find the proper wine for a meal of Chinese stir-fry, a taco, shredded pork, Italian sausage, fried chicken and over-cooked salmon? We usually have ice tea at our buffets.)

The more popular buffets and the cheaper ones often suffer long waiting lines, which seems ironic since this keeps people away from the machines and tables. To avoid the wait, go very early or very late. A few buffets, like Fitzgeralds downtown, use a waiting list, so you're free to wander about the casino until you're called for supper.

If you've never been to a Las Vegas buffet before, the ritual is simple. You stand in line, pay the cashier and then you're escorted to a table. (All buffets have non-smoking and smoking areas.) Once you're assigned a table, make note of where it is—we've been known to forget—and head for the serving lines. About the time you return with your first heavily-laden plate, a server will come by and take your drink order. A few buffets have self-service drink areas.

Ten Buffet Survival Tips

1 Unless you enjoy standing in long lines, listening to your stomach growl, avoid buffets on Friday or Saturday nights. If you're in town only on those nights, try some of the outlying casino buffets, which often are less crowded. Some may have better food at lower prices than popular downtown and Strip resorts, although this isn't the rule. Despite a popular local notion that neighborhood casinos offer better deals, we've found some pretty mediocre food in the hinterlands.

2 Before committing your appetite and your cash, slip into the buffet and check the variety and quality of the food. If the prepared dishes look tired and dried out, move on. (You generally can get into the buffet through the exit and mingle unnoticed with the paying customers. However, it is not cool to sample the food.)

3 Once you've chosen a buffet and are assigned to a table, reconnoiter the food line again to determine what items you'd like to try. Some larger buffets have thirty or more different dishes, so remind yourself—as your mother once did—that your eyes are probably bigger than your stomach. Buffet novices tend to take everything they see on the first pass, overloading their plates and tummies. There's no room left for dessert or new items that may be added to the line later.

4 Don't fill up on ordinary stuff. We're often surprised to see buffet patrons piling on leaf salads, mashed potatoes and beans. Good grief, guys, you can get that stuff at home! Part of the fun of a buffet is sampling a variety of dishes, particularly ethnic entrées.

5 Please don't embarrass yourself by taking a lot more than you can possibly eat.

6 If you really like seafood, don't eat any of it at a buffet. We've rarely found seafood that hadn't been cooked to the consistency of an artgum eraser. Delicate fish is particularly susceptible to steam table trauma. You might have better luck at an all-seafood buffet, where the chefs may be more focused on proper fish preparation. Also, the dishes turn over more quickly, so they aren't overcooked while languishing on the serving line.

7 You're expected to use a clean plate each time you go back for a refill, but don't leave your silverware on your used plate. It may be scooped up while you're gone and you'll wind up eating with your fingers.

8 Ignore the sugar free offerings at the dessert table, which virtually all buffets feature, and go for the real sweets. If you were serious about your diet, you wouldn't be at a buffet.

9 Tip your server about a dollar or two per person. All they really provide is beverage service, so the usual fifteen percent tip isn't expected.

10 Try not to stare at the fat lady inhaling a heaping plateful of food.

THE TEN BEST CASINO BUFFETS

In selecting our ten favorite buffets, we've limited ourselves to dinners for more consistent comparisons. Since one steam table pork chop is pretty much like another, we considered not only food quality and variety, but setting, ambiance and service in making our choices. Price was not a factor here; we list the Ten Best cheap buffets in the next chapter. Finally, we do not regard buffets as a numbers game; we prefer those with a few good entrées over those with dozens of choices. After all, how many different salads and hot dishes can a person eat?

As we reviewed the town's many buffets, we gained considerable insight into the Las Vegas food scene—and about ten pounds each.

1 **FIESTA CASINO HOTEL** ● *2400 N. Rancho Dr. (at Lake Mead Boulevard); (702) 631-7000. Festival Buffet: Breakfast Monday-Friday 7 to 11, $3.99; lunch Monday and Wednesday 11 to 2:30, and Tuesday, Thursday and Friday 11 to 3:30, $6.49; dinner week nights 3:30 to 10 and weekends 3 to 10, $8.99; weekend champagne brunch 7 to 3, $7.99.*

This is the best buffet in town, both in the variety and the quality of the food. Yet, it's surprisingly inexpensive and it's served in a cheerful Mexican village setting with hanging piñatas, strings of lights, Spanish arches and murals. The food is exceptional for a buffet, and most of it is issued from live serving stations. You can get Chinese stir-fry, freshly carved meats, fresh-sizzled hamburgers and even a variety of pizzas by the slice. Other offerings include Cajun specialties, rotisserie or fried chicken, barbecued ribs, an excellent shredded pork and even a gourmet coffee and espresso bar. The dessert section is extensive and tasty; we particularly liked a boysenberry pie, assorted Neapolitans and tasty peanut butter cookies.

2 **BALLY'S LAS VEGAS** ● *3645 S. Las Vegas Blvd. (Flamingo Road); (702) 739-4111. Big Kitchen Buffet: Breakfast 7 to 11, $8:95; lunch 11 to 2:30, $9:95; dinner 4:30 to 10, $13.95.*

The Big Kitchen Buffet is aptly named, since the food line is inside a working kitchen, where servers are on hand to replenish the hot dishes and carve fresh slices of meat. This is one of a few buffets in town that has a view; ask for seats in the lower section near windows on the boulevard, or at the railing above. The Big Kitchen Buffet has the usual huge selection of American salads, hot foods and desserts, plus Asian stir fry at Wong's Wok, which is off to the right of the main serving lines. Service is very attentive at the Big Kitchen, and you can get wine or beer from your server, without waiting for a cocktail waitress to show up. Some of our favorite entrées were stir-fry Italian sausage with onions and peppers, a spicy rotisserie chicken and, for desert, hot bread pudding with brandy sauce.

3 **BOOMTOWN HOTEL, CASINO & RV RESORT** ● *3333 Blue Diamond Rd. (I-15 exit 33); (702) 263-7777. Blue Diamond Buffet: Breakfast 7 to 11, $3.99; lunch 11:30 to 3:30, $4.99; dinner 4 to 10, $8.99.*

We like the cutely rustic Western décor of this buffet, as well as the large selection of well-prepared foods. The dinner buffet is built around all-you-can eat prime rib, although many other hot entrées also are available. They range from Swedish meatballs, stuffed bell peppers and chicken fajitas to Asian stir fry, rice pilaf and country fixin's such as fried chicken and gravy. The salad bar is generous, offering ambrosia, crab salad, pasta salad and the usual leafy things. The dessert selection is small but tasty; our favorites were apple pie, a lemon cherry tart and build-it-yourself strawberry shortcake.

4 GOLDEN NUGGET HOTEL & CASINO • 129 Fremont St.

(at Casino Center Boulevard); (702) 385-7111. The Buffet: Breakfast 7 to 10:30, $5.75; lunch 10:30 to 3, $7.50; dinner 4 to 10, $10.75; Sunday champagne brunch 8 to 10, $10.95.

Salad and seafood lovers will want to line up this elaborate food fest, simply called "The Buffet." A perennial favorite among Las Vegans, it features a huge salad bar plus all-you-can eat shrimp and oysters. The main dish selection isn't as extensive as some other large buffets, although selections are varied and well prepared, including several carving table offerings. Choices during our last visit included garlic chicken, lasagna, a wonderfully spicy Santa Fe chicken, grilled swordfish and southern style pork chops with capers. The dessert selection is huge, with a wide range of torts, tarts, pies and cakes. The star of this tasty show is Mamma Wynn's bread pudding. It's so popular that diners request—and get—copies of the recipe, created by the mother of Golden Nugget CEO Steve Wynn. The Buffet setting is an extension of the Golden Nugget's turn-of-the-century elegance, with coffered ceilings, Italian chandeliers and comfortable booths.

5 MGM GRAND • 3799 S. Las Vegas Blvd. (Tropicana); (702)

891-7777. The Oz Buffet: Brunch daily 7 to 2:30, $5.95; dinner nightly 4:30 to 10, $8.95. Theme nights are Italian on Monday, Southwestern on Wednesday and seafood on Friday.

The Oz is one of the quietest, most pleasant and most appealing buffets in town. It has a pleasing Emerald City theme with bright floral carpeting and umbrella canopies over the food service areas. Food quality is excellent for the price, with dinner at just $8.95. Service is orderly and prompt without being rushed and the food venues are never crowded, since they are set up as four separate and identical buffet lines. The fresh fruit and salad selections are extensive, including rich seafood salads, ceviche, marinated mushroom salad and unlimited peeled shrimp with a very spicy sauce. (We have been known to eat here and never get beyond that glistening pile of chilled shrimp.)

The hot entrées, while not extensive, are interestingly varied. Choices during our last visit included Chinese shrimp fried rice, beef stroganoff, chicken enchiladas, pork picante, baked cod amandine and ribeye steak. Turkey, prime rib and ham are sliced at the carving station. Wine service is available and a bar is located within the buffet. Desserts are excellent, including do-it-yourself cherries jubilee and strawberry shortcake, flan, canoles, carrot cake, pies and cakes, parfaits, tortes and tarts and a tasty apple cobbler.

6 **THE MIRAGE** ● *3400 S. Las Vegas Blvd. (adjacent to Caesars Palace); (702) 791-7111. Mirage Buffet: Breakfast 7 to 10:45, $7.50; lunch 11 to 2:45, $8.95; dinner 3 to 10, $12.95; Sunday champagne brunch 8 to 10, $13.95.*

A pleasing tropic floral décor, interesting food variety and attentive service earn the Mirage Buffet a spot on our Ten Best list. Cold selections are excellent and creative, including pasta pesto salad, artichoke hearts, spicy Chinese chicken salad, seafood pasta salad with dill, Thai beef salad and a really fine smoked turkey salad. A cold strawberry soup was tasty enough for dessert. Mounds of peeled shrimp will attract seafood lovers, although the sauce was a bit bland.

Fresh, custom-prepared ethnic fare emerges from the pasta, fajita and stir-fry stations, while prime rib, turkey and ham are served at the carving station. Other hot entrées vary from one dinner to the next. They may include stuffed flounder, seafood Veracruz, Chicken fricassee, meatballs with mushrooms in demi sauce and a nicely seasoned Southwest chicken. The dessert table is quite elaborate, offering assorted cookies, pies and cakes, cheesecake, bread pudding, apple and peach cobbler. Personally, I go for the macaroons and usually manage to smuggle a few out.

7 **MONTE CARLO RESORT & CASINO** ● *3770 S. Las Vegas Blvd. (north of Tropicana); (702) 730-7777. Monte Carlo Buffet: Breakfast 7 to 11, $5.49; lunch 11 to 4, $6.49; dinner 4 to 10, $8.49.*

Although the food selection isn't as extensive as at some of the larger buffets, the Monte Carlo earns a spot on our Ten Best list for two appealing reasons—the fare is quite tasty and the setting is one of the most attractive in town. The buffet is isolated from the main casino and the designers have created an appealing Moorish setting with fluted arches and domed coffered ceilings. The service is attentive yet quiet, with none of the clamor of some of the larger food fests. Fresh fruit and dip veggies share the small salad bar with several well-prepared chicken and seafood salads.

Among the entrées offered during our last visit were Oriental seasoned steak with red pepper strips, an excellent Italian sausage, very good barbecued short ribs, an Oriental spiced white fish, chicken fajitas, chimichangas and linguine Alfredo. All service stations were manned and the food was rotated frequently, even on a slow night. The dessert section was interestingly varied and tasty.

8 *RIO SUITE HOTEL & CASINO* • *3700 W. Flamingo Rd. (at Valley View Boulevard, opposite the Gold Coast); (702) 252-7777. Carnival World Buffet: Breakfast weekdays 8 to 10:30, $4.99; lunch weekdays 11 to 3:30, $6.99; dinner weeknights 3:30 to 11, Saturday dinner 3:30 to 11:30, Sunday dinner 3:30 to 10:30, all $8.99; weekend brunch 8:30 to 3:30, $8.99.*

Measured in total acreage, the Rio's Carnival World is the largest buffet in town, with the most food selections, and it certainly deserves a spot on our Ten Best list. However, food quality can be uneven and we found the service to be rather chaotic during our visits, with servers dashing about to cover this large domain. But enough of that; this is a fun place. The décor is a kind of Brazilian geometric swirl, and the food stations comprise a virtual restaurant row. They include American fare at USA, pasta at Ludovico's Trattoria, Asian fare at Mani Yen's, build your own tacos and other Mexican grub at the Lazy Lizard, ribs and steaks at Bolo's Western Barbecue, sushi and Japanese fare at the Golden Crane, plus a deep-fry Fish and Chips bar and Glitter City Diner with burgers and related items.

The best of these food outlets is Rico's Amazon Grille, where you can select veggies, shrimp, beef and chicken and have them stir-fried before your eyes. Diners can get inexpensive drinks at Bar Rio, in the center of this massive food fair. With all of these gustatorial largess, the salad bar is rather small, but who needs it? Most of the desserts are quite tasty. Save space for custard pie, cannoli, apple pie and pecan pie.

The Rio also has the only daily seafood buffet in Las Vegas, at the far end of the Masquerade Village casino; it serves lunch and dinner.

9 *SAM'S TOWN HOTEL & GAMBLING HALL* • *5111 Boulder Highway (at Nellis Boulevard); (702) 456-7777. The Great Buffet: Breakfast Monday-Saturday 8 to 11, $4.99; lunch Monday-Saturday 11 to 3, $6.99; dinner Saturday-Thursday (except Wednesday) 4 to 9, $8.99; Wednesday steak night 4 to 9, $11.99; Friday seafood 4 to 10, $12.99; Sunday brunch 8 to 3, $7.99.*

Sam's serves good American grub plus regional fare such as Cajun and Southwest on specific nights. Look for these specials on a chalkboard out front. We're partial to the spicy fish dishes served on Cajun night which, when we last visited, was on Tuesdays. Kids will like the cooked-to-order hamburger station, complete with French fries, and the fudges, pralines, candied apples and other sweets. You can watch them being made in a little demonstration candy kitchen behind the sweet bar. The dessert section also has a full range of cakes, pies, pastries and cream puffs.

The buffet also offers a good salad bar and a separate fresh and

canned fruit bar. On the serving table, look for such American standards as ham hocks and pinto beans, breaded pork chops, potato
wedges and broiled salmon, with smoked turkey and roast beef at the
carving station. All of this is served in a pleasant country kitchen atmosphere, with lots of high backed booths.

10 SUNSET STATION HOTEL-CASINO • *1301 W. Sun-
set Rd. (just west of I-515 interchange), Hendersn; (888) SUNSET-9 or
(702) 547-7777. Feast Around the World Buffet: Breakfast weekdays 7
to 10:30, $3.99; lunch weekdays 11 to 3, $6.49; dinner 4 to 10, $8.99;
weekend brunch 7 to 3:30, $7.99; Friday-Saturday late night feast 11 to
6, $4.49; Wednesday seafood night 4 to 10, $12.99; Friday-Saturday
steak night 4 to 10, $11.99.*

International fare and international façades set the theme for this
large, attractive buffet in the new Sunset Station. Names of the venues
aren't very original, although they get their point across: Chinatown,
Viva Mexico, Mama Mia, Country Barbecue, Farmers Market and
Sweet Dreams Desserts. Every station is manned and we found the
food to be fresh and piping hot. Farmers Market features typical
American fare, including steaks cooked to order, while the Mexican
station offers made-to-order fajitas, several types of chili and even
warm tortillas. Our favorite venues were the Country Barbecue, with
barbecued ribs and chicken, and smoked turkey, chicken and brisket of
beef; and Chinatown, where the spring rolls were amply stuffed and
quite tasty, and the stir-fried veggies were crisp—a rarity for a buffet.

Cold food fans will like the good selection of fresh veggies, assorted
salads and fresh and canned fruits. The dessert section also is generous, with pies, cakes, cream puffs, struedels, napoleons and cobblers.

SPECIAL MENTION: THE STRATOSPHERE • *2000 Las
Vegas Blvd. (Main Street); (702) 380-7777. Breakfast daily 7 to 11,
$5.49; lunch daily 11 to 4, $6.49; dinner Sunday-Thursday 4 to 9 and 4
to 10 Friday-Saturday, $8.99.*

If calories were no object and we wanted to satisfy our sweet tooth
once and for all, we'd walk into the Stratosphere buffet with its cheerful hot air balloon theme, and we'd head straight for the dessert table.
While the overall buffet is quite good, with lots of international selections, the dessert section may be the best in town. Start with bananas
Foster with whisky or raisin sauce and a dollop of soft ice cream. Then
move on to the bread pudding topped with either of the above sauces,
the apple-walnut compote, assorted pies and cakes, chocolate balls,
spiced pears, rich fudge, ice cream with a choice of toppings, and really tasty peanut butter cookies.

Should you want to precede dessert with a real meal, we recommend the cleverly fashioned "Picnic Basket" area for its tasty barbecued ribs, spicy pulled barbecued pork, Southern fried chicken and

good old fashioned hot dogs. Other venues feature Chinese, Southwest and typical American fare. The international station changes entrées frequently, ranging from Italian pasta to Swedish meatballs.

THE TEN BEST SHRIMP COCKTAILS

Inexpensive shrimp cocktails are part of a Las Vegas legend that goes back to 1959. In that year, the downtown Golden Gate Casino offered shrimp cocktails served in tulip glasses to lure patrons. It's still doing so, twenty-five million shrimp cocktails later, and many other casinos now do the same.

Picking the best can't be very scientific since they're all pretty much the same. These are cooked and chilled peanut shrimp served either in a tulip glass or a simple plastic container, with a dollop of red sauce poured over. They're previously frozen shrimp and most of them probably come from the same supplier. So how can we judge one cooked-frozen-thawed peanut shrimp cocktail against another? About the only factors we can employ are the generosity of the serving, spiciness of the shrimp sauce and the atmosphere in which it is served.

And so, the winner is...

1 GOLDEN GATE CASINO • One Fremont St. (at Main); (702) 385-1906. Served at the San Francisco Shrimp Bar and Deli.

Although this is where the shrimp cocktail tradition began, we aren't picking the Golden Gate for historic or nostalgic reasons. What makes its shrimp cocktail Number One is its generosity of size, served with spicy cocktail sauce in a sundae glass for a mere 99 cents. Other elements that tilted the scale in the Gate's favor are a pleasant environment in a little dining area beside the casino, and the availability of inexpensive wine or beer at the snack bar deli. And one final nice touch: a pianist entertains diners in the late afternoon and evening.

2 ARIZONA CHARLIE'S HOTEL & CASINO • 740 S. Decatur Blvd. (near west Charleston); (702) 258-5200.

Served at the Sports Bar Deli, this generous sized 99-cent shrimp cocktail arrives in a flared plastic glass over a thin bed of lettuce, with a slice of lemon and crackers. The sauce is spicy and generous. You can enjoy your repast at a sitting area between the deli and the casino.

3 BARBARY COAST • 3595 S. Las Vegas Blvd. (Flamingo Road); (702) 737-7111.

Barbary Coast's $1.50 shrimp cocktails are the most expensive on our list, and easily worth the extra fifty cents. They're prepared in advance and allowed to chill in a cooler at the bar, from where they're dispensed. These are quite generous, served in a fluted glass with a lemon wedge and plenty of sauce. There's a tiny dab of diced celery at the bottom, just enough for a nice finishing crunch. Our only complaint—the sauce needs to be livelier.

4 CALIFORNIA HOTEL & CASINO • *12 Ogden Ave. (First Street); (702) 385-1222.*

If you're looking for volume in your shrimp cocktail, walk a block north of Fremont Street to Ogden and First, step into the "Cal" and get in line at the Cal Club Snackbar. It's a small, appealing 1930s style deli is just inside the door. The large $1.25 shrimp cocktail is pre-packaged with an equal amount of shredded cabbage in two fused-together plastic tumblers. You dump them into a bowl (which is provided) and stir in your own sauce. The cabbage, like celery used in other shrimp cocktails, adds a nice crunch. The sauce is rather bland pre-packaged Kraft's, although you can lace it with tabasco sauce, which you'll find at every table. You'll also find soy sauce, although we didn't care for its effect on chilled shrimp.

Why soy sauce? The Cal Club serves mostly Asian dishes, so you can accompany your shrimp cocktail with sashimi or a hot tempura entrée, and you have the option of chopsticks over plastic tableware. No other shrimp cocktail takeout in town can make this claim.

5 FREMONT HOTEL & CASINO • *301 Fremont St. (between Third and Casino Center); (702) 385-3232.*

Served at the Lanai Express snack bar, the Fremont's 99-cent cocktail comes in a flared plastic glass, served over minced celery and doused generously with a very spicy sauce. Crackers and a slice of lemon complete the creation. Carry it to one of the snack bar seats, from where you can watch the casino action as you dine.

6 GOLD SPIKE HOTEL & CASINO • *400 E. Ogden Ave. (at Fourth Street); (702) 384-8444.*

Gold Spike's shrimp cocktail arrives unadorned in a humble plastic cup. Look, whaddaya want for four bits? Served at the Gold Spike's snack bar, this 50-cent shrimp cocktail swims under a generous dollop of sauce. We haven't measured, but it's probably more than half the size of all of those 99-cent shrimp cocktails. The only flaw; the sauce could be a bit more spicy.

7 HOLIDAY INN BOARDWALK HOTEL & CASINO • *3750 S. Las Vegas Blvd. (near Harmon Avenue, between the Excalibur and the Bellagio); (702) 735-1167.*

The Boardwalk's generous $1.29 shrimp cocktail arrives in a fluted plastic glass, with a bed of chopped celery beneath, and a moderately lively sauce. The shrimp cocktails are sold at The Deli, which has a small sitting area. However, we like to pack ours out to the Boardwalk's sidewalk tables on Las Vegas Boulevard and dine while watching the passing Glitter City parade.

8 JACKIE GAUGHAN'S PLAZA • *One Main St. (at Fremont); (702) 386-2110.*

This is downtown's other 50-cent special and again, you get a generous little heap of shrimp for the price, plus a couple of packages of crackers. Pick it up at the snack bar just inside the left entrance to the casino (Main at Carson). You'll find several other good food bargains here as well; see Chapter five, page 96.

9 SAM'S TOWN: The Final Point Sports Bar • *5111 Boulder Highway (at Nellis Boulevard); (702) 456-7777.*

Head for the best sports bar in Las Vegas (Chapter seven, page 124) to get this generous 99-cent shrimp cocktail. Although it's served over a deep bed of lettuce, it comes in a large plastic glass, so the shrimp count is equal to any in town. A wedge of lemon and crackers accompany this hefty snack and the medium-spicy red sauce is served on the side. You can order your shrimp cocktail at the bar, or from a waitress at one of the tables. You're surrounded by TV sets and sports memorabilia; this is one of the town's more pleasant settings for consuming shrimp.

10 WESTWARD HO • *2900 S. Las Vegas Blvd. (between Circus Circus and the Stardust); (702) 731-2900.*

Ignored by most other insider guides, Westward Ho's 99-cent shrimp cocktails earns a spot on this list for several reasons. The portions are generous, with a big dollop of spicy sauce and they're served in a flared plastic glass over a bed of diced celery, adding that nice bit of crispness. Another plus: At the same snack bar where you purchase the shrimp, you can get a small tumbler of beer for a mere 75 cents.

Being poor is no disgrace, but it's no great honor, either.

— Will Rogers

Chapter five

PROUD PAUPERS
A BUDGET GUIDE

I t is being said of late that Las Vegas is no longer bargain city; that visitors can't have a princely time on a pauper's budget. That is absolutely not true. In the highly competitive atmosphere of gaming, some casinos are practically giving away the store to lure patrons. Las Vegas still offers 50-cent shrimp cocktails, 59-cent breakfasts, cheap buffets and hotel rooms under $25.

It is true that the major shows are expected to carry their own weight these days; ticket prices have escalated for the top "big room" extravaganzas and leading artists. It is further true that rooms at some of the posh casinos are as expensive as those in San Francisco and New York, and that a glass of designer beer in some places will set you back $4.25 plus tip. However, you can get an equally tasty beer for a dollar if you know where to go and a really nice room for less than the price of a Motel 6.

Only in Las Vegas can you find such a wide price range for essentially the same items and services. Some of the pricing extremes are in the same establishments. For instance, you can get a 99-cent shrimp cocktail at Arizona Charlie's Sports Bar Deli, or pay $6.95 for a shrimp cocktail appetizer at the casino's Yukon Grille.

THE POSSIBILITIES OF LINCOLN'S PORTRAIT

Let's say you've come to Glitter City with a wrinkled green portrait of Abraham Lincoln in your pocket—a five-dollar bill. What can you get with it? Depending on where you go, you can get:

● A glass of designer beer, or five to ten glasses of ordinary beer.

● A single cocktail, about two-thirds' payment on a fancy tropical drink, or five cocktails.

● An hour's lounge entertainment for the price of a drink.

● An appetizer at a fancy restaurant, a full meal at a cheap restaurant, or an all-you-can eat buffet.

● A shrimp cocktail in a gourmet room or five to ten shrimp cocktails in one of several casinos.

● You can get a box or two of buttered popcorn at one of the better movie theaters, or you can all the free popcorn you want at Slots A Fun and keep your five dollar bill.

Finally, you can do what many people do with their five dollar bills in Las Vegas. You can change it to nickels, quarters or tokens and feed these into slot or video poker machines. Now, the possibilities of Honest Abe's portrait become almost limitless. Your five dollar investment may bring you nothing (most likely) or several million dollars if you hit one of the Mega-Bucks machines (most unlikely).

No matter how you spend it, a five dollar bill offers more possibilities in Glitter City than anywhere else on the planet.

Despite price increases, Las Vegas is still America's cheapest tourist destination. We aren't just talking about discount coupon books, which are available on virtually every street corner, at tourist bureaus and at many hotel and motel check-in desks. Many of these coupons require you to do something in order to get something—to buy a certain amount of chips to get free ones (which can't be exchanged for cash), or to gamble for a certain period time. You can get a free pull on a special slot machine that never seems to hit anything, or discounts on souvenir shop curios that you probably don't want in the first place. However, you will find some real freebies in most of these coupon books—generally drinks and discount food deals.

This chapter addresses bargains with no strings attached, in food, drink, amusement and lodging. We also list low-roller joints for the benefit of timid gamblers. There will be, of necessity, several duplications on our budget lists. Casinos with low table limits and lots of nickel slots also tend to offer cheap food, drink and rooms.

THE TEN BEST FREE ATTRACTIONS

Who says you can't get something for nothing? There are plenty of freebies in Las Vegas and the best one—some unkind souls call it tacky—is the liveliest sound and light show you'll see anywhere.

1 THE FREMONT STREET EXPERIENCE • *Downtown Casino Center between Fourth and Main streets. Sound and light shows nightly on the hour, generally from around dusk to midnight.*

A few years ago the Downtown Casino Center was losing much of its action to the Strip, so casino owners and city officials got together to lure them back. Seventy million dollars and two million colored light bulbs later, the Fremont Street Experience was born. Fremont was turned into pedestrian way between Main Street and Las Vegas Boulevard, and a 100-foot-high space age canopy right out of *Star Wars* was erected overhead. This Fremont Street Experience, opened in late 1995, is both an object and an event. Each night, every hour on the hour until midnight, the casino marquees are blacked out and a wonderfully bombastic sound and light show is presented. Themes range from country and western to "Viva Las Vegas!" which honors the town's legendary performers.

The new pedestrian pavilion also is the venue for a variety of outdoor concerts and other special events. With its landscaping, benches and umbrella tables, it's a great place to hang out and watch the passing parade of human traffic, day or night. And don't worry, Fremont Street traditionalists. The famous Vegas Vic neon sign has survived, although the mesh of the overhead canopy gives him a rather mottled complexion on sunny days.

2 CIRCUS ACTS: Circus Circus Casino • *2880 S. Las Vegas Blvd. (Riviera Boulevard); (702) 734-0410. Daily 11 a.m. to midnight.*

Circus Circus started out as just that in 1968—a permanent big top without a casino or hotel. Folks paid admission to see the elephant, aerialists, clowns and—good grief!—topless dancers. (However, Nevada residents could get in free.) The elephants and dancers are gone and Circus Circus has ballooned into a huge resort with casinos and hotel towers. Free circus acts happen periodically above the main casino. They range from aerialists and clowns to comic trampoline artists and jugglers. A mezzanine carnival midway surrounds the "tent."

3 FESTIVAL FOUNTAIN SHOW: The Forum Shops at Caesars • *3570 S. Las Vegas Blvd. (at Flamingo Road); (702) 731-7110. Performances daily on the hour from 10 a.m.*

The Forum Shops at Caesars are anchored by two Roman style fountains. One is static and quite stylish, while the other becomes animated periodically to present a laser show. A pudgy polyurethane Bacchus "statue" is awakened (perhaps from a hangover) by a lightning storm in an overhead skydome. He glances about, blinks a couple of times and then utters a great opening line: "Let the festivities begin!" Three other deities come to life and utter equally banal dialogue, while a laser show flashes and dances in the sky dome. The whole thing is so corny that it's cute. And it's free.

4 *IMPERIAL PALACE AUTO COLLECTION* • *3535 S. Las Vegas Blvd. (between Sands Avenue and Flamingo Road, opposite Caesars Palace); (702) 731-3311. Daily 9:30 to 11:30.*

Although there's a $6.50 admission charge for this fine collection of 200 antique, nostalgic and "personality" cars, the price is often waived. When we last visited, a gentleman out front was passing out free tickets. Room guests, sincere slot players and others are generally comped here. At various times, you may find free coupons in the show guide magazines. You might even be able to walk up to the Palace's third floor premium booth wearing a wistful expression and get a free pass. (We got one recently, plus a souvenir visor.) For details on the exhibit, see Chapter nine, page 152.

5 *PIRATE SHIP BATTLE: Treasure Island* • *3300 Las Vegas Boulevard (Spring Mountain Road); (702) 894-7111. Daily at 4, 5:30, 8:30 and 10, plus 11:30 shows Friday and Saturday. Hours may change with the seasons; they're posted at the lagoon.*

Called the "Buccaneer Bay Show," this elaborate tableaux in a large lagoon in front of Treasure Island combines special effects and live actors to create a realistic battle between pirates and Her Majesty's Royal Navy. Two full-sized ships, *HMS Brittania* and the renegade frigate *Hispañola* fire broadsides at one another while pirates and Limeys rattle their sabers and fall frequently into the water. The effects are quite impressive, right down to the sinking of the loser—and guess who that is? To see this free outdoor show, you must find your niche along the two-tiered sidewalk or lagoon bridge well before the announced time, since it draws big crowds. A better vantage point, right beside the *Brittania*, is on the terrace of Treasure Island's Battle Bar. To get a seat, however, plan on arriving an hour or two before show time and nurse your drinks.

6 *MASQUERADE SHOW IN THE SKY: Rio Suite Hotel & Casino* • *3700 W. Flamingo Rd. (Valley View Boulevard); (702) 252-7777. Daily except Wednesday at 1, 3, 5, 9 and 11 p.m.*

This free show, suspended from the atrium ceiling of the Rio's Masquerade Village Casino, out-glitters them all. Musicians, singers and dancers whoop it up while riding aboard several dazzling lighted floats suspended from tracks above the casino. Other singers, dancers and acrobats—some resembling escapees from *Alice in Wonderland*—perform on a stage at casino level. A giant "talking head" acts as mistress of ceremonies for this splashy Mardi Gras festival, while a huge balloon float of Satchmo looks on in approval. The best place to catch the action is from the balcony above the casino, which puts you eye-level with the floats. The talking head, with video camera eyes that pick up and project images of onlookers, works the audience before and after the show.

Masquerade Show in the Sky doesn't get as crowded with onlookers as the Treasure Island pirate ship battle, although you should find a place along the balcony railing twenty minutes or so before the action starts. You can pass the time kibitzing with the talking head.

7 SPORTS HALL OF FAME: Las Vegas Club Sports Hotel & Casino • 18 Fremont St. (at Main Street); (702) 385-1664. Open 24 hours.

Your first clues that the Las Vegas Club is a sports-minded casino are the pin-striped baseball jerseys on the dealers and the cheerleader outfits on the drink and change girls—even the ones pushing Social Security. The club displays the world's largest private collection of sports memorabilia. It includes World Series bats, photos, baseballs and footballs autographed by sports stars, jerseys of famous players, plus assorted trophies, historic photos and Maurey Wills' bronzed base stealing shoes. Some items line the corridor leading to the John D's Grill and Sports Bar; others are scattered throughout the casino, including two second floor restaurants, the Dugout and Upper Deck.

8 SUNSET STAMPEDE: Sam's Town Hotel & Gambling Hall • 5111 Boulder Highway (at Nellis Boulevard); (702) 456-7777. Shows at 2, 6, 8 and 10 p.m.

It isn't a stampede and it doesn't always happen at sunset, but never mind that. This free sound-light-water-laser show in the 25,000 square foot Mystic Falls Park is worth the short drive out the Boulder Strip. It begins when a stuffed coyote emerges somewhat stiffly from a cave at the top of a waterfall and issues an authoritative howl. Then as the critter watches—somewhat expressionless—water dances and gushes from a pool below and lasers flicker off the rocks, all to a rather thunderous musical sound track. For interesting aerial views, catch it from a windowed corridor leading from Sam's second floor casino to Parking Barn Two, or from the top (ninth) floor corridor of the hotel towers, reached by windowed elevators.

Although the first show is in the afternoon, wait until dark for the best effects, since daylight dims the colored lights and lasers. The interplay of lasers on spraying water is quite impressive at night.

9 VOLCANO ERUPTION: The Mirage • 3400 S. Las Vegas
Blvd. (adjacent to Caesars Palace); (702) 791-7111. Every fifteen minutes from dusk until about midnight; hours posted at the site.

It begins with a warning hiss, and then a throaty grumble. Suddenly, flames and "lava" hurl a hundred feet skyward, lighting up the already dazzling Las Vegas Boulevard. Steve Wynn's erupting volcano was Glitter City's first free resort spectacle, setting the stage for shows such as the Sam's Town Sunset Stampede, Rio's Masquerade Show in the Sky and Wynn's own pirate ship battle at the next-door Treasure Island. The volcano literally was a traffic stopper when it first erupted in 1989, causing jams along Las Vegas Boulevard. Locals have gotten used to it, so it no longer slows the vehicle flow. However, the show is even more flamboyant than before. Engineers recently added more fire and pretend brimstone for a bigger eruption.

10 WHITE TIGER LAIR: The Mirage • 3400 S. Las Vegas
Blvd. (adjacent to Caesars Palace); (702) 791-7111.

Several handsome white Bengal tigers are the stars of the Mirage's Siegfried and Roy show. Between engagements, they lounge in an imposing playpen fashioned like a gleaming Indian temple with a lagoon, off the main casino. These are tigers under glass; a window wall permits visitors to watch them play in the water or just hang out, which is what they do most of the time. When they're off doing their show, folks can watch video tapes of the tigers at play on monitors hanging above the lair.

THE TEN BEST CHEAP PLACES TO GAMBLE

They call them low roller joints—casinos that appeal to timid folks who don't want to commit too much money to gaming. Their table limits are low and they have lots of nickel slots and even penny ones. Conservative gamblers can spend hours worrying a roll of coins and—even with a streak of bad luck—not lose much more than lunch money. These places used to be called sawdust joints, a reference to the early days when sawdust was spread on the floor of seedy saloons to soak up yesterday's spilled beer. However, most of today's low roller places are quite nice, although some of them tend to be on the smoky side.

Many casinos with low-denomination machines and table limits also claim to offer very liberal odds. However, as we pointed out in Chapter three, the Nevada State Gaming Commission does not require casinos to confirm the odds they set on their machines. Thus, claims of loose slots cannot be verified, although we *can* verify that all of the places listed below have lots of nickel slots and video games, and some even have penny ones. Also, these ten places have low table limits.

Most of our selections are downtown, since that's where most of the low-denomination casinos are focused. However, our Number One choice is right in the middle of the Strip.

1 HOLIDAY INN BOARDWALK CASINO • 3750 S. Las Vegas Blvd. (near Harmon Avenue, between the Excalibur and the Bellagio); (702) 735-1167.

The Boardwalk is one of our favorite casinos in Glitter City and definitely our favorite budget casino. Originally a friendly sawdust joint, it was purchased by the Holiday Inn corporation, dismantled and completely rebuilt, with a cute and cheerful East Coast amusement park look, complete with a mock-up rollercoaster and Ferris wheel. Fortunately, the corporations retained its status as one the best bargain places on the Strip for food (see below) and it's still a low-roller joint, with slots and videos ranging from a nickel to a quarter (we found none higher), plus $1 minimums for blackjack and roulette, and $2 for craps. It also tops our Ten Best lists for budget buffets and other cheap casino food; see below.

2 ARIZONA CHARLIE'S HOTEL & CASINO • 740 S. Decatur Blvd. (near west Charleston); (702) 258-5200.

We adjourn to a newly remodeled neighborhood casino for our next low-roller joint. To reach it, follow Charleston west from downtown and turn right onto Decatur Boulevard. Among its promises are 99.6 percent payback on designated poker machines and 90 percent-plus payback on some slots. For low rollers, it features 25-cent craps, $1 roulette and table limits around $2. Naturally, it has an abundance of nickel slot and video poker machines.

3 CASINO ROYALE • 3419 S. Las Vegas Blvd. (opposite the Mirage, between Sands Avenue and Flamingo Road); (702) 737-3500.

This is a good place for both the budget and the beginning gambler, and that's often the same person. Free roulette, blackjack and craps lessons are available, and the tables have some of the lowest limits in town. Timid gamblers can try 25-cent craps and roulette, or slip into seats at blackjack tables with $1 minimum bets. The place of course abounds with nickel slot and video machines. However, no signs claim particularly low odds; Casino Royale is noted mostly for its low limits.

4 *EL CORTEZ* ● *600 Fremont Street (at Sixth Street); (702) 385-5200.*

The venerable El Cortez sits all by itself at Fremont and Sixth, well away from the glitter of Glitter Gulch. Yet it's hardly lonely inside. Popular with locals and tour bus groups, the recently remodeled casino is quite busy most days. (Incidentally, it's the oldest casino in Las Vegas, dating from 1941.) Signs proclaim that the slots are liberal, and gamblers on a budget will find plenty of nickel machines and even rare dime ones. Table limits are low; you can play blackjack or invest in a keno ticket and risk only a dollar.

5 *GOLD SPIKE HOTEL & CASINO* ● *400 E. Ogden Ave. (at Fourth Street); (702) 384-8444.*

Exceedingly friendly and only slightly scruffy, the Spike has been a favorite low roller joint for years. All tables have a dollar minimum and you can play keno for 40 cents or roulette and electronic keno for a dime. Nickel slot machines? Are you kidding? It has ranks of penny ones! If you work up a thirst or an appetite trying to work through a two dollar roll of nickels or bucketful of pennies, you can get a drink or shrimp cocktail for fifty cents, or a roast beef or ham dinner for $2.50.

6 *GOLDEN GATE CASINO* ● *One Fremont St. (at Main); (702) 385-1906.*

This is one of the more appealing small casinos in town, with an old San Francisco theme. Its snack bar is noted for its shrimp cocktails (which we picked as our winner in Chapter four, page 81) and excellent deli sandwiches. The Golden Gate has been here since 1906 which is ironic, since that's the year that San Francisco was nearly destroyed by an earthquake. Within this pleasant atmosphere you'll find lots of nickel slots and videos, a few penny ones, 70 cent keno and single deck blackjack with low table limits.

7 *JACKIE GAUGHAN'S PLAZA* ● *One Main St. (at Fremont); (702) 386-2110.*

The Plaza earns a spot on our list as largest and most attractive downtown casino for low rollers. It offers all the amenities of the large Strip casinos, plus an abundance of nickel slots and videos and even a few penny ones. Historically and visually, the Plaza occupies the premier spot downtown, anchoring the west end of the Fremont Street Experience. It was here that agents of Senator William Clark stood on May 15, 1905, to auction off the first lots of the Las Vegas townsite.

Later, it became the site of the historic Union Pacific railroad station. Shy gamblers will find lots of nickel slots and videos and even a few penny ones, plus 85-cent keno and low table minimums.

8 LADY LUCK CASINO • 206 N. Third St. (downtown, at Ogden Avenue; (702) 477-3000.

Will luck be your lady tonight? Only the fates can tell. However, this bright and cheery low roller joint a block north of Fremont Street gives you a head start by offering the most generous coupon book in town. It's reportedly worth $350, if you go through the ritual of using all fifty-one coupons. The thick book is available only to out-of-staters and you can pick it up—after showing proof of non-residence—at the Mad Money Booth at the rear of the casino. After you've gotten your free foot-long hot dog, subsidized shrimp cocktail and two-for-one bar drink, you can adjourn to any of the dozens of nickel slot and video machines and start investing your money. Most table games start at two dollars and you can play keno for a dollar. Incidentally, Lady Luck is one of several casinos claiming to have "the world's loosest slots."

9 SILVER CITY • 3001 S. Las Vegas Blvd. (opposite the Stardust, south of Riviera Boulevard); (702) 732-4152.

This is one of the most cleverly decorated low roller places in town. Timbered rafters above the table games area are busy with old Western mining memorabilia, including mannequin miners, ore buckets, dynamite kegs and rusty tools. Nickel machines are abundant and blackjack and craps table limits are a dollar. You can play roulette for 25 cents a spin. Another Silver City plus—it's one of the few casinos in town with a no smoking gaming area. Originally, it was entirely smoke free, but that apparently didn't work. (You will note that an alarming number of gamblers smoke.) Both Silver City and Slots A Fun (below) are owned by Circus Circus Enterprises.

10 SLOTS A FUN • 2880 S. Las Vegas Blvd. (beside Circus Circus); (702) 734-0410.

Next door to Circus Circus and owned by it, Slots A Fun is a fine, noisy little place for timid gamblers. It has five-cent and rare ten-cent slot and video poker machines, one dollar table limits and a 25-cent roulette wheel. It also makes Ten Best lists for cheap food and drink.

THE TEN BEST CHEAP PLACES TO DRINK

Several casinos advertise a specific drink to lure patrons, such as a 99-cent margarita or one dollar draft beer. We list only places with cheap prices on all of their basic beers and well drinks.

1 **ORLEANS HOTEL & CASINO** • *4500 W. Tropicana Ave. (a mile west of the Strip); (702) 365-7111.*

Surprisingly, one of the cheapest places to drink is one of the nicest, and it thus earns the top spot on our list. The imposing new Orleans, with its monumental sculptures of alligators and Mardi Gras maidens, has four theme bars in its large main casino. At each, you can get 75-cent draft beer and bottled beer and well drinks for a dollar.

2 **BARBARY COAST** • *3595 S. Las Vegas Blvd. (Flamingo Road); (702) 737-7111.*

Like the Orleans, the Barbary Coast also is an exceptionally pleasant place for cheap drinking, all done up in 19th century San Francisco-style leaded glass and crystal. You can get a frozen margarita or bloody Mary for $1.25, well drinks for $1.50 and beer for a dollar.

3 **CASINO ROYALE** • *3419 S. Las Vegas Blvd. (opposite the Mirage, between Sands Avenue and Flamingo Road); (702) 737-3500*

Although prices aren't posted, this is a cheap drink venue, with bottled beer and well drinks for just 75 cents. A dollar-fifty will get you hot dog and a draft beer. It's one of the liveliest places on the Strip, jumping to the beat of loud rock music.

4 **GOLD SPIKE HOTEL & CASINO** • *400 E. Ogden Ave. (at Fourth Street); (702) 384-8444.*

Well drinks and draft beer at this friendly little downtown casino were fifty cents the last time we checked. It is thus the cheapest drinking establishment in town.

5 **IMPERIAL PALACE** • *3535 S. Las Vegas Blvd. (between Sands Avenue and Flamingo Road); (702) 731-3311*

Most of the large and rambling Imperial Palace is set well back from Las Vegas Boulevard, although a small satellite casino sits on the Strip. At its Kanpai Bar, you can get well drinks and bottled beer (including Heineken and Corona) for 99 cents. Draft beer is 49 cents.

6 **JACKIE GAUGHAN'S PLAZA** • *One Main St. (at Fremont); (702) 386-2110.*

All well drinks and beers are a dollar in this large casino hotel at the end of Fremont Street. Combine a drink with a 50-cent shrimp cocktail and you have a very cheap lunch.

7 **O'SHEAS CASINO** • *3555 S. Las Vegas Blvd. (just north of the Flamingo Hilton); (702) 697-2711.*

This tiny casino, popular with low rollers along the Strip, also is popular with budget drinkers. Sipping prices are 75 cents for domestic draft beer and $1.25 for other drinks.

8 **SASSY SALLY'S CASINO** • *32 Fremont St. (at First); (702) 382-5777.*

This small downtown establishment's single bar focuses on beer, and it earns a spot on our Ten Best beer pubs in Chapter seven. It's also one of the cheapest places in town to drink, with $1.25 bar drinks and bottled beer, and 16-ounce tap beer for a dollar.

9 **SILVER CITY** • *3001 S. Las Vegas Blvd. (opposite the Stardust); (702) 732-4152.*

This little casino with its clever Western mining theme is a cheap place to drink, eat and gamble. Mixed drinks are a dollar and beer is 75 cents. You can get a bag of popcorn for a quarter and inexpensive food at its 24-hour café.

10 **SLOTS A FUN** • *2880 S. Las Vegas Blvd. (beside Circus Circus); (702) 734-0410.*

In addition to being a good place for novice gamblers with its low-limit machines and tables, Slots A Fun offers cheap beer as well as rather inexpensive mixed drinks. Domestic and imported beers are only 75 cents, frozen drinks are $1.25 and well drinks are $1.50.

THE TEN BEST CHEAP CASINO EATS

Cheap food is one of the most popular devices used by casinos to lure patrons. Some of the food at the places we've selected is free, or it can be earned by joining a slot club and making a required amount of plays. Food come-ons change constantly, so we won't list too many specifics here. What appears instead is a list of the ten casinos that are most generous with their food price specials. Many of the best food bargains come in the middle of the night or at breakfast time. Obviously, casino bosses want to keep you at their machines as late as possible, and then lure you back there first thing in the morning.

Incidentally, most casino-subsidized food may be good for your budget, but not for your body. Many of the food specials would drive a cholesterol-counting nutritionist to hysteria—steak and eggs, shrimp cocktails, bacon, sausage and hot dogs.

1 SLOTS A FUN • 2880 S. Las Vegas Blvd. (beside Circus Circus); (702) 734-0410.

This small, noisy casino has some of the best food bargains on the Strip, earning it the top spot on our list. Start with free popcorn just for the asking, plus free coffee and doughnuts in the morning and finger sandwiches in the afternoons, served from carts that travel about the casino. Over at the snack bar, you can get bacon, egg and cheese on an English muffin, a breakfast burrito, shrimp cocktail or half-pound hot dog, each for 99 cents; plus a beef burrito for $1.29 and chili for $1.49.

2 ARIZONA CHARLIE'S HOTEL & CASINO • 740 S. Decatur Blvd. (near west Charleston); (702) 258-5200.

In addition to a rather cheap buffet (see below), Charlie's Sports Book Deli features a 99-cent shrimp cocktail (one of our winners; see Chapter four, page 81), $1.50 chili, $1.75 hot dog; and potato, pasta or tuna salad for $1.25. Coffee and soft drinks are 50 to 75 cents. From midnight to 7 a.m. weekdays, you can get 59-cent breakfasts at the Sourdough Café.

3 AZTEC INN • 2200 S. Las Vegas Blvd. (at Baltimore, opposite the Stratosphere); (702) 385-4566.

This tiny casino draws folks to its few slot and video machines with specials such as 69-cent beef stew or ham and eggs, plus dinners of chicken fried steak, meatloaf and fried chicken under $6. In keeping with its Latin theme, its small café also offers several Mexican dinners for under $6.

4 FREMONT HOTEL-CASINO • 200 Fremont St. (at Casino Center Boulevard); (702) 385-3232.

This venerable downtown casino, a serious gambling venue for decades, lures the budget hungry to its Lanai Café. Offerings include 99-cent shrimp cocktails; ham steak and eggs for $2.49; two eggs with bacon, hash browns, biscuits and gravy for $1.99; steak and lobster tail for $9.99; prime rib dinner for $4.95; and several other dinner entrées under $5.

5 GOLD SPIKE HOTEL & CASINO • 400 E. Ogden Ave. (at Fourth Street); (702) 384-8444.

Start with a fifty-cent shrimp cocktail drowning in sauce, follow with a roast beef or ham dinner for $2.50, or a chili dog for $1.75.

These are regular prices, not special come-ons. The tidy little diner in the Gold Spike is definitely one of the cheapest places in town to eat.

6 GOLDEN GATE CASINO • *One Fremont (at Main); (702) 385-1906.*

The Golden Gate's Bay City Diner is not only inexpensive, it's quite attractive. Frosted glass, art deco chandeliers and wall sconces, laminated wood paneling and black and white tile give it a pleasing 1930s San Francisco look. Seated in comfortable booths or at a long counter, customers can chose from among several evening entrées for under $5, including chicken fried steak, pasta dinners and fried chicken.

7 HOLIDAY INN BOARDWALK CASINO • *3750 S. Las Vegas Blvd. (near Harmon Avenue, between the Excalibur and the Bellagio); (702) 735-1167.*

The Boardwalk rivals Slots A Fun as the cheapest place to eat on the Strip. It has a $1.29 shrimp cocktail, which is hardly unusual. However, you also can get great little "Castleburgers" (mini-hamburgers) at three for $1.29, a 24-hour bacon and egg breakfast for $1.49, tasty potato cakes for under a dollar, and the list continues. These are issued from the Boardwalk's New York style deli.

8 JACKIE GAUGHAN'S PLAZA • *One Main St. (at Fremont); (702) 386-2110.*

Gaughan's Plaza Diner is one of the more appealing budget eating place in the city, with a pleasing early 20th century look. Start with a "pound of pig" for breakfast—ham steak, two eggs, hash browns, toast and coffee for under $2, and then move on to inexpensive lunch and dinner menus. Among budget dinner items are baby beef liver, chicken breasts, trout amandine and sirloin, all for under $6. If your budget's really tight, you can get a 50-cent shrimp cocktail and $1.50 hot dog at the snack bar.

9 NEVADA PALACE • *5255 Boulder Hwy. (at Harmon, just south of Sam's Town, eight miles from downtown Las Vegas); (702) 458-8810.*

If you plan to visit Sam's Town, the largest outlying casino in the area, continue next door to the midsize Nevada Palace casino for some of the best food prices in the area. Two dollars will get you several kinds of breakfasts, a "super sub" sandwich or enchilada "a la grande." For $2.99, you can get a barbecued rib dinner. The Palace has one of the cheapest buffets in town, with all-you-can-eat dinner for a mere $5.99.

10 WESTWARD HO • *2900 S. Las Vegas Blvd. (between Circus Circus and the Stardust); (702) 731-2900.*

The "Ho" features some of the cheapest breakfasts in town—scrambled eggs, biscuits and gravy for 49 cents, or throw in sausage and it's 99 cents. Other gustatorial bargains are a half-pound hot dog and beer for 99 cents; shrimp cocktail for 99 cents (which makes our Ten Best list in Chapter four, page 83); and prime rib dinner, $5.95. Soft drinks are 50 cents, coffee and tea 45 cents, and draft beer 75 cents. Night owls can get a New York dinner with soup or salad, fries and garlic toast for $3.95, from 11 p.m. to 6 a.m. All of this is served at an informal snack bar in the southwest corner of this small gaming parlor.

THE TEN BEST CHEAP BUFFETS

In the previous chapter, we selected the ten very best buffets in Las Vegas. We follow here with the Ten Best budget buffets, for which we've set an arbitrary upper limit of $8 for dinner. There is a common belief among locals that the best budget buffets are in the outlying casinos, although our taste buds tell us this just isn't the case. Four of our top ten selections are right on the Strip and a fifth is downtown.

Budget priced buffets—particularly those on the Strip—generally attract longer lines than the more expensive ones. The only solution, other than standing for an hour, is to get there very early or very late. However, many foods suffer from excess steam table exposure as closing hour draws near. You'll often find shorter lines at outlying casinos.

1 HOLIDAY INN BOARDWALK • *3750 S. Las Vegas Blvd. (near Harmon Avenue, between the Excalibur and the Bellagio); (702) 735-1167. Surf Buffet: Breakfast 7 to 11, $3.69; lunch 11 to 4:30, $4.69; dinner 4:30 to 10, $5.69.*

This new entry, started in 1997, tops our list as the best budget buffet in town for several good reasons. Food selection is varied and tasty, the setting is quite pleasing and it's one of the least expensive buffets in town. The Surf Buffet is less than a dollar higher than the town's cheapest buffet at Circus Circus, and it's much better.

The food selection, while small, is tasty and remarkably versatile, including several American hot dishes, fresh-sliced meats from the carving station, plus Italian, Mexican and Chinese fare. Particularly savory during our last visit were a peppy chicken enchilada and meatballs with onions. The salad bar is quite versatile, with several pasta salads and a good assortment of fresh veggies. The dessert selection is the best in the budget price range, with various napoleons, cute little swan cream puffs, carrot cake, pineapple upside down cake and other cakes and pies, plus soft ice cream. Service is prompt and friendly. The atmosphere is pleasing, with murals of windsurfers, bright and cheery colors and even recorded sounds of the surf, in keeping with the buffet's name.

2 ALADDIN HOTEL & CASINO • *3667 S. Las Vegas Blvd. (below Flamingo Road, opposite Bellagio); (702) 734-3583. Marketplace Buffet: Breakfast 7:30 to 10:30, $4.95, lunch 11:30 to 3, $5.95; dinner 4 to 10, $6.95.*

The Aladdin rivals the Boardwalk for the town's best budget buffet. Both are excellent for the price, although the setting is more appealing at the Boardwalk. Aladdin offerings range from veal Parmesan to catfish to seafood jambalaya, with ham, turkey and prime rib at the carving station. Most entrées are creatively seasoned and quite tasty, particularly for a budget buffet. Another budget buffet rarity—unlimited shrimp. The cooked veggies are properly crisp—very unusual for a buffet at any price. The salad and dessert selections are small yet tasty, and several soups are available. Among dessert standouts are lemon cheesecake and spicy pumpkin pie.

The Aladdin Marketplace won't win any designer awards; the setting is rather spartan, resembling an oversized coffee shop. But never mind that; we go there for the good, inexpensive food.

3 ARIZONA CHARLIE'S HOTEL & CASINO • *740 S. Decatur Blvd. (near west Charleston); (702) 258-5200. Wild West Buffet: Breakfast 7 to 10:30, $3.50, lunch 11 to 3:30, $4.50; dinner 4 to 10, $6.50; Monday crab night 4 to 10, $7.95.*

Charlie's buffet is a simple, unadorned place that sets out a fair feast for very little money. The buffet is rather small, although it contains some interesting items and we found most of them to be quite tasty. Among the cold offerings, we favored a chunky ham, cheese and cherry tomato salad and a marinated three-bean salad. The spicy chicken Marco Polo and sweet and sour pork were quite good and the Cajun catfish was one of the few buffet fish dishes we've found that wasn't overcooked. Charlie's has the usual fried chicken and cooked veggies, plus turkey, ham and beef at the carving station. It has a self-service drink station with soft drinks, coffee and tea; you can get iced tea on request. From the small dessert section, we pigged out on very good eclairs, cream puffs, apple crumb cake and carrot cake. You'll also find jello, butterscotch pudding, pies and cakes.

4 FITZGERALDS CASINO • *Molly's Coffee Shoppe and Buffet: 301 Fremont Street (at Third); (702) 388-2400. Breakfast 7 to 11, $4.99; lunch 11:30 to 4, $5.49; dinner 5 to 10, $7.99; weekend champagne brunch 7 a.m. to 4 p.m., $7.99.*

The best feature of this buffet is that it's served in Fitzgeralds' café; instead of standing in line, patrons leave their name at the maitre 'd desk and wait to be called. Out there on the food line, Fitzgeralds strongest suit is its selection of prepared salads—tuna salad, chicken salad, coleslaw, pasta salad, seafood salad and such. No tired lettuce here! The selection of hot dishes is quite good, including sirloin steak cooked to order, ham and chicken, plus Asian dishes like steak teriyaki and Chinese stir fry. Dessert selections are extensive as well, although most items are rather conventional cakes, pies and pastries.

5 *GOLD COAST HOTEL & CASINO* ● *4000 W. Flamingo Rd. (about half a mile west across I-15); (702) 367-7111. Coast Buffet: Breakfast 7 to 10:30, $3.45; lunch 11 to 3, $4.95; dinner 4 to 10, $6.95; Wednesday seafood buffet 4 to 10, $7.95; Sunday brunch 8 to 3, $6.95; (most meals include a frozen drink).*

The Gold Coast's buffet is small enough to be both manageable and comfortable, while still providing a good selection of food. The atmosphere is simple—like an oversized coffee shop filled with booths, which are quite comfortable. It's quiet in here, well away from the casino area. Service is attentive and the twin serving lines receive frequent attention from cooks and their assistants. We liked the creativity in the salad bar, with offerings such as a spicy kidney bean and pimento salad and a cubed ham and mixed cheese salad. You'll find the usual leafy salads, three-bean, pasta, tuna, coleslaw and other standards, plus a big brick of cheese and a small fruit selection. The hot dishes include several international entries. Among its better entrées were shepherd's pie and ox tail stew, plus a fine Santa Fe breast of chicken fillet with cheese and a mild chili laid over. Roast beef, ham and barbecued chicken emerge from the carving station.

The dessert selection is good although it's not self-service, perhaps to protect us from over-indulging. A pleasant gentleman in a chef's hat will fill your plate with tasty pies, eclairs, napoleons and pecan tarts. Our favorites were the cookies—peanut butter and oatmeal-raisin. Because of the presence of the guy in the chef's hat, we had to stifle the temptation to fill our pockets.

6 *IMPERIAL PALACE* ● *3535 S. Las Vegas Blvd. (between Sands Avenue and Flamingo Road, opposite Caesars Palace); (702) 731-3311. Emperor's Buffet: Breakfast 7 to 11:30, $4.99; lunch 11:30 to 4, $5.99 and dinner 5 to 10, $6.99.*

The Palace food selection isn't large, although it's creative and tasty for the price. We like the salad bar variety, which includes a good assortment of canned and fresh fruits, plus garnishes like sunflower seeds and chopped black olives. After salad, I like to head for the build-your-own taco stall. Roast beef, turkey and ham generally are available at the carving stations, and hot dishes range from sweet and sour pork to hot pastas and seafood Newburg. The dessert selection is small and interesting—a lemon-filled chocolate eclair, mince pie and raspberry cheesecake were quite tasty. All of this is served in a pleasant, comfortable environment, with mostly booth seating and a kind of South Seas Maori décor. Soft drinks, coffee and tea are self-service; you have to bring your our own liquor from an adjacent cocktail bar.

7 ORLEANS HOTEL & CASINO • 4500 W. Tropicana Ave.; (702) 365-7111. Market Buffet: Breakfast weekdays 7 to 10:30, $3.45; lunch weekdays 11 to 3:30, $4.45; dinner Tuesday-Sunday 4 to 10, $6.95; weekend brunch 8 to 3, $6.95; Monday night seafood buffet 4 to 10, $7.95.

This is one of Glitter City's top inexpensive buffets, rivaling the Boardwalk and Aladdin. In fact, for lovers of Creole and Cajun fare, it's one of the best buffets at any price. The hot table offers a treasure of New Orleans style food, including cornbreaded catfish, jambalaya, pork loin in whiskey sauce, blackened turkey breast in Creole mustard sauce and Cajun smoked sausage in cabbage. These may not equal the creations of Emeril Lagasse, but the entire buffet is less than the price of an appetizer at his famous New Orleans Fish House. Further, the Orleans buffet has one of the best salad tables in town, featuring marinated baby corn, fajita salad, pasta vegetable salad, crab salad, ambrosia, black bean and corn salad, rainbow ratolli and a tasty Oriental salad with shrimp, baby corn, bamboo shoots and water chestnuts.

The dessert section is small and select, with napoleons, tarts and cream puffs added to the usual cakes and pies. We particularly liked the butterscotch nut bars and apple crumb cake. Wine service is available from the servers, for a modest $2 a glass. The look of the dining area is French New Orleans, with old brick, green iron grillwork and bright floral print booths.

8 SANTA FE HOTEL & CASINO • 4949 N. Rancho Dr., Las Vegas, NV 89130; (702) 658-4900. Lone Mountain Buffet: Breakfast Monday-Saturday 7:30 to 10, $3.95; lunch Monday-Saturday 11:30 to 2:30, $4.95; dinner Sunday-Wednesday 4 to 9 and Friday-Saturday 4 to 10, $6.95; Thursday seafood night 4 to 9, $8.95.

What's your preference? The large and attractive Lone Mountain Buffet has different dinner themes each night—Southwest on Monday, Italian on Tuesday, American on Wednesday, seafood on Thursday, international mix on Friday, "steak-out" on Saturday and country barbecue on Sunday. It has quite a variety of entrées for its modest price, and its one of the few buffets at any price that includes red or white wine with dinner. Food quality can be a bit uneven, although it's generally quite good. We found that cooked meats such as chicken and pork chops were often overdone, even though the serving stations are manned and food is rotated frequently. The best bets are the various prepared dishes.

Among entrées during a recent American night were pork chops with onions, trout amandine, braised short ribs, baked marinated salmon, beef stew and fried chicken. The salad bar is extensive, with such specialties as fresh fruit salad, a generously endowed antipasto salad and spicy Mexican corn salad. The dessert section is rather small, consisting mostly of pies and cakes, plus a yogurt station with assorted toppings. All of this variety is served amidst an appealing Southwest décor with pole beam ceilings, stucco walls, desert plants and painted tile accents. Most seating is in comfortable booths and some are adjacent to the Santa Fe's ice rink.

9 SHOWBOAT HOTEL, CASINO & BOWLING CENTER •
2800 Fremont St. (at Charleston, two miles east of downtown); (702) 385-9123. Captain's Buffet: Lunch Monday-Friday 10 to 3:30, $4.95; dinner nightly 4:30 to 10, $6.15; steak and seafood nights $7.95; weekend brunch 8 to 3, $6.45.

This busy buffet, popular with locals, features a baked potato bar with twelve toppings, build-your-own tacos and nachos, plus a variety of pizzas. Otherwise, the fare is tilted toward regional American, with offerings such as oven roasted game hen with sage stuffing, pork chops with baked apple slices, salmon with hollandaise and old fashioned pot roast and leg of lamb. The salad section is rather small, although the dessert section is rather extensive, with Neapolitans, cream puffs, pies, cakes and an ice cream station. This is one of the more handsome neighborhood casino buffets, featuring a pink and white Southern antebellum décor with latticework accents and floral patterns.

10 CIRCUS CIRCUS • 2880 S. Las Vegas Blvd., (upper Strip,
south of the Sahara); (702) 734-0410. Circus Buffet: Breakfast 6 to 11:30, $2.99, lunch noon to 4, $3.99, dinner 4:30 to 11, $4.99.

Dead last but finished category: This is supposedly the world's largest buffet, feeding up to 1,200 people a day. With four serving lines, it operates with the efficiency of a military messhall—and it's about as appealing. (Or perhaps a school cafeteria. Signs admonish you not to waste food.) The service in this large, barn-like place is rather noisy and chaotic. It's on our Ten Best list only because it's among the cheapest in town, with a choice of fifty different food items. Unfortunately, forty-nine of them are garbonza beans.

Just kidding, of course. However, there isn't much originality in all of this variety. Among its offering when we last visited were conventional salads, fried chicken, sliced beef and ham and overcooked fish. The dessert section was limited to cakes, pies and pastries; we found no fancy torts or tarts. There's lots of Jello for the kids, plus a soft ice cream station with a variety of toppings. The most tasty items we found among the fifty food selections were spicy Italian sausage with red peppers and a quite good slice of apple pie. (Much better than Mom's, but then, my mother was a terrible cook.)

THE TEN BEST CHEAP CASINO SLEEPS

Compared with San Francisco, New York and certainly Tokyo, Las Vegas room rates are a bargain. However, a nice room in one of the major resort hotels will still cost $80 to $100 and well beyond. Yet, there are several casino hotels—both large and small—that offer bargain prices, and we list ten of them below.

Room rates in Las Vegas can gyrate wildly, changing with the seasons, the weather, the presence of a big convention, the days of the week and perhaps at the whim of a manager. Prices at many places are so unstable that clerks can't quote you a rate unless you give a specific date. The hotel computer then determines if this is a cheap date or an expensive one.

Rates are almost always cheaper Sunday through Thursday and higher Friday and Saturday. There's a third level for three-day weekends and other peak holiday periods. The highest prices and toughest times to find rooms are the two weeks of Christmas Vacation, Superbowl Sunday weekend, spring break (the weeks before and after Easter), and during big conventions, which tend to hit in spring and fall. Spring and fall also are peak tourist seasons.

If you do hit town during a major convention and you haven't made reservations in advance, check out some of the smaller casino hotels in town and out, since they usually don't block convention space. Generally, hotel rates are cheaper in midsummer, although this is changing as Las Vegas becomes more of a family destination. The slowest periods of the year? The first half of December and January, but definitely *not* during Superbowl weekend. After the Superbowl, business slows down through February and March, then starts picking up speed in April.

If we didn't already live here, we'd stay at a casino hotel, since that's where the action is. If our recommended places are full, you can find inexpensive rooms at some outlying casinos, particularly along the Boulder Highway that runs through next-door Henderson to Boulder City; it's an extension of downtown Fremont Street. Two places that have very nice, large rooms for $29 Sunday-Thursday and $49 Friday-Saturday, are on either side of Boulder City. Check out Railroad Pass Hotel & Casino on the west side, (800) 654-0877; and Gold Strike Hotel & Gambling Hall on the east side, (800) 634-1359.

What follows is our picks for affordable rooms right in Las Vegas. Remember that listed prices are subject to change, probably upward. Most of the rates shown are for weekdays during non-peak periods.

1 **GOLD SPIKE HOTEL CASINO** • *400 E. Ogden Ave. (at Fourth Street), Las Vegas, NV 89101; (800) 634-6703 or (702) 384-8444. Couples $20, mini-suites $30; rates include breakfast or two-for-one meal coupons.*

The Gold Spike qualifies for several of our budget lists in this chapter and it's our top choice for cheap lodgings. It features the best room buys in town; they're small yet neat and clean units with balconies, TV and phones.

2 **ARIZONA CHARLIE'S HOTEL & CASINO** • *740 S. Decatur Blvd. (West Charleston), Las Vegas, NV 89107; (800) 342-2695 or (702) 258-5111. Couples and singles from $30.*

A neighborhood casino popular with locals, Arizona Charlie's recently expanded, adding several ranks of hotel rooms. It has a full casino, pool, buffet and other facilities and it's only minutes from downtown. Head west on Charleston and turn right onto Decatur.

3 **BINION'S HORSESHOE HOTEL & CASINO** • *128 Fremont St. (at Casino Center Boulevard), Las Vegas, NV 89101; (800) 622-6468 or (702) 382-1600. Couples and singles $28 to $60.*

This is one of the least expensive large hotels right on Fremont Street, with 380 rooms. A rooftop pool occupies one of its 26-story towers.

4 **EL CORTEZ HOTEL** • *600 Fremont St. (Sixth Street), Las Vegas, NV 8 9101; (800) 634-6703 or (702) 385-5200. Couples and singles from $23.*

El Cortez is in a slightly scruffy neighborhood and the casino is a bit dusty, although the rooms were refurbished recently and are quite tidy. Boasting the oldest original casino in Las Vegas, the hotel is three blocks east of the Fremont Street Experience.

5 **GOLDEN GATE BED & BREAKFAST** • *One Fremont St. (at Main Street), Las Vegas, NV 89101; (800) 426-1906 or (702) 385-1906. Rooms for one or two $38 Sunday through Thursday and $53 Friday and Saturday, including a full breakfast.*

The oldest and one of the smallest downtown casino hotels, the Golden Gate dates from 1906 and it's named in honor of San Francisco. The busy casino and its 106 rooms have a 1930s San Francisco art deco look. Rooms go quickly, so make reservations very early.

6 *JACKIE GAUGHAN'S PLAZA* • *P.O. Box 760 (One Main Street), Las Vegas, NV 89125; (800) 634-6575 or (702) 386-2110. Couples and singles from $30.*

Located at the head of the Fremont Street Experience and offering full resort facilities, the Plaza is one of the better downtown hotel buys. Rooms get down to $30 during slow periods, and prices aren't too expensive during the rest of the year.

7 *LADY LUCK CASINO HOTEL* • *P.O. Box 1060 (206 N. Third Street at Ogden Avenue), Las Vegas, NV 89125; (800) 523-9582 or (702) 477-3000. Couples and singles $30 to $75.*

This large hotel sits just a block off the Fremont Street pedestrian mall, and it has full casino facilities. Room amenities include TV movies, radios and refrigerators.

8 *STARDUST HOTEL* • *3000 S. Las Vegas Blvd. (Stardust Road); Las Vegas, NV 89109; (800) 634-6757 or (702) 732-6111. Couples and singles starting at $18 in the off-season; $18 to $20 per person double occupancy the rest of the year.*

The Stardust is one of the least expensive major Strip hotels, with its older motel rooms going for under $20 a night during slow seasons, such as early December and January into March. Guests get all the facilities and conveniences of one of Glitter City's legendary resorts, which has been here since 1955.

9 *VACATION VILLAGE* • *6711 S. Las Vegas Blvd. (far end of the Strip), Las Vegas, NV 89193; (800) 658-5000 or (702) 897-1700. Couples and singles $20 to $45.*

The rooms are basic but neat and attractive in this pleasant complex, which offers a full casino, restaurants and a pool. It's at the far end of the Strip, although it's served by city buses (CAT) that run along Las Vegas Boulevard.

10 *WESTERN HOTEL/CASINO* • *899 E. Fremont St. (at Ninth Street downtown), Las Vegas, NV 89202; (800) 634-6703 or (702) 384-4620. Couples from $20.*

This small, slightly scruffy casino hotel is about six blocks east of the Downtown Casino Center. The rooms, while not fancy, are neat and clean.

They talk about the dignity of work. Bosh. The dignity is in pleasure.
— **Herman Melville**

Chapter six

DIVERSIONS AFTER DARK

SLEEPLESS IN LAS VEGAS

Whoever called New York "the city that never sleeps" obviously hadn't been to Las Vegas. The people here sleep, but not the city. And they sleep in shifts; they take turns, to ensure that the city stays awake. Their time to sleep may come in the middle of the day, because they worked the night shift at a casino or rounded up predawn revelers in their cabs. The city itself doesn't even nod off.

Las Vegas is unlike any other city in the world for two major reasons. The first, obviously, is that it contains the world's largest collection of gaming parlors. The second is that it offers more nightlife than any other place on the planet. Of course, "nightlife" isn't quite the right word for the city that never nods. Lounge shows can happen in the middle of the afternoon or the wee hours of the morning. Visitors will find one combo working a cocktail bar as the sun rises, and another as the sun goeth down.

The entertainment scene has changed through the years, however. No longer can you catch the "Summit Show" of Frank Sinatra, Dean Martin, Joey Bishop, Peter Lawford and Sammy Davis, Jr., at the Sands Copa Room for $5.95, *including* dinner. Still, the town features some of the greatest entertainment bargains on earth. Although some of the new high tech shows cost more than $80 a pop, you can enjoy a lounge show for the price of a drink.

Las Vegas nightlife—whenever it occurs—ranges from headliners and lavish production shows to cabaret shows to cocktail lounge entertainment to piano bars. Since headliners and cocktail lounge acts come and go, this chapter will address only the longer-running production shows and performers. We group them into two broad categories—the elaborately staged "big room" productions and the smaller shows. To find out what else and who else is happening where, consult one of the many free show guides available in racks all over town. Our favorite is *What's On* because it contains maps to help you locate casinos on the Strip, downtown and in the outlying areas. It also has a TV log, but what visitor watches television in Glitter City?

THE TEN BEST "BIG ROOM" SHOWS

Originally, all "big room" shows were either headliners (major stars) or dance revues. Bugsy Siegel opened his Fabulous Flamingo with Jimmy Durante and Rose Marie. The greatest stars of Hollywood and beyond have since followed them to Las Vegas, from Frankie to Elvis to Barbra. However, Siegel wasn't the first to import entertainers, nor was Las Vegas the first Nevada city to do so. The practice started way out in Elko, way back in 1941. Casino owner Newton Crumbly decided to clean up his sawdust joint, serve food to his patrons and hire showbiz celebs, starting with bandleader Paul Whitman. "WHITMAN GOES STIX," read a front page headline in *Daily Variety*.

Las Vegas quickly followed suit, first with "name" stars and then with Parisian style dance revues. It was soon apparent that Elko, Nevada, would not become the entertainment capital of the world.

The current trend is toward high tech productions such as the Mirage's Siegfried and Roy and MGM Grand's "EFX," although dance revues still draw crowds. They remain the most enduring signature of the local entertainment scene, with leggy showgirls wearing elaborate head dresses, feathers on their fannies and little else. Lasers and other special effects have been added, although these spectaculars generally follow a fixed format. Expect to see big, splashy production numbers with draped and semi-draped singers and dancers, a magician, a brace of acrobats or jugglers and perhaps an animal act. Most magicians will have a shapely female assistant. Her primary function seems to be the removal of excess doves from the stage, which have been produced from hankies, balloons and the ear canals of audience volunteers.

However, some of the best shows in town aren't girlie revues.

Danny Gans brings a large cast to Rio's Copacabaña Showroom—himself, impersonating more than a dozen personalities. Siegfried and Roy present a dazzler of an animal and magic act at the Mirage, and next-door Treasure Island offers the hauntingly beautiful Mystère circus performance. MGM Grand's "EFX" (which is supposed to be pronounced "Effects") is a multi-million dollar high tech show currently starring David Cassidy.

If you haven't been here for a few years, you'll note some changes in the big room shows. First, prices have escalated considerably, since some shows cost millions of dollars to produce. Second, dinner shows are going the way of the dodo birds which I think they used to serve. Most shows now offer cocktails only, with one or two drinks included in the ticket price. Some have eliminated drink service. Patrons go to an adjacent bar for their libations, which may or may not be included in the ticket price.

Four "dining shows" remained at this writing and only one is a traditional dinner show, the Flamingo Hilton's "Great Radio City Spectacular." Tropicana's "Folies Bergere" offers an optional dinner buffet for the early show, "Caesars Magical Empire" at Caesars Palace is half dinner and half show, and an eat-with-your-hands medieval dinner is served at "King Arthur's Tournament" at the Excalibur.

Another major change in the big shows. Most now have pre-assigned seating; you buy your ticket in advance as you would for a concert or ball game back home. The days of slipping a ten-spot to a *maitre d'* to get a seat in the bald headed row are slipping away fast. Obviously, this suggests that you should buy your tickets as far in advance as possible to get good seats. Some shows charge higher prices for better seats; others have a single-price policy. (Either way, you probably won't get the *best* seats; those go to high rollers and other favored casino guests.) And finally, good news for fresh-air fans—nearly every show in town is now smoke-free.

We rate the shows as **adult** (topless); **all-family** (with particular appeal to kids) and **adults and teens** (kids admitted, although pre-teens probably won't find it interesting).

1 SIEGFRIED & ROY • *The Mirage, 3400 S. Las Vegas Blvd. (adjacent to Caesars Palace); (702) 792-7777. Friday-Monday 7:30 and 11, dark Wednesday-Thursday; $89.35 including tax and two drinks. All-family show.*

Glitter City's first high tech production is still the most impressive, earning our top spot as the best "big room" show in town. It's a one-of-a-kind spectacular performed on a $25 million set—a dazzling blend of animal act, magic, dynamic special effects, brilliant lighting and big production numbers. The free-form stage juts into the audience, surrounding pods of patrons and drawing them into the action. And that action is nonstop, flowing smoothly from one episode to the next, in a dizzying netherworld of lasers, smoke, fire and probably even brimstone.

The opening is awesome—a haunting, quiet prelude that suddenly explodes into high tech action. A formless hologram floats below a black canopy of stars, squirming and writhing soundlessly like a jellyfish suspended in space. A huge, rotating circle of colored spotlights and lasers appears from above. Then, as a swelling soundtrack rattles the room, two asteroids float onto the stage and in a flash of smoke and fire, Siegfried and Roy appear, surrounded by a whirling cast of sixty wildly costumed dancers. From that point on, the intensity never yields. Our heroes, who have been performing together for three decades, match magical wits with a lovely sorceress, battle a mechanical fire-breathing dragon, disassemble and reassemble beautiful women, impale themselves on spikes, vanish and unvanish, evaporate elephants and nuzzle beautiful white tigers—who share their mansion in the suburbs.

A recent addition to their act—and to their home—are several rare white Timbatavi lions. Both white tigers and lions are now extinct in the wild and Siegfried and Roy have had considerable success in breeding them. They hope eventually to return some to their native environment.

At nearly $90 a pop, the Siegfried and Roy show is the most expensive in town. But never mind, just do it! No other production on the Strip—or on the planet—offers this mix of technical wizardry, magic acts, big production numbers and cuddly kitties.

2 DANNY GANS • *Rio Suite Hotel, 3700 W. Flamingo Rd. (West across I-15, at Valley View Boulevard); (702) 252-7776. Wednesday-Sunday at 8, dark Monday-Tuesday; $44.95 including two drinks and tax. Adults and teens.*

Danny Gans is a one-man amusement machine, currently the hottest ticket in town and one of the few performers—in this era of entertainment overkill and jaded audiences—who earns standing ovations. Gan's press release calls him "The man of many voices," which is an understatement—a rare occurrence for a press release. He is a man of many men, a few women and at least one frog.

Working with a simple lighting and a small combo, he brings a world of personalities to his stage. For most of his hour and 45 minute show, his only props are his face, his gestures and his voice. He not only mimics famous singers; he parodies their songs. As a laconic Randy Travis, he sings "I'm going to bore you forever, amen." Then, he is Willie Nelson, lamenting: "Just like the IRS, I made my life a mess." Next, he imitates several rock singers whose words nobody understands. With a blink of that single spotlight, he's a hundred-year-old George Burns doing a rap number, which turns into a touching tribute to the legendary entertainer. A spotlight blink later, Jimmy Stewart and Kermit, the Frog, sing "Rainbows," and then Nat and Natalie Cole reach across the generations for an "Unforgettable" duet. Henry Fonda and Katherine Hepburn present a touching scene from *On Golden Pond.* Just when the audience is mellowing out, Neal Diamond appears to sing "Perot, my friends Perot," followed by political promises from Ronald Reagan and Bill Clinton. From Gan's versatile voice box, Dean Martin and Jerry Lewis sing "That's Amore" and a dozen noted entertainers recall the "Twelve Months of Christmas."

At show's end, he becomes Danny Gans, to sing Garth Brooks' sanguine song about life's challenges, "The River."

3 *EFX* • *MGM Grand, 3799 S. Las Vegas Blvd. (Tropicana); (702) 891-7777. Tuesday-Saturday 7:30 and 10:30, dark Sunday-Monday; $70 preferred seating, $49.50 regular seating, kids 5-12, $35; tax and beverages extra. All-family show.*

There's more ham than Hamlet here, although this show will blow you out of your seat and its special effects will blow your mind. The plot is as thin as a newlywed's nightie and the dialogue is corny. However, with star David Cassidy's likable antics, unbelievable special effects and an earth-rattling soundtrack, who needs art? Cassidy flits about on flying saucers and beams of neon light, appearing as a young King Arthur, a futuristic P.T. Barnum, the Great Houdini and an Indiana Jones character in an imposing jungle temple scene.

The show begins as the giant, disembodied head of James Earl Jones—with his rich Darth Vader voice—invites the audience to join him in a flight of high-tech fancy and fantasy. Dancers in outerworldly garb flit about the theatre, setting the mood for this supernatural voyage, to the beat of flashing lights and assorted pyrotechnics. And then—talk about an Ecederin headache—the talking head explodes.

Then Cassidy is plucked from the audience, where he's supposedly working as a busboy, and sent on a journey through time and space to try and recover his lost love. He replaced the show's original star, Michael Crawford of *Phantom of the Opera* fame. Crawford had a stronger singing voice for this high tech musical, although Cassidy is more animated and the better actor of the two. Interestingly, one of the best episodes in "EFX" is not technical at all. The Flying Kaganovitch, a group of aerialists with the show's "Intergalactic Circus of Wonders," perform stunts we've never seen before. They launch themselves from trapeze bars, do triple somersaults and land on the clasped hands of compatriots to form human pyramids.

4 *ENTER THE NIGHT* • *Stardust Hotel, 3000 S. Las Vegas Blvd. (Stardust Road); (702) 732-6111. Tuesday-Thursday and Saturday 7:30 and 10:30, Sunday-Monday 8, dark Friday; $26.90 plus tax, including two drinks. Adults only.*

Stunning ladies, slinky costuming, precision choreography, dazzling laser dances and fine specialty acts flow together to create this fine production show. Although the theme is adult frolic after dusk, the current version is more upbeat and lively than the earlier edition that premiered in 1991. The dancers—some topless, others in dazzling costumes—are as sexy as before, although they move to a faster tempo. This is no stately chorus line strut, but a contemporary song and dance revue. Old fashioned runways bring performers into the audience. Although it isn't ultra high tech, it employs very sophisticated lasers and lots of moving sets, including an entire ice rink. (In fact, one of the show's most sensuous numbers is a wriggling, writhing laser dance.)

The lead dancer is Aki, the quintessential Las Vegas showgirl—a slender, sensuous blonde kitten. Lead singer Jennifer Page belts out popular songs in the style of Whitney Houston. The Scott Brothers perform several jittery, disjointed yet precision comedy dance numbers they describe as "cartoon dancing." The Las Huincas Gauchos from Argentina whirl their bolos, rattle the house with their drumbeats and crack their whips, along with a few good jokes. Perhaps the best specialty act is a near flawless ice skating routine by Cindy Landry and Bart Lancon. It's as good as you would see in any major ice show. Their costumes are so sexy and scanty that if they'd won first prize, there'd be no place to pin their medals.

5 THE BEST OF THE FOLIES BERGERE • *Tropicana Resort & Casino, 3801 S. Las Vegas Blvd. (Tropicana Avenue); (702) 739-2411. Nightly except Thursday at 8 and 10:30; $45 for table seating, $55 for booth seating, plus $11.75 for the Island Buffet (8 p.m. show only). Adults.*

The new Folies Bergere is, in a word, gorgeous. From the brilliant sets to the flawless choreography to the good-looking cast—male and female, it's one of the best musical revues in town. The show flows easily from one scene to the next, tracing the history of song and dance from a 19th century Paris music hall through the American flapper era to a Western hoedown and contemporary hits. It's accomplished with a pleasing mix of acrobatic dancing, jitterbug, modern dance, ballet and even a Strauss waltz, all supported by an excellent sound system.

As you enjoy this seamless river of song and dance, of color and glitter, you realize that the productions are deceptively simple and uncluttered. No lasers, no tin dragons, no fire and brimstone. This isn't high tech; it's simply high entertainment.

"The Best of the Folies Bergere" begins with a rear-screen projection of historic music hall scenes and yesteryear entertainers, and then goes "live" with a stunning night scene of Paris and a great "Can-Can" music hall number. You're transported to a grand ballroom in Versailles and then to the French Riviera for a cute "By the Sea" number in which modestly clad sea nymphs disrobe behind candy-striped beach umbrellas. The show dances through early Hollywood with a wonderful kaleidoscopic number, moves into the jazz era, then hops into a lively Western saloon scene with "Belly Up to the Bar" from *The Unsinkable Molly Brown*. As the singers and dancers gather for the finale—"Can You Feel the Love Tonight?" and "The Circle of Life" from *The Lion King*—you realize with a start that an hour and a half has slipped past.

6 JUBILEE! • *Bally's Las Vegas, 3645 S. Las Vegas Blvd. (Flamingo Road); (702) 739-4567. Sunday-Monday at 8, Tuesday-Thursday and Saturday 8 and 11, dark Friday; $60 preferred seating, $49.50 regular seating, including tax. Eighteen and older.*

While Siegfried and Roy and "EFX" may be more technically advanced, "Jubilee!" is the best musical revue in town—and it has some technical tricks of its own. Maybe it's the best revue that ever was. The girls are gorgeous, the sets are monumental, the staging is glittery and the numbers are brilliantly choreographed. BIG is written all over this show in capital letters—BIG cast, BIG sets and BIG production numbers. Samson brings a pagan temple to the ground, the Titanic sinks into the sea before your very eyes and, in a fine magic segment, a gleaming Lamborgini disappears into the sky. The only thing small in "Jubilee!" is the size of the dancers' costumes. While covering very little, they are elaborate bouquets of feathers, fans and floral puffs.

Technically impressive pageantry—notably the Samson and Delilah and Titanic episodes—alternate with lavish dance numbers and fine specialty acts. Bally's Delilah shows more than Liz Taylor was ever permitted to reveal in the film version, and her seduction of Samson is—well—rather seductive. The collapse of the pagan temple is the technical highlight of the show. (Samson topples the giant temple pillars even before his hair grows back, but of course, it would have been an awfully long show otherwise.) A close technical rival to the temple scene is a larger-than-life Titanic engine room set, which crumples to the cadence of broken, hissing steam pipes and fractured, fire-belching boilers as the ship self-destructs after hitting an iceberg.

The show ends with a musical tribute to Hollywood as the full cast prances about in their glittery costumes, singing such classics as "I Married an Angel." However, is the world really ready for a topless angel with a rhinestone halo, wings and G-string? No, but Las Vegas is.

7 KING ARTHUR'S TOURNAMENT • *Excalibur, 3850 S. Las Vegas Blvd. (Tropicana); (702) 597-7600. Nightly at 6 and 8:30; $29.95 including dinner and tax. All-family show.*

You might call this fun family show "King Arthur meets Darth Vader," since the Black Knight looks suspiciously like the *Star Wars* bad guy. This jousting tournament is all in jest; the horsemanship is good, the balsa wood lances shatter dramatically and no one gets hurt. However, the swords are real and you'll see some well-choreographed, realistic looking sword play.

While you hiss the bad guy and cheer your appointed hero (each seating section is assigned a good guy), you eat rock Cornish game hens with sticky fingers and pretend you're at a decadent medieval banquet. However, you are not encouraged to throw the bones at the Arthurian Darth Vader. The show features a bit of high tech wizardry as laser beams bounce around the sawdust arena and ringmaster Merlin struts about, setting off puffs of smoke.

This arena also is the setting for a pleasing afternoon show of horsemanship, "An Evening in Vienna," featuring the prancing, dancing and leaping Royal Lipizzaner Stallions. Brightly costumed riders put their steeds through complex paces. The show runs daily except Friday at 2 p.m.; adults $7.95; seniors and kids under 12, $5.95.

8 LANCE BURTON • *Monte Carlo, 3770 Las Vegas Blvd. (north of Tropicana); (702) 730-7000. Tuesday-Saturday 7:30 and 10:30, dark Sunday-Monday, $34.95 balcony and $39.95 main floor, including tax; drinks extra. All-family.*

He strolls onstage, amiable and almost shy, wearing a tuxedo that looks out of place beneath his tousled black hair; he talks to his audience with a soft Kentucky accent. There is no sense of mystery to Lance Burton; no intense David Copperfield gaze or Houdini haughtiness. His show is classic and low key, a study in old school magic. The few high tech effects that he employs seem almost to be a distraction. Yet, this is the most astounding magic show we have ever seen. There is nothing up his sleeves, for he keeps them rolled up. Burton vanishes and unvanishes, produces flights of doves and herds of geese, flirts casually with his bevy of seven beautiful girls and makes them disappear in a cute "Air Lance Burton" episode. (Fortunately, they all return to finish the show.) We stared until our eyes hurt, trying to figure out his levitation tricks. As he ended the show by flying off into space in his white Corvette—with the wheels folding up like the *Back to the Future* Delorean, we gave up trying.

Although Burton is funny in a down-home way, serious comic relief is provided by his featured performer, Michael Godeau. Posing as a clumsy juggler, he staggers and giggles and stares and drops things and wobbles around on a unicycle. Then he wows the audience by juggling a bowling ball, a lighted torch and a running chain saw.

This is one of the best shows in town because it is not high tech—except for that flying Corvette. Most of its visual miracles are performed not by multi-million-dollar computer-driven machines, but by humans. It all happens in a comfortable, plush turn-of-the-century style theater, built especially for Burton.

9 **MYSTÈRE by Cirque du Soleil** • *Treasure Island, 3300 S. Las Vegas Blvd. (Spring Mountain Road); (702) 894-7722. Wednesday-Sunday 7:30 and 10:30, dark Monday and Tuesday; adults $64.90, kids under 12, $32.45. Drinks and snacks extra, available at snack bar. All-family show.*

We have seen the Cirque du Soleil performance several times, and we always come away intrigued and pleased. The current edition, "Mystère," is essentially a circus show, staged in a big top style arena with steeply tiered seating. However, this is a circus like you've never seen before. Created by the French-Canadian Cirque du Soleil troupe, it's a hauntingly enchanting, wildly costumed production using only people. There are no snarling big cats, plodding elephants or dog and pony acts. The outerworldly costumes, strange music and fog effects create a Wagnerian scene as performers bounce about on trampolines, juggle assorted objects, pop themselves into the air from teeter totters and defy everything but gravity in high wire acts.

Mystère has its light moments as well. A fat, over-sized "baby" waddles about, babbling in French gibberish, tripping over props, bouncing a huge rubber ball into the audience and generally disrupting the performance. The show's funniest moments come even before the main program starts. Keep your eye on a tuxedo-clad character resembling a deranged Albert Einstein. He does the greatest warmup act you'll ever see as he helps escort people to their seats. If you're not seated and he offers to assist, we hope you've brought your sense of humor along with your popcorn. You might lose both.

10 **SPLASH!** • *Riviera Hotel, 2901 S. Las Vegas Blvd. (Riviera Boulevard); (702) 477-5274 or 794-9433. Nightly at 7:30 and 10:30, $39.5 or $49.50 plus tax; includes one drink. All-family early show; topless adults only late show.*

The current rendition of this popular aquatic-theme show is more wiggle than wet. While the first two versions focused on synchronized swimming in a giant onstage tank, most of the performers in this rendition don't go near the water. The show opens with a striking black-lighted Neptune set, with two mermaids undulating in that big tank while dancing waters and lasers "perform" in the foreground. However, for the rest of the evening, "Splash" features lively, highly charged and well executed dance numbers and specialty acts. The early show is suitable for families although it's probably more interesting for teens and adults. Some of the ladies drop their tops for the late show; their dances are sexy but not really bawdy.

Production numbers move quickly from one theme to the next—from a Chinatown scene for a kind of *West Side Story* setting to a scene from *Evita* featuring a very convincing Madonna mimic. Equally effective Janet and Michael Jackson facsimiles pop in and out of several numbers, including the *West Side Story* bit. (Michael meets Maria?)

Specialty acts range from Clint Carvalho's talking parrots and macaws that strafe the audience to low-key comic Mark Cornhauser who identifies audience members' hometowns by their zip codes. (He even knew that 95310 was Columbia, California, our second home—even though it's a tiny mountain town of only 90 people.) The best specialty performers were Joe Trammel, a highly charged comic-dancer-mime who galloped through a wild slapstick routine; and Anderson's Power Riders, four motorcyclists who buzzed around like angry hornets inside an iron ball and somehow avoided tangling handlebars.

THE TEN BEST SMALL SHOWS

These are shows in smaller theaters or cabarets, usually with a much smaller cast and cost than the big room productions. Our selections dance from magical dinners to celebrity impersonators to country dancers. The winner is a lively one-woman show in the only star-owned theater in town, presented by a spunky lady who has lived in Las Vegas for three decades:

1 THE DEBBIE REYNOLDS SHOW • *Debbie Reynolds Hollywood Hotel and Casino, 305 Convention Center Dr. (between Las Vegas Boulevard and Paradise Road); (702) 733-2243. Monday-Friday at 7:30, dark Saturday-Sunday; $39.95 including tax and two drinks. All-family show.*

Move over, "EFX" and Siegfried and Roy. At least for those of us who remember her innocent, cheery and upbeat films, the Debbie Reynolds Show is one of the most entertaining productions in town. It is definitely Glitter City's best "small room" show. Although Ms. Reynolds recently qualified for Social Security and Medicare, the voice, the body and certainly the spirit are still intact. She struts on stage in a slinky, sequined gown and wows her audience for an hour and a half without taking a break or even pausing to catch her breath. Her only "production" elements are a fine pianist and drummer and a rear projection screen that shows a few of her film clips.

Barely over five feet tall, she carries on with all of the spunk and energy that won her an Oscar nomination for *The Unsinkable Molly Brown*. Her patter is down-home friendly, sometimes cutely sexy but never bawdy. "I show a little leg for the boys," she says of her sparkling gown that's slit up to the thigh. "The rest of the body is shot." (It isn't.) And she jokes about her struggle to keep her little hotel afloat among the mega-resorts that surround her. "We only have two hundred rooms here," she says. "But it's a friendly place and I answer room service." Friendly, indeed. After each show, Ms. Reynolds chats with her guests, autographs their programs and has her photo taken with them.

Although we're familiar with Debbie's fine singing voice, we were surprised by her fine skills as a comedienne. Her mimicry of Jimmy Stewart, Barbra Streisand, Willie Nelson, Zsa Zsa Gabor and Katie Hepburn were hilarious. She tickled her Fiftysomething audience with a cornball country version of "Singing in the Rain" and a rap variation on "Down in the Meadow." And then to prove that the old vocal chords were still in tune, she closed the show beautifully with her only Top Ten hit, "Tammy."

2 *AMERICAN SUPERSTARS* • *The Stratosphere, 2000 Las Vegas Blvd. (Main Street); (702) 380-7711. Nightly except Thursday at 7 and 10, dark Thursday; adults $22.95, kids 4-12, $16.95, plus tax. Adults and teens.*

This fast-paced, impressively staged show would be excellent even if it weren't an impersonator gig. The clones of such stars as Madonna, Charlie Daniels and Michael Jackson are fine entertainers in their own right. They perform on attractive sets, backed up by an excellent six-woman chorus line called the "Superstar Dancers" and some of the most creative lighting effects we've seen in town. As an added bonus, the show features outstanding camera work. The acts are videotaped and simultaneously projected on screens flanking the stage. With the skilled use of lap dissolve, freeze-framing and other special effects, the audience sees two shows at once.

The production we caught featured a Gloria Estevan mimic doing several of her specialties, backed up by the chorus line, which she led through the audience with a bouncy version of "On Your Feet." A Charlie Daniels look-alike could have shaved his stage-grayed beard, shed his dark glasses and emerged from the clone closet; he was one the best fiddle players we've ever heard. Diana Ross and the Supremes didn't quite copy the originals in appearance and voice, although they were a fine act in their own right. Perhaps the best look-alikes were a believable Michael Jackson (although he couldn't quite reach the real Michael's high, feminine notes) and a pretend Madonna, an exact replica from the ground up, from shapely legs to shapely hooters to a fine voice. The full cast appeared at show's end for a group finale and then adjourned to the lobby to sign autographs and pose for pictures.

3 *CAESARS MAGICAL EMPIRE* • *Caesars Palace, 3570 S. Las Vegas Blvd. (Flamingo Road); (702) 731-7333. Nightly 4:30 to 10:30; $75 including dinner, magic shows & tax; $10 discount for early and late seatings; kids 5 to 10 half price. Adults and kids 5 and over.*

Leave it to Caesar to combine an elaborate underground catacomb and intriguing special effects with a Roman banquet. The Magical Empire is a 66,000-square foot complex beneath Caesars Palace where dining, magic and humor are crafted into an evening's entertainment. Think of it as "Indiana Jones Meets the Spirit of Caesar," without the scary part. Small groups of diners are escorted into the "Chamber of Destiny," which shudders and sinks into an underground grotto, taking them into the spirit world of Caesar. They are greeted by a centurian who escorts them into one of ten elaborately decorated, dungeon-like yet cheerful dining halls. Here, a three-course dinner is hosted by a sorcerer who conjures up magic and music. It's like having one's own personal magician at an intimate, lively dinner party. As the sorcerer performs his mystical feats, a nubile maiden serves food and pours wine or flavored iced tea (nectar of the gods) from Roman vessels.

"Nice jugs," our host-magician quipped as the wine maiden appeared. "Try the chardonnay. Vintage 84 B.C.—a very good year." Our "Roman" magician had a soft English accent and a great sense of humor. "This is better than working the streets," he said, glancing up at the vaulted stone ceiling.

After dinner, guests are escorted into the imposing seven-story *Sanctum Secorum* for more magic, fire and occasional dashes of brimstone. They then wobble and giggle through the "Forbidden Crypt"; the floor is stable but a revolving cylinder creates a dizzying sense of motion. From here, guests attend two magic shows, in the Secret Pagoda Theater and Sultan's Palace Theatre. (One of the featured magicians is Jeff McBride, voted by the *Las Vegas Review-Journal* staff recently as the best magician in town. He doesn't work every night, so check before you go.)

If all of this activity and entertainment works up additional thirst, bars are placed strategically about the catacombs. Guests can remain in Caesars Magical Empire for as long as they wish. They can linger and admire the complex dungeon-like décor, or catch the magic shows a second time and try to figure out how that lady disappeared into the thin, subterranean air.

4 *COUNTRY FEVER* • *Golden Nugget, 129 Fremont St. (Casino Center Boulevard); (702) 386-8100. Nightly except Friday at 7 and 9:45; $22.50 plus tax, including one drink and "country fixin's." Adults and teens.*

Add a neon cactus or two and the small, elegant Golden Nugget showroom becomes a country theater for one of the fastest-paced, most tightly-packaged productions in town. Fever, indeed! A scantily clad chorus line in cut-away Levi's opens the show, scampering about a Western barroom set and rocking the room with lively singing and dancing. (They didn't dress like that in *Annie, Get Your Gun!*) Don't get the wrong impression; this isn't "Grand Ole' Oprey Goes to the Follies." It's a wholesome, upbeat country show and the featured singers—fully clad, of course—could hold their own on any Nashville or Branson stage. A country band called "The Posse" provides lively musical backup. The show runs the rural music gamut from Corrie Sachs' rendition of "Whose Bed Have Your Boots Been Under?" to some lively country choir numbers by the Golden Nugget Gospel Singers. Soft-spoken Kirby St. Romain ("Think of a vacuum cleaner and French lettuce") provides comic relief. This big, good-looking guy is one of the town's funniest performers, alternating between droll, down-home humor and hilariously realistic sound effects.

"You ever been awaken at 5 a.m. by the garbage truck?" He then proceeds with the entire audio scenerio.

"How can a guy win at keno in this town?" he asks, kidding his employers. "They've got a million dollar computer and they give us a piece of paper and a crayon..."

5 CRAZY GIRLS • *Riviera Hotel, 2901 S. Las Vegas Blvd. (Riviera Boulevard); (702) 477-5274 or 794-9433. Tuesday-Friday and Sunday 8:30 and 10:30. Saturday 8:30, 10:30 and midnight, dark Monday; $18.95 plus tax; includes two drinks. Adults only.*

A more appropriate name for this fast-paced, well-executed cabaret show would be "Naughty Girls." The ladies of the chorus certainly aren't crazy or even silly; they *are* very sexy. The song and dance numbers are mostly topless, rather erotic and sensual. The lady emcee was, in a word, rather raunchy. (However, the show we saw featured a guest emcee, so the regular may or may not be quite as graphic.) The singer-dancers are all strikingly attractive and it's likely that some of their attributes have been given a silicon boost. (A recent *Las Vegas Review-Journal* poll voted them best-looking showgirls.)

The show is cute if you're broad-minded and no pun intended, guys. It opens with the dancers wriggling in, over, under and through a giant pair of lips and moves briskly from one song and dance act to the next. A number based on the famous Marilyn Monroe air vent scene from *The Seven-Year Itch* was really cute, with four matched Marilyns wearing the same style of billowy skirt and little else. The show's best number was a sensuous Gypsy Rose Lee style strip, well executed by a showgirl clad entirely in red. Between dances, the emcee kidded the gents in the bald-headed row about their private parts and how they employed them. This is mostly a guy show, although several couples were in attendance.

6 AN EVENING AT LA CAGE • *Riviera Hotel, 2901 S. Las Vegas Blvd. (Riviera Boulevard); (702) 477-5274 or 794-9433. Nightly except Tuesday at 7:30 and 9:30, plus an 11:15 p.m. show Wednesday; VIP seating $32.16, regular seating $21.95, plus. Adults only.*

If you're ready for Whoopi Goldberg and ten singing nuns in drag, or an overweight Cher waddling about the stage like a happy hippo, then you're ready for an evening in this "cage" of female impersonators. This may be the most cutely outrageous show in town, led by a nasty talking Joan Rivers replica played by Frank Marino. What's remarkable about these male performers is that—with one exception— they impersonate female stars. They often do a more convincing job than the same-sex mimics at "Legends in Concert" and "American Superstars." In fact, some of the guys of La Cage play more than one female character.

Marino, who launches this fast-paced, glittery show by singing "One of the Girls Who's One of the Boys," keeps the audience howling with his off-color jokes. He introduces the evening's ten impersonator acts, appearing each time in a new, strikingly gorgeous gown. Numbers are lavishly staged and brilliantly lighted in this large but cozy theater. A pretend Whoopi Goldberg and the show's chorus line whoop it up as nuns in a scene from *Sister Act*, then a very convincing Whitney Houston belts out "I Will Always Love You" from *The Body Guard*. A look-alike Judy Garland warbles "Over the Rainbow" and pretender daughter Lisa Minelli follows with a tremendous dance number to the tune of "City Lights" from *Forty-second Street*.

Others prance, dance and sing in a glittering blur of personality parody: Diana Ross, Dionne Warwick, Bette Midler and—the only guy-guy in the cast—Michael Jackson, portrayed by Lane Lassiter. His snap-wiggle dancing style is as good as the real Michael's. Chubby Marvin Nathan carries the show to a high level of silliness with his parodies of Cher and country singer "Tammy Spraynet." Logan Walker, who portrays Judy Garland, creates one of the show's finest moments. To the tune of "What Makes a Man a Man," he sheds his womanly stage makeup and garments to become male again, complete with hairy chest.

7 *FOREVER PLAID* • *Flamingo Hilton, 3555 S. Las Vegas Blvd. (Flamingo road) (702) 733-3333. Nightly except Monday at 7:30 and 10; $19.95 plus tax; includes two drinks. Adults and teens.*

This little four-man show is the darling of nostalgia buffs. A harmonic quartet sings popular melodies of the 1950s and 1960s, interlaced with comedy that falls just short of slapstick. It's the *premise* that makes this show appealing: In a flashback, the audience learns that members of a small-town quartet called Forever Plaid were en route to their first big gig in 1964 when they were broadsided by a bus full of Catholic teenage virgins headed for a Beatles concert. The teens were unhurt but the crash sent the quartet to heaven. As the show opens, they've come back to earth in a kind of cosmic *Brigadoon* cum *Carousel* schtick, and given one last chance to perform before a big audience. The tunes are predictable and pleasing—those songs of innocence just before the music scene went rock-crazy, such as "Catch a Falling Star", "Heart and Soul", "Three Coins in a Fountain" and "Love is a Many Splendored Thing." Fans of the Four Aces and Four Lads will love it.

"Forever Plaid's" best moment is an *Ed Sullivan Show* spoof. As one member of the quartet plays "Lady of Spain" on an accordion, the others perform—in three and a half minutes—every kind of dog-and-pony act, vocal and dance number ever seen on the Sullivan stage.

8 SHOWGIRLS OF MAGIC • *Hotel San Remo, 115 E. Tropicana (opposite the MGM Grand); (702) 597-6028. Nightly except Monday at 8 and 10:30; $19.95 plus tax; includes one drink. Family show at 8, adults only at 10:30.*

These three lady magicians are so clever they make their own clothes disappear! However, they drop their tops only during the late show; the early production is suitable for families. Although the concept of topless lady magicians suggests more gimmick that substance, the show actually is a delight—and not just because magicians Cheryl, Julie and Helen are awesome looking ladies in or out of costume. They're also good magicians and you certainly know that there's nothing up their sleeves! They are more or less clad for most of their magic acts. They go topless only for a couple of very good dance numbers, and one of them does a fine Janet Jackson impersonation.

This little show offers big variety, in addition to the mix of magic, singing and dancing by the featured trio. The Los Latin Gouchos spin their bolos, stomp their spurred boots and keep the audience laughing with their lively patter, and Japanese magician Luna Shemada mystifies them with her disappearing and reappearing bamboo umbrellas. Two-and-a-half-foot-tall Antonio Hoyos and 400-pound Steve Daley do a Sonny and Cher bit that's strictly slapstick and pretty humorous. Perhaps the show's funniest bit is Daley's portrayal of a woman chariciture artist. He does a hasty cartoon sketch of a member of the audience, and it somehow becomes animated and starts talking.

9 LEGENDS IN CONCERT • *The Imperial Palace, 3535 S. Las Vegas Blvd. (between Sands and Flamingo); (702) 794-3261. Nightly except Sunday at 7:30 and 10:30; $29.50, including two drinks and tax. Adults and teens.*

Bring in the clones. The original Las Vegas impersonator show has been jazzed up with a glittery set, lasers and a bevy of rather shapely and sexy dancers. Most of the "stars" are remarkably matched to the originals in appearance, voice and gestures. Video screens on either side of the stage show clips of the original performers, allowing onlookers to compare real stars and their pretenders. The performers vary from night to night, drawing from a cast of about a dozen impersonators.

On our last visit, we were entertained by a *faux* Neal Diamond (a near twin to the original), Sammy Davis, Jr. (good voice, although a bit chubby), Dolly Parton (anatomically complete), Elton John (who tended to slip in and out of a Jerry Lewis character), Diana Ross (very believable), the Four Tops (animated and excellent), and—hands down—the best Elvis in town. His highly-charged, laser-laced "Viva Las Vegas!" finale was excellent.

10 *VIVA LAS VEGAS!* • *The Stratosphere, 2000 Las Vegas Blvd. (Main Street); (702) 380-7711. Monday-Saturday at 2 and 4 p.m., dark Sunday; $10 plus tax. All-family.*

This small afternoon revue may be the best entertainment buy in town, particularly when the Stratosphere periodically offers coupon specials admitting two people for the price of a drink apiece—about $6 plus tip. Look for them in *What's On* and other local entertainment guides. Even at ten dollars a pop, this afternoon show is a bargain. Seasoned professionals prance, dance and do funny bits in the same technically advanced showroom used for the Stratosphere's evening show, "American Superstars."

The last time we took an afternoon break, the show opened with standup comedian Dave Swan from Wales. ("If your wife's overweight, have her walk two miles every morning and two miles every night. At the end of the week, she'll be twenty-eight miles away.") Other acts, alternating with a fine, cheerfully costumed dance troupe, included vocalist Laurie Caceres, who could really belt out the pop tunes; magician Valentino, who produced from thin air—among other things—two entire ducks; and David Iannaci, a classic slapstick vaudevillian comic. His act ranged from a one-armed violinist and an inept Indian rainmaker to an absolutely mad chicken.

THE OTHER TEN BEST PLACES FOR AMUSEMENTS

1 THE BEST PLACE FOR NIGHT OWLS: **Cleopatra's Barge** • *Caesars Palace, 3570 S. Las Vegas Blvd. (Flamingo Road); (702) 731-7110.*

Cleo's Barge presents proof positive that Las Vegas never sleeps. This cleverly fashioned lounge—a replica of an Egyptian barge floating on its own pond—has never seen the light of day, for it doesn't open until 9 p.m. You can enjoy live entertainment and dance until 4 a.m., while rocking gently above the mist and fog.

2 THE BEST PLACE TO DANCE: **The NightClub** • *Las Vegas Hilton, 3000 Paradise Rd. (Riviera Boulevard); (702) 732-5422. Open 3 p.m. to 4 a.m., with live music and entertainment usually from about 9 to well after midnight.*

This 450-seat club is the town's most inviting dance venue, with live bands playing Top Forty numbers and an occasional oldie. This is no nostalgic swing era club with big band sounds, however. The music, the beat and the look of the place are contemporary, although it's a bit quieter than a disco. You can even find a relatively secluded corner in this large two-tiered lounge. The NightClub is home to dynamic dance diva Kristine W., who performs nightly.

3 THE BEST PLACE TO DANCE IF YOU'RE WEARING COWBOY BOOTS: Western Dance Hall & Saloon • *Sam's Town, 5111 Boulder Highway (Nellis Boulevard); (702) 456-7777.*

Wanna-be cowboys can kick up their heels every night but Sunday from 9 to 3 a.m. in Sam's Western dance hall. Free country dance lessons are offered nightly from 7:30 until 9; seniors dance lessons are Wednesday and Friday from 4 to 5:30. (*"Finally, Martha, we can learn to line dance!" "Okay, Zeke, but take off those dang spurs first."*)

4 THE BEST PLACE TO GRAB THE MIKE: Ellis Island Casino • *4178 Koval Lane (Flamingo Road); (702) 733-8901.*

Some of the would-be performers who take the mike at this karoake bar probably should have been kept at the *real* Ellis Island. On the other hand, many are quite entertaining. Every night is amateur night at this casino bar, from 9 until 3 a.m. It's part of a Super 8 complex immediately south of Flamingo Road.

5 THE BEST PLACE FOR A CHEAP LAUGH: Holiday Inn Boardwalk • *3750 S. Las Vegas Blvd. (near Harmon Avenue, between the Excalibur and the Bellagio); (702) 730-3194.*

Las Vegas suffers no shortage of comics, although most shows go for more than $20 a ticket. The Boardwalk's "Unknown Comic" performs at 9 nightly except Monday for a mere $9.95, and that includes a drink. If you want to keep on laughing, catch a second comedian Tuesday-Saturday at 10:30, for just $5.95. You have to buy your own drink for that one.

6 THE BEST PLACE TO GET THE BLUES: Sand Dollar Blues Lounge • *3355 Spring Mountain Rd. (Polaris Avenue); (702) 871-6651.*

Most live music in town is either rock or country. However, you can catch some fine blues at this pleasantly scruffy 24-hour bar just west of the Strip. Live performers do the blues thing from Wednesday through Sunday from 10 to 5:30 a.m. You'll find it on the outer corner of a strip mall less than a mile west of Las Vegas Boulevard. The look is weather-beaten nautical; the mood is strictly cool blues.

7 THE BEST PLACE TO CATCH HOT ROCK: The Joint • *Hard Rock Hotel and Casino, 4455 Paradise Rd. (at Harmon); (702) 226-4650 for show schedule; (702) 474-4000 for tickets (Ticketmaster) or stop by the Hard Rock Hotel box office, generally open noon to 9.*

This flashy and hip 1,200-seat showroom carries the Hard Rock theme into the concert hall, featuring appearances by such groups as REO Speedwagon, Grand Funk and Dog Star. However, the shows aren't all hard rock. Fortysomethings can catch the likes of Mary Chapin Carpenter, Gordon Lightfoot and Boz Skaggs.

8 THE BEST PLACE TO LIMBO: La Playa Lounge • *Harrah's Las Vegas, 3475 S. Las Vegas Blvd. (opposite the Mirage); (702) 369-5000.*

The newly redecorated Harrah's features a "fantasy beach lounge" with beach style chairs, tropical trim, palms and lots of good Caribbean music. The place never closes and its bamboo walls ring with live reggae and calypso sounds daily from 2 p.m. until 3:30 a.m.

9 THE BEST PLACE TO CATCH A FLICK: Showcase 8 **Theatre** • *At the Showcase, Las Vegas Boulevard and Tropicana; (702) 740-2468.*

It's difficult to find a big screen theater these days. Most are chopped into several viewing rooms with screens the size of bed sheets. The new Showcase, although it's a multi-screen theater, has large screens and Dolby digital stereo, to maximize enjoyment of the high tech special effects films being produced today. It's just off the Strip next to the MGM Grand, reached via the new Showcase complex through catwalks and elevators.

10 THE BEST PLACES TO PIG OUT AT MIDNIGHT: **Boulder Station and Sunset Station** • *4111 Boulder Highway (near I-515 interchange), (702) 432-7777; and 1301 W. Sunset Rd. (just west of I-515 interchange), Henderson, NV 89014; (888) SUNSET-9 or (702) 547-7777.*

Has all of this nighttime activity worked up an appetite? There are plenty of 24-hour restaurants and late night dining specials in Las Vegas but—the last time we checked—only two late-night buffets. Boulder Station and Sunset Station offer all-you-can-eat spreads at 11 p.m. Saturday and Sunday, and you can keep eating until 6 a.m. for a mere $4.49.

A man's got to believe in something. I believe I'll have another drink.
— **W.C. Fields**

Chapter seven

PUB CRAWLING
...BAR HOPPING AND BEER SIPPING

The souls of the departed Mormons who founded the first settlement at the oasis of Las Vegas must be having a fit. It is against the Mormon faith to touch alcohol. Yet, more booze is probably consumed here each day than in any other city on earth, except possibly vodka-soaked Moscow.

On the positive side—if you aren't a Mormon—Las Vegas also may offer more interesting places to drink than any other city, from cutesy theme bars to industrial-strength brewpubs. Many are inside casinos; others are scattered about the area's neighborhoods.

THE TEN BEST CASINO BARS

Casino resorts offer some of the most interesting cocktail lounges and bars in Las Vegas. Many of them are great places for people watching or relaxing, to take a break from the gaming action or—in come cases—to continue the action if you perch at the "plank," since most have video poker machines built into their bartops.

1 HOUDINI LOUNGE: Monte Carlo • 3770 Las Vegas Blvd.; (702) 730-7777.

This elegant, clubby lounge with its warm woods, glossy black tile floor and overstuffed burgundy chairs and couches is the most appealing cocktail lounge in Glitter City. It's a grand place in which to settle back, drink in hand, and watch the activity in the adjacent gaming area. Or pick up that drink and take a slow stroll along the walls. They're covered with old posters, handbills and other memorabilia relating to Harry Houdini and other master magicians and illusionists of yesterday. Why a magicians' theme inside the Monte Carlo, which is styled after the posh casino in Monaco? It pays homage to prestidigitator Lance Burton, who is performing, apparently indefinitely, in the casino's main showroom. We say indefinitely because it's called the Lance Burton Theatre.

2 THE BAR AT TIMES SQUARE: New York New York • 3790 S. Las Vegas Blvd. (Tropicana Avenue); (702) 740-6969.

Weary of the glitter and commotion of the casino? Retreat into this Manhattan style drinking establishment, step up to the main bar with its handsome mirrored, wooden arch back bar and place your foot on a real brass rail. Or you can settle at an old fashioned wooden table beside warm, wood paneled walls. Except for the sounds of the casino pouring in through the open doors, you can believe for a moment that you're in your favorite neighborhood pub back in the Big Apple. To make the transition more believable, there are no gaming devices in here, not even the ubiquitous bartop video poker machines. The walls are decorated with black and white photos of old New York.

3 BATTLE BAR: Treasure Island at the Mirage • 3300 S. Las Vegas Blvd. (Spring Mountain Road); (702) 894-7111.

This large bar with an appealing colonial-Caribbean look is situated between Treasure Island's main casino and the outside lagoon, where periodic high-tech battles are staged between a British frigate and a pirate ship. Sippers can sit near the casino action, find a quiet corner, or adjourn to the deck and relax in the fun atmosphere of a pretend South Seas pirates' lair. It is a great place to watch the ship battle, although you'll have to take up position an hour or so before showtime.

4 THE FINAL POINT: Sam's Town Gambling Hall • 5111 Boulder Highway (at Nellis Boulevard); (702) 456-7777.

This is one of the town's best sports bars, with the requisite TV monitors, including several king-size ones, plus sports memorabilia and proper fare such as hamburgers, hot dogs, jalapeña poppers and spicy chicken wings. It's a participatory sports bar as well, with several pool tables and table hockey. It even has a small basketball shooting cage inside and a volleyball court outside, beside Sam's swimming lagoon.

5 **HARD ROCK HOTEL AND CASINO** • *4455 Paradise Road (at Harmon, just east of the Strip); (702) 693-5000.*

If you really like to be in the middle of things, find a seat at the circular Hard Rock Casino Bar, or a table on the edge. The Hard Rock Casino is laid out in a circle and the bar is at ground zero. From here, you can watch the casino action swirling about you, check MTV rock videos or the latest game on monitors hanging from the central bar structure, or just sit and admire this virtual museum of rock star memorabilia.

6 **IPANEMA BAR: Rio Suite Hotel & Casino** • *3700 W. Flamingo Rd. (at Valley View Boulevard, opposite the Gold Coast); (702) 252-7777.*

This cheerful, open bar with its Brazilian festival decor is a fine place for people-watching, since it's located between the Rio's two large casinos. You can sit on the rail and watch the action in the casinos, or retreat inside to quieter corners. The bar serves the usual libations plus several tropical specialties and they're served by the prettiest cocktail waitresses in town.

7 **LAGOON SALOON: The Mirage** • 3400 S. Las Vegas Blvd. (adjacent to Caesars Palace); (702) 791-7111.

This lushly decorated tropical theme bar is adjacent to the 90-foot canopy of the Mirage's indoor rainforest. Patrons can sit near the "forest" and listen to the pleasant sounds of a waterfall (and even crickets at night), find a quiet corner or sit on the casino side and watch the action while they sip.

8 **LA PLAYA LOUNGE: Harrah's Las Vegas** • *3475 S. Las Vegas Blvd., Las Vegas, NV 89109; (702) 369-5000.*

Think of this spirited place as a psychedelic beach bar. As part of Harrah's brilliant new Mardi Gras theme, the lively La Playa cabaret is a rainbow study in multi-colored beach style chairs, Technicolor palm trees and splashy carpeting. Dozens of glittering stars dangle from a darkened ceiling. The place is open 24 hours and live entertainers offer reggae, calypso and rock sounds from 2 p.m. until 3:30 a.m. When you've overdosed on all that singing and wriggling, you can seek refuge at an outside patio table, beside a pretend waterfall spilling over a pretend rock wall.

9 MARDI GRAS BAR: Orleans Hotel & Casino • 4500 W. Tropicana Ave.; (702) 365-7111.

This flashy new resort with a Mardi Gras theme has several intriguing casino bars. The most impressive is the circular Mardi Gras Bar, with four huge figureheads of masked Mardi Gras queens thrusting from an drop ceiling. The ladies are accented by violet and red neon and amber twinkle lights; the effect is quite smashing. It's the casino's most centrally located bar. You can sit before one of the maidens, or grab a table on the large outer rim, either near the race and sports book, the table games or the slot and video machines.

10 TROPICS LOUNGE: Tropicana Resort & Casino • 3801 S. Las Vegas Blvd. (Tropicana Avenue, opposite the Excalibur); (702) 739-2222.

We'll call this the most cheerful bar in Glitter City. In keeping with the Tropicana's "Island of Las Vegas" theme, its done up tropic decor, with a brilliant carpet of purple orchids and green fronds, pretend rocks sprouting plastic jungle plants, with bamboo decorator accents. Of course you can get tropical drinks here. Among the bar's occupants are a toucan named Pinnochio and several other critters on perches; more are a short squawk away, down a corridor called the "Wildlife Walk."

THE TEN BEST OTHER BARS

The Glitter City drinking scene certainly isn't limited to casinos. Las Vegas has some of the most interesting bars and cocktail lounges west of the Pecos and maybe even the Hudson. Our Ten Best choices are listed in no particular order, except by personality.

1 THE BEST PLACE TO DRINK: Drink • 200 E. Harmon Ave. (Koval Lane); (702) 796-5519.

Remember the quote from W.C. Fields, at the beginning of this chapter? "A man's got to believe in something. I believe I'll have another drink." It's a pity he didn't live long enough to visit a bar where his favorite pastime is capitalized. At Drink, he could have chosen from seventy-five different beers, twenty kinds of vodka libations and just about anything else alcoholic. Drink isn't just one bar; it's seven, each with a different theme. If you feel like being rilly silly, belly up to the Bucket Bar, where booze is served in tiny buckets.

Between rounds, step onto the courtyard dance floor and swivel your hips to Thirtysomething sounds. The look of Drink is trendy distressed disco, with floral splashes on rough walls, exposed heating ducts and shards of neon. Incidentally, don't come to drink at Drink too early. This is a nighttime drinking person's venue. The doors don't open until 8 p.m. and the last drink is poured around 4:30 a.m. It's tough to find space in this place on Friday and Saturday nights, since Drink draws droves of locals who come to do just that.

2 **THE BEST PLACE TO PARTY: The Beach** • *356 Convention Center Drive (at Paradise Road); (702) 731-1925.*

When you hit this Beach, you hit one of the liveliest party clubs and sports bars in town. You'll think you've walked into a casting call for a beer commercial. Think of this as an overgrown beach shack, with a dance floor below and a large, noisy sports bar above, with more TV monitors than Mission Control. The cocktail waitresses wear cutoffs and swimsuit tops; the bartenders look like Malibu lifeguards. The median age here is somewhere between twenty-one and 500 SL. The Beach is a happening as well as a place, with a busy schedule of dances, margarita parties and live bands. A sign out front describes it best. The Beach is "A place to party." My only problem, as I enjoyed the camaraderie, the big-screen TV and the happy hour buffet, was that the bikini-topped cocktail waitress kept calling me "sir."

3 **THE MOST ROMANTIC BAR: Fireside Lounge** • *At the Peppermill Inn, 2985 S. Las Vegas Blvd. (opposite the Stardust and beside Silver City); (702) 735-7635.*

Fireside is the most sensuous cocktail lounge in town, and possibly in the country, with soft red and blue lighting, soft bar chairs and soft music. A sunken seating circle with a gas flame rising from a burbling water fountain forms a stunning centerpiece. Cozy couches are tucked into darkened corners, inviting hushed conversations. The walls are mirrored, repeating this lush setting again and again, blurring the distinction between reality and reflection. Curiously, all of this sensuality is housed in a rather ordinary looking building with an ordinary restaurant up front.

4 **THE BEST NEIGHBORHOOD PUB: Four Kegs West** • *276 N. Jones Blvd. (Aberdeen); (702) 870-0255.*

This pub is a bit off the main visitor track, although it's easy to reach. Head north on Freeway 95, take the Jones Boulevard exit to the right and you'll see it within a block, in a strip mall on your right, behind a Del Taco. Four Kegs West is neither trendy nor fancy, but a pleasant, rather quiet pub decorated mostly with neon beer signs. It's noted for its camaraderie and good, inexpensive food. Patrons pick up pizzas, sandwiches, finger food and other savories from a takeout window, and adjourn to one of the large seating areas. It recently won the "best bar food" category in the annual *Las Vegas Review-Journal* poll.

5 THE NEATEST THEME PUB: Lucky Dog's • *2396 Lamb Blvd. (Sahara Avenue); (702) 431-3991.*

It's okay to go to the dogs as long as you have a sense of humor about it. Another creation of the Holy Cow people (see below, under "The Ten Best beer pubs), this is the doggonest bar in town. As you step inside, you're greeted by dog statuary and dog photos, murals, prints and paintings. A huge stuffed hound rides a motorcycle and paw prints mark a drop ceiling above the bar. This is both a lively pub and a pizza parlor and of course it features lucky dog salad and hula hound pizza (with pineapple and ham).

This doggie place is a bit out of the way, but worth the drive if you're dogged about it. Head east from the Strip on Sahara for about four miles, turn left onto Lamb Boulevard and there it is, on your right. Look for the red, white and blue building with the big dog statue on the roof, and the marquee sign that reads: *I'm lookin' for the man that shot my paw."* But enough of this doggerel.

6 THE COOLEST THEME BAR: The Bombardier • *4213 Sahara Ave. (in Liberty Square, just west of Las Verdes Street, about 2.5 miles from the Strip); (702) 365-8988.*

This bar and steak house is dressed in World War II aviation memorabilia, although it's rather subdued and sensuous, instead of bright and cheery. Model aircraft dangle from the ceilings and others fill several display cases. Two particularly clever design elements are a wall tapestry portraying a dogfight, complete with travel lights for gunfire; and ceiling fans fashioned as nose cones of fighter planes. A backlighted glass painting of a P-40 Flying Tiger accents the large central bar. This cozy place serves mesquite grilled steaks, chickens and other fare, in addition to lots of drinks and nostalgia.

7 THE BEST COLLEGIATE BAR: Tom & Jerry's Grub & Pub • *4550 S. Maryland Parkway (at Harmon, in Runnin' Rebel Plaza); (702) 736-8550.*

This large and lively bar is the chosen hangout of the Runnin' Rebels, whose University of Nevada Las Vegas campus lies immediately west. It's decorated mostly with beer banners, a large mural with faces of regular patrons, and an imposing stack of beer pitchers. A sunken bar with a small bandstand and a huge TV screen, alternates as a live music venue and a place to catch the latest game. More than a dozen pool tables reside in an adjacent room. As required for a decent college bar, it offers nine beers on tap including Samuel Adams, Harp, Red Hook and Guinness, plus a dozen or so others by the bottle. It serves the usual 'burgers and deep fried pub grub.

8 THE BEST NOSTALGIA BAR: Play It Again Sam's •
4120 Spring Mountain Rd. (Wynn Road); (702) 876-1550.

Ingrid Bergman never said "Play it again, Sam" in the film classic *Casablanca*, although this cozy and comfortable bar and restaurant can be forgiven for its historical inaccuracy. It could be a setting for that film, with its dark corners, subdued lighting, candlelit tables and Moorish arches. It lacks only beaded curtains and beady eyed Peter Lorre. Black and white blow-ups of Bogart and Bergman decorate the walls, and a silhouette of Ingrid leaning over the piano forms the backdrop to a small bandstand, where jazz and soft rock combos occasionally perform.

Incidentally, what Bergman *really* said as she leaned toward the pianist was: "Play it, Sam, for old time's sake." However, that's an awfully long name for a cocktail lounge.

9 THE BEST JIMMY BUFFET MEMORIAL BAR: Tommy Rocker's Cantina • *4275 S. Industrial Rd. (across Flamingo, just south of the Rio, reached by Hotel Rio Drive); (702) 261-6688.*

Local entertainer Tommy Rocker created this place for young, upwardly mobile adults and fans of Jimmy Buffet, whose songs are often sung and whose "Boat Drinks" are consumed here. The look is sort of industrial strength *Latino* Key West, with high ceilings, exposed ventilation ducts, corrugated walls, plastic palms, cyclone fence partitions and half a VW bus impaled into a wall. It has the necessary ingredients for a hip bar—pool tables, a small dance floor, occasional live music, good food and TV monitors airing current games. El Grill issues barbecued ribs and chicken, sandwiches and Mexican fare. A patio invites patrons into the fresh air, although the view is of I-15 and the backside of the new Bellagio resort.

10 THE BEST GLORIA STEINHAM MEMORIAL BAR: Hooter's • *5675 W. Sahara Avenue (in Westview Plaza between Decatur and Jones, about 2.5 miles from the Strip); (702) 248-4668.*

Several years ago, a group of guys got together in Clearwater, Florida, and created a lively party bar called Hooters. It caught on quickly and soon spread to other parts, including Las Vegas. The name supposedly refers to wide-eyed owls, although there is some suspicion that it was inspired by the slang expression for a woman's upper anatomy. The barmaids at Hooters are generously proportioned and dressed in tight-fitting T-shirts and bright orange brief gym shorts. The National

Organization for Women became incensed by this brazen display of womanhood and filed a lawsuit against the chain a few years back, insisting that Hooters was discriminating by not hiring male cocktail servers.

We aren't sure of the lawsuit's current status, although the Las Vegas Hooters is amply staffed by amply endowed young women. It's a lively place, done up in knotty pine, exposed heating vents and Hooter logos. In addition to plenty of booze and camaraderie, it serves buffalo wings and shrimp, assorted seafood, salads and sandwiches.

THE TEN BEST BEER PUBS

Perhaps it's the hot summer weather, or maybe the fact that Las Vegas lures a lot of serious Midwestern beer drinkers. The town has developed a serious reputation for beer pubs and micro breweries. Here are the ultimate places in which to sip suds, both within and outside of casinos:

1 MONTE CARLO PUB & BREWERY • *Monte Carlo Hotel & Casino, 3770 Las Vegas Blvd.; (702) 730-7777.*

So who said themes in Las Vegas have to be consistent? The town's best beer pub—looking very much like a working brewery with its high ceilings, copper steam kettles and exposed plumbing—sits inside the Monte Carlo Casino, on a quaint Monaco alleyway called the Street of Dreams. The brewing kettles here are immense, suggesting that serious work goes on behind that tall glass wall.

One can sit at the bar or ask for a table, and request a setup of five designer brews. They're placed on a place mat with descriptions of what you're sipping. The five servings are generous; we'd suggest sharing them with a friend. You can of course get individual glasses of the local brew and assorted other drinks. Typical light and spicy brewpub fare is served here as well, such as grilled sausages, stir-fried chicken, pasta, sandwiches and salads.

2 BARLEY'S CASINO & BREWING COMPANY • *In the Town Center mall at 4500 E. Sunset Road (several blocks east of Green Valley Parkway), Henderson; (702) 458-BREW.*

Although most brewpubs have a few gaming devices, Barley's is more of a small casino with a microbrewery attached. Housed in an attractive urban shopping center in Henderson's Green Valley area, it has dozens of slot and video machines, a small race and sports book and even a keno game.

Barley's creators are serious about beer, however. Stainless steel brewing tanks glisten beyond the ranks of slots. Offerings include hand-crafted Mahi Bock, Blue Diamond, Black Mountain and Red Rock beers. Since this is near our Henderson home, I can attest that they're all quite good. Barley's serves typical brewpub fare such as chicken wings, chicken tenders, onion rings and assorted sandwiches. Regulars can join Barley's Brew Club and earn points toward logo items by getting a card punched for each beer consumed. However, if you're here only for a week's vacation, don't try to earn the hundred points required for a Barley's denim jacket.

3 CROWN & ANCHOR PUB • *1350 E. Tropicana Blvd. (just beyond Maryland Parkway); (702) 739-8676.*

Heading east from the Strip on Tropicana, look to your left just after crossing Maryland Parkway and you'll see a white stucco cottage with a double-barreled smokestack. Inside is Glitter City's most popular British pub and, for beer drinkers, it is suds heaven. It has thirty international brews on tap and another fifty-five by the bottle. These are mostly ales, pilsners and stouts from the British Isles and the rest of Europe and a few American specialty beers.

These brews can be accompanied by traditional fare such as bangers and mash, shepherd's pie, fish and chips, and Cornish pasties, plus American food. (For the uninitiated, a banger is a large, spicy sausage, and "mash" refers to mashed potatoes. Pasties are small "pocket pies" stuffed with meat and veggies.) The Crown & Anchor serves an all-you-can-eat buffet lunch daily for $5.95. The place has a pleasantly weathered Old English aquatic look, with rope-entwined beams, navigational charts on the walls and brass ship regalia.

4 DRAFT HOUSE BARN & CASINO • *Rancho Drive at Craig Road; (702) 645-1494.*

Located several miles out Rancho Drive, the Draft House is another of the "Holy Cow" group's creations. This pub and restaurant features fourteen international and domestic beers on tap, including our favorite Anchor Steam Beer from San Francisco. Not surprisingly, it pours several of the Holy Cow brewpub products. In addition to the tap beers, it has a couple of dozen bottle beers, plus a full bar. Tequilas are another specialty, with fourteen available. The adjacent restaurant offers basic American barbecue, plus pasta, sandwiches and salads. The overall look of the place is rural American barn.

5 GORDON BIERSCH BREWING COMPANY • *Sunset Station Hotel-Casino, 1301 W. Sunset Rd. (just west of I-515 interchange), Henderson, (702) 547-7777; also at Flamingo and Paradise, 312-5247.*

The Sunset Station Hotel-Casino, opened in mid-1997, has a Spanish-Mediterranean theme, although its Gordon Biersch Brewing Company has a pleasing "industrial modern" look with lots of brickwork and stainless steel. A second free-standing Gordon Biersch opened in 1997 at Flamingo and Paradise, just off the Strip.

Sunset Station's large Gordon Biersch occupies a good portion of the new Henderson resort, with several dining and drinking areas, including a section projecting into the main casino. Home-brewed offerings include a full-bodied pilsener; a curiously soft and mellow Märzen; and Dunkles, a medium flavored malty brew. If you're undecided, the bar offers gratis sips of each. Once you've made your decision, you get a good honest pint for around $3.50.

6 HOLY COW • 2423 S. Las Vegas Boulevard (at Sahara); (702) 732-COWS.

Is this Holstein heaven? Probably not, although it certainly is a serious beer drinker's *haven*. With a decor best described as "industrial Holstein," this cheerful high-ceiling place produces several microbrews in stainless steel kettles lining a balcony above the main bar. "Free tours" are offered, which means that you can walk along that balcony, stare at the brewing kettles and read graphics about the brewing process.

Holy Cow also is something of a sports pub, with several TV monitors dangling over the main bar. An adjacent dining area serves beer pub fare such as spicy chicken wings, chicken fingers and fish and chips, plus complete meals. The main bar is often rather chaotic, so serious beer aficionados might prefer to adjourn to a small bar to the left of the main entrance. Here, the in-house brews such as Ambler Gambler Pale Ale and Rebel Red Ale can be sipped in relative quiet. Try the brewmaster's weekly special, which can be something as strange as raspberry wheat.

7 HOUSE OF BREWS • In Sassy Sally's Casino, 32 Fremont St. (at First); (702) 382-5777.

Although the bar at this small downtown casino looks nothing like a microbrewery, it has more than 250 international beers. Most of them are displayed on shelves behind a long mirrored backbar. On any given day, five or more interesting microbrews and/or international beers are on tap, with generous servings selling for $2.

8 TRIPLE SEVEN BREWPUB • In Main Street Station Casino, 200 Main Street (Ogden); (702) 387-1896.

The Boyd Group, one of the more successful casino conglomerates in town, recently purchased the dead Main Street Station and brought it back to life. As a catheter, they built a pedestrian walkway across Main to tie it to the California Casino, the Boyd Group's flagship. They brightened the place up and installed one of the best brewpubs in Las Vegas.

Triple Seven, featuring "meals, music and micro-brews," has high ceilings, copper kettles and other microbrewery decor, with turn-of-the-century Victorian touches. Like any decent brewpub, this also is a lively sports bar, with a dozen or so TV screens hanging about. It also has a raw bar and sushi bar, plus a lunch and dinner menu ranging from Philly steak and cheese to Cajun crawfish pasta. The five locally brewed brews run the usual gamut from light High Roller Gold to assertive Marker Pale Ale. You can get a sampler of each for about four dollars.

9 SCHULER'S ROADHOUSE • 4755 Spring Mountain Road (at Wilmot, just east of Decatur Boulevard); (702) 252-7427.

Nineteen domestic and international draft beers and another half dozen in bottles attract locals to this appealing neighborhood bar two miles west of the Strip. Arrive during the 3 to 6 happy hour and you can get a glass of domestic beer for a dollar, or imports for two.

The bar occupies a handsome cross-timbered and stucco Normandy style building, with an interior to match. Patrons can pull a long-legged captain's chair up to the well-worn plank or retire to a window table. Schuler's is a locally popular restaurant as well, noted for its barbecued ribs, hamburgers and other sturdy American fare.

10 YE IRISH PORKER • 1945 S. Las Vegas Blvd. (in St. Louis Square, just north of the Stratosphere); (702) 731-0066.

In Ireland, a proper pub must close around midnight. In Las Vegas, however, the Irish in all of us can celebrate around the clock, sipping beer, tossing darts and swapping lies. This large bar on the upper end of the Strip has a pleasing 19th century pub look with rough-hewn beams and print wallpaper.

On tap are Bass ale, Harp lager, Guinness stout, Newcastle brown ale, Watney's red ale, Double Diamond and a couple of wimpy American beers. And of course you can get a good Irish whiskey, along with assorted other mixed drinks. If elbow-bending causes your appetite to rise, try the bangers and mash, corned beef and cabbage, shepherds pie and peas, or Irish stew.

The most romantic thing any woman ever said to me in bed was: "Are you sure you're not a cop?"
-- **Larry Brown**

Chapter eight

ROMANCE

...AND OTHER PRIMAL URGES

Many large Glitter City resorts are working to draw vacationing families by building amusement parks and video arcades with virtual l reality games. However, the *real* reality is that the town is still primarily a playground for consenting adults.

Thousands, including a few of the rich and famous, come each year to get married, or to spend their honeymoons. Thousands more—guys, of course—come to ogle the pretty girls in the dance revues and topless bars. Many go beyond ogling, since there's no shortage of party girls in this party town.

Put the kids to bed for the night, folks. This chapter is strictly for adults.

THE BEST PLACES TO BE ALONE TOGETHER...
...IN A CASINO?

There aren't really too many places to be alone in this party town, other than 100,000 hotel rooms and perhaps the back seats of limos. However, there are a few quiet corners where the two of you can withdraw from the crowd and perhaps do a bit of ear-nibbling. Virtually all of our choices are casino cocktail lounges. Although most casino bars are in the middle of the gaming action, a few provide quiet retreat.

1 THE BAR AT THE BARGE: Caesars Palace • 3570 S. Las Vegas Blvd. (at Flamingo Road); (702) 731-7110. Open noon to 4 a.m.

This is the coziest corner in town, although other couples may beat you to its coziest table. Cleopatra's Barge is a floating nightclub, featuring live entertainment and dancing nightly from 10 p.m. to 4 a.m. Just to its left is the small Bar at the Barge, which keeps much longer hours. One of its tables is tucked into a darkened corner, between the bar and the barge. To get there, step into the bar and turn right. If the corner is occupied, you'll find a few other quiet tables on the left side of the bar, although they aren't nearly as secluded.

2 BATTLE BAR DECK: Treasure Island • 3300 S. Las Vegas Blvd. (Spring Mountain Road); (702) 894-7111.

One of the more appealing quiet spots in town, at least between pirate ship battles, is the outside deck of Treasure Island's Battle Bar. Got a dockside table and you can hear the water lapping in the lagoon. It's quite romantic, and never mind that it's created by a wave machine. You'll find no quietude during the lagoon battle, of course. In fact, unless you arrive an hour before the conflict, you won't even get a table out here.

3 BUGSY'S DELI: The Flamingo Hilton • 3555 S. Las Vegas Blvd. (Flamingo Road); (702) 733-3111.

What! You're going to snuggle with your sweetie at a deli? Not the deli itself. Part of the seating area is set well apart from the deli and away from the commotion of the casino, with several tables for two. A nice mural of an Italian vineyard fills the wall above, so you can pick up a couple of glasses of wine at the deli and imagine that you're alone somewhere in Tuscany. Only Inglenook table wine is offered, so you'll just have to pretend that it's a rare chianti classico.

4 FISHERMAN'S PORT BAR: Aladdin Casino • 3667 S. Las Vegas Blvd. (opposite Bellagio); (702) 734-3583.

A tiny bar just to the left of the entrance to Fisherman's Port Restaurant is one of the coziest in town, dimly lit with plush seating. You'll find it in the far northern side of the main casino, a bit beyond the clatter of machines. Enter the Aladdin's most northern portal and turn left.

5 *IPANEMA BAR: Rio Suite Hotel* • *3700 W. Flamingo Rd.* *(at Valley View Boulevard); (702) 252-7777.*

The circular Ipanema is the largest bar at the Rio and it opens onto the lively casino. However, you'll find a few quiet tables on the back side, toward the bar's piano and hotel registration desk. (Of course, it isn't quiet when someone's at the piano.) If you're a lady reading this, tell your companion to keep his eyes off those sexy Rio cocktail waitresses.

6 *KABUKI LOUNGE: Las Vegas Hilton* • *3000 Paradise Rd.* *(Riviera Boulevard); (702) 732-5111.*

This handsomely attired bar occupies a terrace in the Benihana Village restaurant complex, just off the main casino. The bar and two Benihana dining areas rim an elegant sunken Japanese garden with a trickling stream, lanterns, a *tori* arch and tile-roofed temple buildings. The bar's quiet tables, all with views of the garden, are "shaded" by a huge mockup of a traditional Japanese bamboo umbrella.

7 *LAGOON SALOON: The Mirage* • *3400 S. Las Vegas Blvd.* *(adjacent to Caesars Palace); (702) 791-7111.*

Do the two of you yen for a lush tropical getaway? Step into the Lagoon Saloon next to the Mirage's indoor rainforest and stroll—hand-in-hand, of course—to the far right side of the bar. You'll find a few quiet tables tucked into the edge of the "forest," away from the adjacent casino.

8 *MAI TAI BAR: Imperial Palace* • *3535 S. Las Vegas Blvd.* *(between Sands Avenue and Flamingo Road); (702) 731-3311.*

The sign at the Mai Tai bar invites you to "sip into something tropical," such as a piña colada or mai tai. You also can slip into chairs at one of several cozy tables. The seating area extends around a corner from the serving bar, well shielded from casino clamor.

9 *MYSTIC FALLS PARK: Sam's Town Hotel & Gambling Hall* • *5111 Boulder Highway (Nellis Boulevard); (702) 456-7777.*

Mystic Falls, the 25,000 square foot indoor park rimmed by Sam's hotel towers, is a rather romantic spot at night. Tiny white lights twinkle from the trees like fireflies and falling water whispers over the pretend cliffs that are softly illuminated. Find a table at the rear of a cocktail lounge that occupies the center of this indoor park. Sit and sip quietly and you'll transported far from the casino clamor that's just a few dozen yards away. Don't expect quietude at 6, 8 and 10 p.m., for the park erupts into a "dancing waters" and laser light show called the "Sunset Stampede," with a howling coyote and thunderous sound track. However, it lasts for only a few minutes, so enjoy the spectacle and then go back to whatever it was you were doing.

10 TERRACE BAR: *Stardust Hotel* • *3000 S. Las Vegas Blvd. (Stardust Road); (702) 732-6111.*

This pleasant bar with a view of one of the Stardust swimming pools has a couple of cozy alcoves where your whispered thoughts can be shared. The bar is located between the main casino and the hotel registration area, well out of traffic. If you want to ply your companion with drinks, go there between 4 and 7 p.m. or midnight and 4 a.m., when you can get two for the price of one.

THE TEN MOST ROMANTIC RESTAURANTS

1 HUGO'S CELLAR • *Four Queens Hotel, 202 E. Fremont St (Casino Center Boulevard); (702) 385-4011. American-continental fare. Reservations recommended; major credit cards; $$$.*

Although the Four Queens is not the fanciest casino in town, its gourmet restaurant is the most romantic. Seating is cozy, the light is properly dim and each lady is handed a long-stemmed rose as she is escorted to her seat. That, of course, sets the stage for a romantic meal; it is the gentleman's cue to keep the amorous mood glowing. Service is efficient and unobtrusive, so as not to distract those romantic murmurings. The wine list is among the best in town; the gent can ply her with a proper selection. Note that the lady now has the rose in her teeth.

2 BACCHANAL • *Caesars Palace, 3570 S. Las Vegas Blvd. (Flamingo Road); (702) 734-7110. Art-decadent Roman. Prix fixe seatings Tuesday-Saturday at 6 and 9:30. Reservations required; major credit cards; $$$$.*

Is it romantic or is it corny? If the opulent gimmickry of a sensual Roman banquet fails to ignite an amorous mood, perhaps the free-flowing wine poured by nubile, toga-clad maidens will help. Will you, sir, be able to concentrate on your lady's flirtations when one of those maidens is massaging your weary shoulders and feeding you grapes? And will you, madam, try to outshine that wine goddess by first peeling the grapes before feeding him? This bacchanal is fun and a little bit sexy and the food is ample and excellent.

3 *FIORE* • *Rio Suite Hotel, 3700 W. Flamingo Rd. (Valley View); (702) 252-7777. Northern Italian. Dinner nightly. Reservations recommended; major credit cards; $$$.*

...And suddenly, you're in a quiet booth, holding hands and in no hurry for the waiter to arrive. The Rio is one of the flashiest, liveliest casino resorts in town, and the quietly elegant Fiore offers quick escape from all that fun commotion. The look is floral—befitting the name—and quiet elegance, with a high mahogany ceiling, tapestry booths, crisp linens and opulent table settings. Arched windows overlook a pool and terrace, and you can dine beneath the stars on balmy nights.

4 *KOKOMO'S* • *The Mirage, 3400 S. Las Vegas Blvd.; (702) 791-7111. American-continental. Breakfast Sunday-Thursday, lunch and dinner daily. Reservations recommended; major credit cards; $$$.*

If you've ever fantasized fleeing with your lover to Bali Hai but can't afford the plane fare and mosquito netting, Kokomo's offers a suitable alternative, without the mosquitos. The bamboo-trimmed restaurant sits beside the Mirage's indoor rainforest, just beyond the Lagoon Saloon. Ask for a table next to the rainforest, which is right out of a Tarzan movie, Jane, with luxuriant vegetation, orchids, trickling streams and a splashing waterfall. If you seek something more secluded, request one of the brocaded booths on the other side of the restaurant. Here, where you can listen only to your mate's delicate breathing and the distant trickle of that pretend jungle cascade. Pluck the floating orchid from your tropical drink and place it behind your partner's ear. (Right or left? We've forgotten which flowered ear signals willingness.)

5 *MANHATTAN OF LAS VEGAS* • *2600 E. Flamingo Rd. (Topaz Street); (702) 737-5000. Italian-continental. Dinner nightly. Reservations recommended; major credit cards; $$$.*

Never mind that the owners of this place opened their original Manhattan restaurant in La Jolla, California, not New York. This twice-misplaced Manhattan is one of the towns tonier and more romantic dining venues. Slip into the sunken dining room and slip behind a candle-lit table set with fine linens. This *chic* restaurant housed in an upscale tile-roofed cottage is both clubby and elegant, with an etched glass New York skyline to give this misplaced place a sense of place.

6 *MICHAEL'S* • *Barbary Coast Casino, 3595 S. Las Vegas Blvd. (Flamingo Road); (702) 737-7111. American-continental. Dinner nightly. Reservations essential; major credit cards; $$$$.*

This is the town's most opulent restaurant, with flocked wallpaper, high-backed burgundy chairs and a stunning leaded glass canopy overhead. While romantic, it's not quite intimate, since there are no hidden corners and it seems that four waiters are assigned to every table. However, it is not difficult to steal a kiss from behind those high-backed chairs.

7 **MORTON'S OF CHICAGO** • *Fashion Show Mall, 3200 Las Vegas Blvd. (At the rear of the mall, off Spring Mountain Road); (702) 893-0703. American; mostly steaks, plus chops and seafood. Dinner nightly. Reservations essential; major credit cards; $$$$.*

Yes, the lights are dim and seating is divided into cozy partitions. However, is this restaurant with a men's club look really one of the most romantic places in town? It certainly is for regulars, who can have their waiter bring a special wine from their own personal wine locker. For the rest of you, it has an excellent wine list and attentive yet inconspicuous service.

8 **MOUNT CHARLESTON HOTEL** • *Two Kyle Canyon Road (on State Route 157 to Mount Charleston); (702) 872-5500. American; breakfast, lunch and dinner daily. Reservations accepted for dinner; major credit cards; $$$.*

What could be more romantic than a crackling fireplace, a mountain lodge and pure, pine scented air? This handsome lodge on the slope of Mount Charleston resembles one of those monumental log chalets in older national parks. The octagonal dining room with its lofty pitched log ceiling isn't exactly cozy, although the setting is certainly romantic and the tables are well-spaced, permitting hushed conversation.

The mountain and valley views from the restaurant's picture windows and the adjacent Cliffhanger cocktail lounge are grand. However, you're supposed to be gazing into one another's eyes, guys. And should this romantic dinner follow its logical course, the hotel has cozy rooms, a sauna and spa. There's a small gaming area off the lobby, but you didn't drive all the way up here just to poke quarters into a slot machine.

9 **PAMPLEMOUSSE** • *400 E. Sahara Ave. (between Paradise Road and Santa Rita Drive); (702) 733-2066. Classic French; dinner Tuesday-Sunday, closed Monday. Reservations accepted, essential on weekends; major credit cards; $$$.*

Take your significant other to this cozy cottage restaurant and pretend you're in a French countryside café, even though it's mere minutes from the glitz of the Strip. It's cozy and properly dim inside;

dining areas are set off by drapes. Service is quiet and inconspicuous. Ask for a corner table and enjoy the silent flicker of candle light. Everything here is romantic except the name. *Pamplemousse* is French for grapefruit.

10 *PIERO'S • 355 Convention Center Dr. (Paradise Road); (702) 369-2305. Elegant Italian. Dinner nightly. Reservations essential; major credit cards; $$$$.*

This clubby, dark-wood and dimly elegant restaurant offers quiet retreat and unobtrusive—just short of haughty—service. Piero's is a favorite retreat of the city's power brokers; the waitstaff knows and respects the need for privacy. You will be left alone at your dim corner table, although the slightest nod will bring your waiter to clear away dinner's remnants and refill the wine glasses. "Dessert?" he will ask. "No thanks," you say, probing the depths of your lover's eyes. "We have our own."

THE TEN CUTEST WEDDING CHAPELS

Getting married in Nevada is even easier than getting divorced, and a lot more fun. All that is required is a driver's license or other photo ID if you're 18 or older, and a willing partner. There is no waiting period and no blood test requirement.

Las Vegas leads the state and probably the nation in marriages, with more than 100,000 nuptials a year. That's one set of "I do's" every five minutes. Most of these are performed by Marryin' Sams, who work the three dozen marriage mill chapels, and the rest by state-appointed marriage commissioners. You'll be in good company if you come to town for a hasty nuptial fix. Among those who have tied the knot here are Michael Jordan, Joan Collins, Bruce Willis, Bette Midler and Lisa Bonet.

For $35, you can pick up a license at the Clark County Marriage License Bureau at 200 S. Third Street downtown; the phone number is (702) 455-3156 during normal working hours and (702) 455-4415 after 5 weekdays and on weekends; office hours are 8 a.m. to midnight. You can then stroll—hopefully hand-in-hand—one block to the Commissioner of Civil Marriages at 309 S. Third Street. There, a deputy justice of the peace will do the deed for another $35. For something more formal, adjourn to one of the ten commercial chapels we recommend below or any of dozens more you'll find in the Yellow Pages. Several casinos have their own wedding chapels, with honeymoon suites just an elevator ride away.

Commercial wedding chapel prices range from a bare bones $35 to several hundred for packages that include a champagne reception, limo service, photos and a souvenir video of the happy moment. Packaged weddings come with nauseously sweet names like "A Precious

Moment" and "Earth Angel." At the Little White Chapel, you can order the Michael Jordan Special. In addition to package wedding prices, you'll be expected to slip a $35 to $45 gratuity to the minister. The low-end price at most chapels is $35 to $60, which includes use of the chapel, a witness and recorded music. If you hire a limo, a $20 tip for the driver is considered proper—assuming he doesn't run over your foot when he pulls up.

Not all Las Vegas weddings are Levi-clad quickies. Some of the ceremonies at these chapels are quite formal, with brides in silken white gowns and attendants in matching formal wear, just like back home. All of this attire can be rented, either at the chapel or from any of several rental agencies.

Elvis at your wedding?

Newlyweds also can hire singers who'll vocalize such romantic songs as "Can You Feel the Love Tonight" or "The Hawaiian Wedding Song." You can even rent an Elvis impersonator who'll give the bride away and bring tears to her eyes with "Love Me Tender." The firm is called Wedding Singers of Las Vegas; phone (800) 574-4450 or (702) 384-0771.

The cheapest and fastest way to get married—which gives new meaning to the term "quickie"—is at drive-up windows provided by some of the wedding chapels. You can tie the knot without leaving your car, for as little as $25. It is recommended that you shut off the ignition and apply the hand brake before kissing the bride.

Incidentally, just about everyone in the Las Vegas wedding industry except the preacher takes credit cards.

Although many casino resorts have wedding chapels, we've limited our list to independent ones. Many are along upper Las Vegas Boulevard, extending south from Fremont Street to the Stratosphere, where the boulevard and Main Street merge. Curiously, they're all on the east side of the boulevard. Also along this stretch are several small motels, including a couple of adult ones in case you need wedding night inspiration. Two of our wedding chapel choices, including our first choice, are outside this "wedding row" cluster.

1 **LITTLE CHURCH OF THE WEST** • *4617 S. Las Vegas Blvd. (opposite Russell Road, half a mile north of the Signature Flight Support terminal), Las Vegas, NV 89119; (800) 821-2452 or (702) 739-7971.*

It's nice to see a bit of history survive in the ever-rebuilding face of Las Vegas. The cute wood-sided Little Church of the West had been part of the Hacienda Hotel since 1943; many celebrities and ordinary folks have spoken their vows here. When the Hacienda was demolished in 1996, the chapel was saved. It was moved—lock, stock and sanctuary—to a spot farther south on Las Vegas Boulevard. It's listed on the National Register of Historic Places as one of Nevada's oldest wedding chapels. The interior is inviting and warm, with old fashioned pews, lacquered wooden walls and ceilings, with large twin candelabras at the altar. Among notables who were married in this chapel are Cindy Crawford, Richard Gere, Judy Garland, Mickey Rooney and Dudley Moore. Elvis Presley married Ann-Margaret in the chapel in 1964, although that was just for the movie *Viva Las Vegas*.

2 CHAPEL OF LOVE • *1431 S. Las Vegas Blvd. (below Charleston), Las Vegas, NV 89104; (800) 922-LOVE or (702) 387-0155.*

If you like choices, this marriage mill has four different chapels—Rainbow, Peach, Rose and Lavender. It has its own limo fleet and in-house floral service. Although the interior is quite attractive, the building's curved roof and stone wall accents give the exterior the look of a 1950s coffee shop.

3 CUPID'S CHAPEL • *827 S. Las Vegas Blvd. (Hoover Street), Las Vegas, NV 89101; (800) 543-2933 or (702) 598-4444.*

Called "The little chapel with the big heart," this cozy place is done in simple white and green, accented by pretend leaded glass. Its packages have cutesy names like "You Send Me" (the least expensive) and "Unforgettable" (high end). Christian and traditional Jewish ceremonies are available, along with generic weddings.

4 GRACELAND WEDDING CHAPEL • *619 S. Las Vegas Blvd. (Garces), Las Vegas, NV 89101; (800) 824-5732 or (702) 382-0091.*

What a place for an Elvis impersonator and yes, you can hire one. This chapel was named for Elvis' Graceland estate in Memphis, although the two bear no resemblance. It's a cute little New England style chapel done in simple white and green, with church style pews. There's a gazebo out front for those who want to marry in the sunlight. Among notables hitched here were Lorenzo Lamas (Fernando's kid; remember *Falcon Crest?*) and rock star Jon Bon Jovi.

5 LITTLE CHAPEL OF THE FLOWERS • *1717 S. Las Vegas Blvd. (Oakey), Las Vegas, NV 89104; (800) 843-2410 or (702) 735-4331.*

This prim, appealing New England style place with a steeple and shake roof has two chapels—Victorian and Heritage. Folks also can get hitched outside in a lattice-walled gazebo. The chapel's interior look is New England-Victorian, with brass chandeliers, etched glass and cherrywood. As the name suggests, it also has a floral shop.

6 *LITTLE WHITE CHAPEL* • *1301 S. Las Vegas Blvd. (south of Charleston Boulevard), Las Vegas, NV 89104; (800) 545-8111 or (702) 382-5943.*

Michael Jordan and Joan Collins were married in this cute little New England style chapel (not to one another) and two of the packages are named in their honor. The Joan Collins Special fetches a higher price tag than Michael's package. The chapel has a quickie drive-up window, its own fleet of burgundy limos, a lattice gazebo and a putting green-carpeted patio for outdoor weddings.

7 *MISSION OF THE BELLS WEDDING CHAPEL* • *1205 S. Las Vegas Blvd. (Park Paseo), Las Vegas, NV 89104; (800) 634-6277 or (702) 366-0646.*

This is the most attractive hitching facility on upper Las Vegas Boulevard, done up in the style of a Southwest mission. Its large wedding chapel with Spanish tile floors and traditional dark wood pews will seat a hundred guests. It's often used for Catholic weddings. The mission style Thunderbird Motel is adjacent.

8 *PRECIOUS MOMENT WEDDING CHAPEL* • *800 Fourth St. (Gass), Las Vegas, NV 89101; (800) 9-MARRY U or (702) 384-2211.*

Precious indeed. Opened in late 1996, this large marriage mill resembles a New England church outside and within. The burgundy carpeted chapel with a curved wooden staircase for the bride's entry is quite handsome. Most of the packages, even the relatively inexpensive "Special Moment," include limo service. If you're in a hurry to tie the knot, or perhaps in a hurry to get to your honeymoon suite, Precious Moment offers a drive-up wedding window, with a $25 fee.

9 *SILVER BELL WEDDING CHAPEL* • *607 S. Las Vegas Blvd. (Bonneville), Las Vegas, NV 89101; (702) 382-3726.*

Cute is the word for this little chapel with its white wedding parlor and a well tended garden in front with lattice arches for outdoor ceremonies. The church style façade is done in gleaming white and turquoise, with silver and white bells trimmed in neon. Neon? Well, this *is* Las Vegas...

10 *WEE KIRK O' THE HEATHER* • *231 S. Las Vegas Blvd. (Bridger), Las Vegas, NV 89101; (702) 382-9830.*

Tiny Kirk o' the Heather is the simplest of our selected chapels and we include it for historic and personal reasons. No, we weren't married there; we did our deed on a Hawaiian beach. Wee Kirk is the oldest existing marriage mill in town, dating back to 1940. About fifteen years after it opened, I made my first trip to Las Vegas, not to gamble but to stand up for two friends who got hitched here. Refurbished in 1997, it features a cheerful little chapel done in white and green. It's the closest chapel to Glitter Gulch, two blocks below Fremont Street.

EL MACHO GRANDE: THE PRETTIEST VEGAS VIXENS

My wife, while certainly no prude and not really a woman's liberationist, had nothing to do with this section. She said she had better things to do than to watch me stare at pretty girls.

1 THE PRETTIEST COCKTAIL WAITRESSES: Rio Suite Hotel & Casino ● 3700 W. Flamingo Rd. (at Valley View Boulevard, opposite the Gold Coast).

The Rio features a splashy Brazilian fiesta theme and the cocktail waitresses here are authentic beach beauties, as if they just stepped off the sands of Ipanema. They aren't wearing string bikinis, although their costumes are quite sexy, with one bare shoulder and a bloused sleeve on the other, and bikini-cut bottoms.

2 THE SEXIEST COCKTAIL WAITRESS OUTFITS: Imperial Palace ● 3535 S. Las Vegas Blvd. (between Sands Avenue and Flamingo Road, opposite Caesars Palace).

The low-cut, side-slit, mini-skirted gossamer blue *cheongsams* worn by the Imperial Palace drink girls are the sexiest in town. Further, the ladies themselves are uniformly attractive and sufficiently endowed to enhance those plunging necklines.

3 THE CUTEST COCKTAIL WAITRESS OUTFITS: Orleans Hotel & Casino ● 4500 W. Tropicana Ave.; (702) 365-7111.

Sexiest and cutest? We may be stretching a point, although the costumes worn by the Imperial Palace and Orleans cocktail waitresses both deserve mention. The Orleans outfits are skimpy little black and multi-colored lace merry widows that are a frisky step away from being negligee. Glass "throw beads"—the kind tossed to the crowds from floats during New Orleans' Mardi Gras—glitter from their necks.

4 THE PRETTIEST CHANGE GIRLS: Vacation Village ● 6711 S. Las Vegas Blvd. (at the far end of the Strip, below the airport); (702) 897-1700.

Most casino change personnel are morose looking men and women pushing around heavy carts that have little flags on them. We had to travel to the far end of the Strip to find a cadre of uniformly attractive change makers. The young ladies are modestly dressed in black slacks, with blouse and vest tops. Instead of pushing change carts, they wear little change makers around their waists—the kind that street car conductors once used.

5 THE PRETTIEST CIGARETTE GIRLS: Caesars Palace •
3570 S. Las Vegas Blvd. (at Flamingo Road); (702) 731-7110.

The cigarette girl has gone out of style in most places, although not at tradition-bound Caesars. The young women who make the rounds here are very pretty, and quite fetching in their purple, backless micro-miniskirts. If you don't smoke, they'll sell you a lighted yo-yo. Why on earth would you want to buy a lighted yo-yo? It gives you an excuse to talk to a pretty girl in a purple mini-skirt.

6 THE PRETTIEST SHOWGIRLS: The Best of the Folies
Bergere • Tropicana Resort & Casino, 3801 S. Las Vegas Blvd. (Tropicana Avenue); (702) 739-2411. Nightly except Thursday at 8 and 10:30; $28.95 or $38.95 with a buffet (early show only); adults.

Where do they find all of those lovely lasses? Folies Bergere is the longest-running review in Las Vegas and the current version has one of the largest dance troupes in town. Like a matched string of pearls, the ladies are uniformly attractive, particularly in their elaborate new costumes. The show traces the history of musical theater from the "Can-Can" of Paris to modern rock and those leggy lovelies don't miss a step.

7 THE SEXIEST MAJOR REVUE: Enter the Night • Star-
dust Hotel, 3000 S. Las Vegas Blvd. (at Stardust Road), (702) 732-6325. Tuesday, Wednesday, Thursday and Saturday 7:30 and 10:30, Sunday and Monday 8 p.m., dark Friday; $26.90 including two drinks; adults only (21 and over).

Lovely ladies and special laser effects create the sexiest "big room" show in town, with highly charged dance numbers, slinky and often topless costuming. The current lead dancer is Akl, a stunning, sexy, shapely, statuesque showgirl and how's that for alliteration? The show's focus, as suggested by the title, is adult frolic after dusk.

8 THE SEXIEST CABARET SHOW: The Xtreme Scene •
Gaughan's Plaza, One Main St. (at Fremont Street); (702) 386-2110. Saturday-Thursday at 8 and 10 p.m., dark Friday; $19.95 including one drink. Smoking is permitted although the showroom is well ventilated. Adults only.

For guys who like to see performers extremely undressed, Xtreme Scene features scantily clad ladies without the raunchiness of the town's topless clubs. The dance team consists of several women and a guy, all wearing short haircuts and not much else. Their costumes are teasing little bits of colorful fabric. With all of this exposure, Xtreme Scene is still R-rated. Although the dancers writhe and wriggle seductively and flash bare fannies, there's nothing lewd in their moves.

This is a rather low-budget presentation, although we like the show for its wholesome sexiness and the tightly choreographed dance numbers. The single stage set is simple—an aluminum framework like a playground jungle gym, through which the barely clad maidens writhe and twist.

9 THE SEXIEST TOPLESS BAR DANCERS: Girls of Glitter Gulch ● *20 Fremont Street (between First and Main); (702) 395-4774. Two-drink minimum; no cover charge.*

After spending an hour nursing my two-drink minimum, I determined that all of the girls of Glitter Gulch are properly slender and bosomy and some are quite statuesque. They come out in pairs—no pun intended—and dance along a runway bar just above the seated patrons. Well, they sort of dance. Mostly they lean over and wiggle their ample bosoms, inviting the guys to slip paper money into the slim bands of their G-strings. Some particularly frisky men rise to the occasion—pun intended—although they aren't permitted to touch the girls. While some ladies dance in pairs on the runway, others work the room, prancing about and offering brief companionship to gents seated in adjacent booths.

Certainly you can buy a lady a drink or install a five dollar bill into a willing waistband, although I was impressed by the fact that there is very little hustle here. Further, drink prices are reasonable for a topless bar—about $5.75. (I once paid $4.25 for a glass of designer beer at casino pub, served by a fully clad bartender who offered only a smile, and he needed a shave.)

10 THE SEXIEST ADULT ENTERTAINMENT GUIDE GIRLS: Full XXXposure ● *Available in news racks all over town.*

Las Vegas may be the only city in America with X-rated litter. So-called "entertainment guides" filled with nude photos of women who'll get naked in your hotel room are stuffed into free news racks, and many of them get scattered over the sidewalks. They once were thrust upon pedestrians by legions of leaflet distributors, although a recent law ended that practice because they interfered with sidewalk traffic.

Of all the adult literature we collected to research this chapter, the one we found most appealing was called *Full XXXposure*. A fully exposed dark-haired nude lady named Suzette graces the cover of the one we picked up. We've nicknamed her "Peaches" and—even as we write this—she's propped up against our computer for inspiration.

TEN NAUGHTY DIVERSIONS IN LAS VEGAS AND BEYOND

The deadly threat of AIDS has taken much of the momentum out of what's left of the sexual revolution in Las Vegas and elsewhere. However, it's still not difficult to find naughty diversions and naked entertainment here. Call girls who call themselves "entertainers" scatter their literature all over town. Dancers dangle their attributes in topless bars and "gentlemen's clubs." Topless mermaids splash about in the "Splash" revue at the Riviera; showgirls show off their fronts at several main showrooms and cabarets.

With all of this titillation, prostitution is illegal in Las Vegas and the rest of Clark County, although call girls still work their trade. It is legal in Nye County, a short drive west. Several brothels are located there; the town of Crystal exists only to support its cathouses.

This list is intended for harmless titillation, not gratuitous sex. Because of the lethal threat of AIDS, *never* accept the services of a Las Vegas prostitute.

1 ADULT ROOM SERVICE • *Available through flyers or Yellow Pages ads.*

Scores of nubile young ladies and—yes—macho looking men, offer to fulfill your wildest fantasies in the privacy of your hotel room. They advertise in those nudie news rack flyers, and in the Las Vegas phone book, which has forty pages of listings, under the "Entertainers" category. The conservative phone company limits the photos to mug shots. However, the copy leaves little to the imagination, with terms like "young lust" and "hot bodies."

Since prostitution is illegal here, these girls and guys are supposed to limit their activities to strip teases and dances—both exotic and dirty. Or, they simply get naked while you watch. Options include nude aerobics, bondage, whips and chains, and oil wrestling (oil included).

Will they—as we teenagers used to wonder while breathing heavily in the back seats of our Ford Fairlanes—go all the way? The Metro Police vice squad says that 99 percent of these "entertainers" are prostitutes. *Do not* accept their offerings! Unlike the licensed working girls of Nye County, these freelancers are not checked medically. You don't know where they've been or what microbes they may be carrying, including the ones that can kill you. Further, soliciting the favors of a prostitute is illegal here. Las Vegas policewomen have been known to pose as hotel room entertainers and then cuff unsuspecting "johns" who agree to join in the performance.

Our advice: Just watch the dance and stay out of trouble. However, some of these women, upon learning that a dance is all that their johns want, may leave in a huff, taking the $125 to $200 fee or signed credit card slip with them.

2 A MUSEUM OF NAUGHTINESS • Brothel Art Museum, Crystal Springs Bar and Restaurant, Crystal, Nevada; (702) 372-9999. Free; age limit 21 or older.

Touted as the "Only Museum of its Kind in the World," this attraction at Crystal Springs Bar traces the history of prostitution in Nevada and elsewhere. While there, you can pick up free tourist information along with a "sexy souvenir" and buy adult T-shirts. The museum's ad says that tour buses are welcome and you truckers will want to now that there's plenty of room to turn around. (We assume they're talking about your rig.)

3 PACKETS OF SEXY FLYERS FOR A FEE • At news racks around Las Vegas.

Four quarters will get you a "Las Vegas Value Pack" or other packet of adult entertainment literature from a news rack. However, to abuse the old cliché, you can't judge an adult packet by its cover. One such investment yielded a legitimate singles magazine that even touted Christian singles clubs. Another packet contained the *Arizona Swingers* magazine (in Nevada?). It featured "real phone numbers of real people," with photos that achieved new levels of porn. Many of the packets contain the same adult entertainment pamphlets that are available free around town (below).

4 NAKED GIRLIE PICTURES FOR FREE • At news racks, in stacks and littering the sidewalks.

Why pay for pictures of sexy ladies? Just lift the lid of designated free news racks or look for stacks along the sidewalks. These adult entertainment guides, as noted above, are filled with photos of folks who'll come to your hotel room and maybe even your Winnebago and get naked. You'll find proposals from sweet and innocent Shauna, spicy Sarah, charming Chinese Choy, coed Stephanie, Valerie and Vickie together, and of course, hard-body Chad. These are the same people we warned you about in item Number One above. Your mother would probably warn you about them, too.

5 NEVADA CATHOUSE DIRECTORY • "Best Cat Houses in Nevada" by J.R. Schwartz, Straight Arrow Publishing, P.O. Box 1092, Boise, ID 83701.

You may be surprised to learn that Nevada has fewer than forty working brothels, even though prostitution is legal in all but the most populated areas—Clark County, Washoe County (Reno), Carson City and County, and the Lake Tahoe area. Most of them are listed and described in this cathouse directory. However, instead of treating the subject tongue-in-cheek, the author uses too much outhouse humor for our taste.

6 **FANTASY DUNGEON** • *Mistress Ariana's Chambers, 3060 Ali Baba (near Industrial Road); (702) 895-9559.*

Mistress Ariana offers private fantasy sessions by appointment in her three fully equipped dungeons, according to her advertisement in *Full XXXposure.* Equipped with what? You'll have to dial this raven-haired lady and find out; the call is free. Her chambers also feature adult toys, books, videos and "quality leather wear."

7 **"GENTLEMAN'S CLUB" ON THE STRIP** • *Talk of the Town, 1238 S. Las Vegas Blvd. (between Charleston and Oakey); (702) 385-1800. Open 24 hours; live entertainment from 4 p.m. to 4 a.m.; fees vary.*

Located on the north end of the Strip, this club features live table dancing, fantasy booths and something called nude lap dancing. (Use your imagination.) It's one of many "gentlemen's clubs" in the area that cater to male amusements. Talk of the Town invites you to bring your own booze and, says their ad, couples and ladies are always welcome. (Welcome to do what?)

8 **ADULT VIDEO SUPERMARTS** • *Adult Superstores, 3850 W. Tropicana (Valley View), (702) 798-0144; 3226 Spring Mountain Rd. (Polaris), (702) 247-1101; 601 S. Main (Bonneville), 383-0601; and 1147 S. Las Vegas Blvd. (Park Paseo), (702) 383-8326. Open 24 hours; MC/VISA, AMEX.*

Looking for the latest in naughty videos? The Adult Superstore chain is the largest in town, with four outlets. Most have preview theaters so you can peek before you purchase or rent. The outlet at Tropicana and Valley View claims to be the largest adult store in the West, with 50,000 videos. These supermarkets of sex also peddle adult books, toys, games and "marital aids," which probably doesn't refer to marriage counseling manuals.

9 **ADULT LOVE NESTS** • *Upper Las Vegas Boulevard.*

Several motels in Las Vegas feature sensuous furnishings, X-rated movies on the telly and maybe even mirrors on the ceilings. Although we didn't check them out personally, we did note these two, conveniently located along the "wedding chapel row" of upper Las Vegas Boulevard: **Del Mar Resort Motel**, 1411 S. Las Vegas Blvd. (between Park Paseo and Oakey), Las Vegas, NV 88104; (702) 384-5775. It advertises adult movies on a 25-inch screen and, for folks with limited time, hourly rates. **Oasis Motel**, 1931 S. Las Vegas Blvd. (Oakey); Las Vegas, NV 89104; (702) 735-6494. The Oasis has adult movies, spa tubs and "fantasy rooms"; it's conveniently located adjacent to the Hitching Post Wedding Chapel.

10 *SEXY LADY BARBERS* • *A Little Off the Top, 5720 W. Charleston (a block east of Jones); (702) 258-5411.*

When these sexy lady barbers offer to take a little off, they're referring to your hair. However, you gentlemen probably won't be looking in the mirror to check their progress; you'll more likely be watching them work, since they wear scanty lingerie. And if their presence makes you tense, they also do shoulder and neck massage.

The traveler sees what he sees; the tourist sees what he has come to see.
— **Gilbert K. Chesterton**

Chapter nine

WHAT! YOU WANT TO PLAY TOURIST?

WHAT ELSE TO DO IN LAS VEGAS

What else is there to do in Glitter City besides gamble, drink, see live shows and watch pretty ladies get naked? The list of attractions is long and versatile, from the outstanding Clark County Heritage Museum and fine Imperial Palace Auto Collection to the wonderful glitter of the Liberace Museum.

We've selected our ten favorites, followed by ten "only in Las Vegas" attractions. In the next chapter, we pick the Ten Best family attractions, along with the Ten Best family oriented casino resorts. For descriptions of all of Glitter City's attractions, track down a copy of our *Nevada Discovery Guide* and flip to the thick Las Vegas chapter.

THE TEN BEST ATTRACTIONS

This list covers museums and other attractions both inside casino resorts and out. Most charge admission; a few do not. The Ten Best free attractions are listed in Chapter five, starting on page 86.

1 CLARK COUNTY HERITAGE MUSEUM • 1830 S. Boulder Highway, Henderson; (702) 455-7955. Daily 9 to 4:30; adults $1.50, kids and seniors $1.

Plan several hours to explore one of Nevada's finest historic museums. You'll find displays in the *adobe moderne* exhibit center and on the expansive grounds. Displays include a southern Nevada timeline, a Pleistocene diorama with local camels and ground sloths, Anasazi artifacts and an 18th century Paiute camp complete with sound effects. Kids can grind cornmeal with a *metate* and legally feed antique slot machines since there are no payouts. Out on the grounds, you can stroll through period furnished homes, check out the 1931 Boulder City railroad depot and walk the dusty streets of a Nevada ghost town.

2 HOLLYWOOD MOVIE MUSEUM • Debbie Reynolds Hotel and Casino, 305 Convention Center Dr. (between Las Vegas Boulevard and Paradise Road); (702) 734-0711. Weekdays 10 to 10, Saturday 10 to 6 and Sunday 11 to 4. Adults $7.95, kids $5.95.

The irrepressible Debbie Reynolds, who calls Las Vegas her home, has created an appealing museum of Hollywood costumes and other memorabilia in her small casino-hotel. It's actually more than a museum; it's an entertaining show. Patrons are ushered into an old style cinema, where Debbie (on film) presents clips of old movies. Curtains on either side of the screen part to reveal the actual costumes worn by the stars in those films. There's Charlton Heston gritting his teeth in the *Ben Hur* chariot race while a light plays on the armor he wore in the scene. Claudette Cobert (1934) and Elizabeth Taylor (1953) appear in their *Cleopatra* roles as their elaborate costumes are displayed. It's all very clever! After the film, visitors adjourn to an adjacent museum room to inspect more costumes and Hollywood artifacts.

3 IMPERIAL PALACE AUTO COLLECTION • 3535 S. Las Vegas Blvd. (between Sands Avenue and Flamingo Road, opposite Caesars Palace); (702) 731-3311. Daily 9:30 to 11:30. Adults $6.95, seniors and kids (4-12) $3. (Free passes are sometimes being given away out front, or at the third floor redemption center.)

The fifth floor of the Imperial Palace parking garage has been converted into a fine auto museum. Voted one of the top ten auto exhibits in the world, it covers a wide range, from horseless carriages to celebrity cars. More than 200 vehicles are displayed, part of a collection of 700 that's rotated periodically. Among personality cars are the 1937 Cord in which Tom Mix met his doom in 1940; limos that toted Presidents Truman, Eisenhower, Nixon, Kennedy and Johnson; plus Hitler's

1939 armored Mercedes parade car and Marilyn Monroe's 1955 Lincoln Capri convertible. Nostalgia buffs will like the 1954 Chevrolet Bel Air convertible and pair of Ford Mustang Cobras. One room is stuffed with $50 million worth of Duesenbergs; it's regarded as the world's finest collection of these custom-made cars of the Thirties. A bar at one end of the Duesenberg showroom peddles great sinus-clearing bloody Marys and other libations.

4 **LAS VEGAS NATURAL HISTORY MUSEUM** • *900 N. Las Vegas Blvd. (at Washington),; (702) 384-3466. Daily 9 to 4; adults $5, students and seniors $4, kids $2.50.*

After modest beginnings, the Las Vegas Natural History Museum is taking shape as one of Glitter City's better attractions. It has been assembled with wit and imagination, from the *tyrannosaurus* tracks leading from the parking lot, to the mounted colobus monkeys in classic "see no evil, hear no evil, speak no evil" poses. With only private funding, it isn't a high tech museum, yet it's very nicely done. It's an all-family attraction, with exhibits directed toward youngsters as well as their parents. In the Young Scientists Center, kids can learn about nature through "touch and feel" displays and interactive exhibits.

In the main museum, the International Wildlife Room contains mounted specimens from around the globe, including "situational exhibits" such as a pair of lions pouncing an absolutely frantic-looking zebra. In the Marine Life Room, cleverly done with blue lighting, several model sharks and other aquatic critters dangle from the ceiling, while real ones swim about small aquarium tanks. A series of dioramas in the Wild Nevada Room depict the flora and fauna of the desert and mountain regions of Southern Nevada. Our favorite spot is the Dinosaur Den, with full-sized mockups of T-rex and his prehistoric cousins. Here, we learned something to add to our storehouse of worthless information—*tyrannosaurus rex* is Latin for "tyrant reptile king."

5 **LIBERACE MUSEUM** • *1773 E. Tropicana Ave. (at Spencer, in Liberace Center, about three miles from the Strip); (702) 798-5595. Monday-Saturday 10 to 5, Sunday 1 to 5; adults $6.50, seniors $4.50, teens $3.50 and kids $2.*

Although he lived most of his life in Palm Springs, Walter Valentino Liberace loved Las Vegas and the town loved him. Since both were garish and outlandish, they suited one another well, and Liberace performed here for decades. Glittery examples of his flamboyant lifestyle are on display in the most-visited museum in Nevada. Join the other 250,000 annual visitors and enjoy "Mr. Showmanship's" legacy—a sequined, pearl-encrusted, rhinestone-shrouded collection of ostentatious regalia. Check out his jeweled red, white and blue hotpants, his white fox and mink capes, the rhinestone-covered Baldwin piano and million dollar Rolls Royce covered with mirror tiles. Despite his flamboyant extravagance, Liberace was a generous soul and he remains so, even in death. As specified in his will, proceeds from the museum go to the Liberace Foundation for Creative and Performing Arts.

6 MAGIC AND MOVIE HALL OF FAME ● *O'Sheas Casino, 3555 S. Las Vegas Blvd. (north of Flamingo Road, opposite Caesars Palace); (702) 737-1343. Tuesday-Saturday 10 to 6, closed Sunday-Monday. Adults $9.95, kids 12 and under, $3.*

Occupying 20,000 square feet above O'Sheas Casino, this busy blend of magic, movie memorabilia and early day robotics is one of the town's often overlooked attractions. The museum's versatile mix includes artifacts from Houdini and other early magicians, costumes of movie heroines, a huge collection of ventriloquists dummies and antique arcade games. You can listen to the world's largest robot band, play century old arcade games (no atom blasters here!) and practice throwing your voice. Onboard magicians reveal some of their secrets, and you can stock up on prestidigitation items at the gift shop.

7 MARJORIE BARRICK MUSEUM OF NATURAL HISTORY ● *On the UNLV campus, 4505 S. Maryland Parkway (follow Harmon Avenue into the west side of the campus); (702) 895-3381. Weekdays 8 to 4:45, Saturday 10 to 2, closed Sunday; free.*

Don't be misled by the stuffy title. This is one of Glitter City's more interesting museums. Exhibits include live desert critters in glass cages, an excellent display of the early days of Las Vegas and the creation of the Strip, changing art and photo shows, Indian basketry and projectile points, dance masks of Mexico, Navajo rugs, stuffed birds and animals of Nevada, a xeriscape demonstration garden and—for reasons that escape us—a stuffed polar bear.

The exhibit hall for this bio-diverse collection seems rather cavernous, and for good reason: This was home court for the Runnin' Rebels basketball team before construction of the imposing Thomas & Mack Center.

8 NEVADA STATE MUSEUM ● *700 Twin Lakes Drive in Lorenzi Park (Take Bonanza Road west from downtown, across bottom of Lorenzi Park, right onto Twin Lakes then right to museum parking lot); (702) 486-5205. Daily 9 to 5; adults $2, under 18 free.*

An effective mix of artifacts, graphics and photos trace the evolution of southern Nevada from pre-history through the present in this museum operated by the Nevada State Historical Society. Particularly interesting and certainly appropriate is an extensive exhibit on Nevada gambling, with old gaming machines and photos. Other displays cover

Hoover Dam construction, nearby A-bomb testing, wildlife and plant life of the area. Among recent additions exhibits are "Nevada in the Ice Age" and "Gum San: A History of the Chinese in Nevada."

9 **OLD MORMON FORT STATE HISTORIC PARK** ● *908 N. Las Vegas Blvd. (at Washington Street, adjacent to the Las Vegas Natural History Museum); (702) 486-3511. Daily 8:30 to 3:30; free. (Admission fees may be added later as the facility is expanded.)*

The first and oldest structure in Las Vegas, a small adobe built by Mormon settlers, is being expanded into one of the town's best educational attractions. The "Nevada Mission" was established in 1855 and abandoned just three years later. Through the decades, most of the fortress-like complex has disappeared. The single surviving structure has been abused, misused and neglected for decades, serving as a barracks, ranch outbuilding, Hoover Dam concrete testing lab and as a storage shed. It became state park property in 1990 and is being expanded into a major exhibit center tracing the history of early Las Vegas. A bond issue is funding the project.

When we last stopped by, the only exhibits were a furnished room in the surviving adobe building and nicely done graphic displays concerning the early settlement of Southern Nevada. By the time you arrive, you may see a complete fort quadrangle with living history exhibits, a running creek and even crops in the nearby fields.

10 **STRATOSPHERE TOWER** ● *2000 S. Las Vegas Blvd. (at Main Street); (702) 380-7777. Observation levels open daily 10 a.m. to 1 a.m.; various hours for rides. Tower admission $5 for visitors and $4 for Nevada residents; rollercoaster and free-fall rides are $5 each; less with a combination ticket. Tower admission included with reservations at the Top of the World Restaurant.*

Opened in 1995, the Stratosphere is a multiple Las Vegas superlative. Ride one of the elevators to the top while you ponder these facts: At 1,149 feet, it's America's tallest free-standing observation tower, and its 16-level pod is the world's most complex tower viewing area. It contains indoor and outdoor observation platforms, a revolving restaurant, bar, casino, rollercoaster ride, free-fall ride and a wedding chapel. All of the above are either the highest in America or the world. It's the best place in town to watch the sunset, certainly the best place to enjoy the lights of the Strip and—short of chartering a helicopter—it's the best place from which to see the whole dang countryside. During daylight, the view isn't quite as awesome as you would imagine, since Las Vegas is a flat city, looking even flatter from such a high perch. At night, however, it's totally awesome. Go there just before sunset and watch nighttime Glitter City come to life.

The Stratosphere was operating under bankruptcy reorganization as we wrote this. We assume, however, that such an expensive and elaborate facility will not be permitted to fall. We're speaking figuratively, of course.

ONLY IN LAS VEGAS ATTRACTIONS

Look carefully as you wander about Las Vegas and you'll discover several little gems that likely won't be found anywhere else. Many are displays of the wealth that flows through casino halls; others are just quirky little attractions.

1 **SHOWCASE: Adjacent to MGM Grand** • *3785 S. Las Vegas Blvd. (north of Tropicana); (702) 597-3122.*

Completed in 1997, Showcase is many things wrapped up in an intriguing geometric glass and steel architectural package. There's the lively All Star Café, a joint creation of six sports superstars (Chapter four, page 64); the World of Coca-Cola fronted by the world's largest coke bottle; a huge video game and electronic partying complex called Gameworks (Chapter ten, page 163); and M&M's, featuring Ethel M chocolates for those with sweet teeth. From the sidewalk outside, step into the 108-foot Coke bottle and catch an elevator up to three levels of Coca-Cola exhibits. From here, you can take a catwalk over Rue de Monte Carlo, offering views of the Strip on one side and MGM Grand's pool complex on the other. The walk leads to a parking complex and—via an elevator—to the new state-of-the-art United Artists Theater, an eight-screen complex with the world's most advanced sound system.

2 **ANTIQUE SLOT MACHINE EXHIBIT: Sam's Town Hotel & Gambling Hall** • *5111 Boulder Highway (at Nellis Boulevard); (702) 456-7777.*

About a dozen slot machines dating from the 1920s are on display in the main casino at Sam's town, including one that dispensed both nickels and Lifesaver candy. Several are grouped near the entrance to the Players Corral high limit area, and others are along the casino wall opposite the entrance to Mystic Falls Park. Also check out the larger-than-life cowboy and Mexican outlaws with slot machines built into their chests, at the entrance to Willy and Jose's Cantina. These are *really* one-armed bandits!

3 **BRAHMAN SHRINE: Outside Caesars Palace** • *3570 S. Las Vegas Blvd. (at Flamingo Road).*

This four-ton, four-faced, eight-armed shrine is set against the main casino building, behind the main Caesars Palace marquee. It was donated by a Thai millionaire in 1984 to promote good luck, presumably for himself as well as other hotel guests. Passersby often pause and pay homage to the bronze, gold-plated shrine. Many light joss sticks and leave offerings for good luck. When we last checked, the offering dish contained three bags of airline peanuts and a packet of Grandma's oatmeal applesauce cookies.

4 *CHINATOWN* • *Spring Mountain Road and Wynn Road (a mile west of I-15).*

How can a Chinatown rank as an "Only in Las Vegas" item? Most overseas Chinese communities gradually evolved, as immigrants gathered together in a particular neighborhood. Chinatowns of San Francisco, New York, Vancouver and Toronto are good examples. However, the Las Vegas Chinatown is a theme shopping center, created within a few months. It's gaily decorated with turned-up eves on glossy tiled roofs, golden dragons and lots of red for good luck—which can come in handy in Las Vegas.

While hardly a conventional Chinatown, it's interesting for its gaudy décor and its Asian shops. Look for plaques on corridors and columns that discuss Chinese history, art and culture. This modern Asian mall has half a dozen restaurants including one with a barbecue take-out offering glazed ducks and other ethnic fare, plus a couple of import shops and a traditional herb shop. However, my Chinese wife Betty wasn't impressed with the bakery, which has more birthday cakes and cream puffs than mooncakes and beancakes.

5 *CONFECTIONERY CASTLE: Excalibur* • *3850 S. Las Vegas Blvd. (Tropicana Avenue).*

This is a detailed scale model of the Excalibur hotel complex, made entirely of chocolate and *pastilliage,* which is powdered sugar, cornstarch and gelatin. It's the result of a thousand volunteer hours by members of the hotel's food and beverage staff. This candy castle is located on the upper level Medieval Village on Sharing Crossroad just beyond the escalator. It looks good enough to eat, although *pastilliage* is rather chewy and it isn't very tasty.

6 *NEON JUNKYARD: Young Electric Sign Company* • *5119 Cameron St.; (off West Tropicana); (702) 876-8080.*

This junky jewel is a classic "Only in Las Vegas" attraction. Over the years, YESCO has produced most of the town's gaudy and gargantuan electric and neon creations, plus Reno's latest "Biggest Little City in the World" arch. The factory is on the right side of Cameron Street, and a large lot just beyond serves as a junkyard of its yesterday signs. They don't do tours but you can peek through the fence at a scatter of golden arches, marquees from early-day casinos and other businesses.

To reach the "neon junkyard," go west on Tropicana for about a mile and a half, then turn left onto Cameron at a stoplight just beyond the Orleans Hotel. YESCO is a short distance down Cameron Street on your right.

7 ELVIS SHRINE: Las Vegas Hilton • *3000 Paradise Rd. (east of Las Vegas Boulevard, next to Las Vegas Convention Center; (702) 732-5111.*

Occupying a corner near the Hilton main entrance is a bronze of Elvis Presley, who set an all-time record here by performing in 837 consecutive sold-out concerts during an eight-year stint. Also on display are a sequined red, white and blue patriotic costume he wore at some of the concerts and the guitar he used—a six-string Guild.

8 MILLION DOLLAR CURRENCY DISPLAY: Binion's Horseshoe Casino • *128 Fremont St. (between First and Casino Center Drive).*

A million dollars in $10,000 bills is framed behind Plexiglas at the northeast corner of the casino, near the Casino Center Drive entrance. You can't take any home, although you can take home a picture of yourself standing before it, feeling like a million. Casino personnel will shoot a free photo of you with all that loot, daily from 4 p.m. to midnight. And who's face graces a $10,000 bill? Salmon Portland Chase, who was President Lincoln's secretary of the treasury and later chief justice of the U.S. Supreme Court.

9 A REAL GLITTER CITY: Las Vegas Hilton casino • *3000 Paradise Rd. (Riviera Boulevard); (702) 732-5111*

Only in Las Vegas will you find this much glitter dangling from a ceiling. Four huge crystal chandelier strips, each more than 150 feet long, hang above the main table games arena at the Hilton casino. At the far end is a final glitter fling—an imposing circular chandelier that serves as the ceiling to a casino bar.

10 WORLD'S LARGEST PRIVATE GOLD NUGGET DISPLAY: Golden Nugget • *129 Fremont St. (Casino Center Boulevard); (702) 385-7111.*

The gleaming star of this show is the "Hand of Faith," a 875 troy ounce nugget found in 1975 near Wedderburn, Australia. A sign says it's the "world's largest natural nugget on public display." Several smaller nuggets complete this exhibit, which occupies a display case in the left corridor leading from the main casino on Fremont Street to the hotel desk.

In America there are two classes of travel—first class and with children.
— **Robert Benchley**

Chapter ten

WHAT! YOU BROUGHT THE KIDS?

KEEPING THE LITTLE RASCALS OUT OF THE CASINOS

Las Vegas began as an adult playground, a place to pursue the earthly pleasures of wine, women and winning. However, a key to its current success is its shift toward family entertainment. Many old timers disdain this approach. They would like to keep this a town for adults, and possibly for occasional adultery.

The family theme was slow in coming. Even the original Circus Circus, opened by Jay Sarno in 1968, had topless circus ladies; the shows were for adults only. Then Arizona furniture tycoon William Bennett bought the big top in 1974, put tops on the ladies, added a large hotel and amusement arcade and declared it to be a family attraction.

The firm, now Circus Circus Enterprises, followed with a clone in Reno, and then the Excalibur and Luxor in Las Vegas. Suddenly, Glitter City was a place for families to play. The Mirage, Treasure Island, MGM Grand and New York New York all have family-oriented attractions. Even the legendary Tropicana and Flamingo, survivors of the old days on the Strip, have large swimming areas that will appeal to kids. (*"C'mon Dad, it's my turn on the water slide!"*)

With this trend, Las Vegas is becoming a major summer destination, when the little monsters are out of school. Thus, the hottest time of the year is no longer the slowest time of the year, thanks to William Bennett and Willis Haviland Carrier, the inventor of air conditioning.

This doesn't mean that Glitter City is a suitable playground for all ages. There isn't much here for toddlers, who tend to get in the way and occasionally get stepped on in casino crowds. And there's absolutely no reason to bring infants. We often see moms and dads packing them through crowded casinos or lugging them along hot sidewalks; neither parents nor tots appear to be having any fun. State law prohibits minors from loitering in casinos; they're only permitted to pass through, en route to non-gaming areas. So if your kids aren't old enough to be parked in the video games parlor or to safely explore on their own, you need to deal with baby sitting services. These are available, but why would your rug rats want to be cooped up in a hotel room with a sitter while you're out having a good time? We recommend a Las Vegas vacation only for kids age eight or older. As for the rest, isn't that why grandparents were invented?

Incidentally, Las Vegas out-draws Disneyland and Walt Disney World combined. It took Disneyland about three decades to log in its thirty millionth visitor. Las Vegas gets that many every year, although they aren't all families, of course. Most visitors are adults who come looking not for Chip 'n' Dale, but for a good stack of poker chips.

THE TEN BEST FAMILY ORIENTED CASINO RESORTS

If you are bringing the family to Las Vegas, these are the Ten Best places to stay, or to explore with your younsters if you've selected lodgings elsewhere in town:

1 CIRCUS CIRCUS • 2880 S. Las Vegas Blvd. (upper Strip, south of the Sahara); (800) 444-CIRC or (702) 734-0410.

Glitter City's first family resort is still the best, from the giant pink lollipop-clutching clown outside to the free circus acts inside. While mom and pop gamble, the kids can be upstairs watching trapeze or trampoline acts or trying to win a stuffed panda at the large carnival midway. A covered amusement park, Grand Slam Canyon, can keep both kids and parents amused. It is, incidentally, the world's largest fully enclosed amusement park, housed under five acres of pink solar glass. Circus Circus is geared for family budgets. Rooms start as low as $39 for four people and the buffet is one of the least expensive in town. The casino is a low roller haven, with lots of nickel slots and low table limits. (Many parents can't afford $10 table limits when they're trying to feed a bunch of hungry kids at the table at home.)

2 **EXCALIBUR** • *3850 S. Las Vegas Blvd. (Tropicana Avenue);* *(800) 937-7777 or (702) 597-7777.*

This multicolored bundle of Arthurian towers was the largest hotel in the world when it was opened in 1990 by Circus Circus Enterprises. Like its shiny sister up the Strip, it's primarily a family destination, with a large amusement arcade called the Fantasy Faire, a pretend jousting match called King Arthur's Tournament and Wizard's Video Arcade. It's a visual treat for youngsters as well, with its Technicolor towers, medieval drawbridge and its Arthurian décor inside.

3 **LUXOR HOTEL & CASINO** • *3900 Las Vegas Blvd. (Tropicana); (800) 288-1000 or (702) 262-4000.*

From the folks who brought you the circus and King Arthur's castle comes an incongruous marriage of ancient Egypt and family amusement center. Opened in 1993 by Circus Circus Enterprises, the Luxor features a large video arcade, "Virtua Land" virtual reality venue, a new 3-D IMAX theater, Secrets of the Pyramid "movie magic illusion" and more. All of this is on the Attractions Level, which is basically the roof of the casino. King Tut's Museum, originally in the basement but closed at this writing, may reopen here as well. The Luxor joined the growing list of Las Vegas superlatives when it opened, offering the world's largest atrium. The best place to see this great hollow space, with its hanging balcony rooms, is on the Attractions Level. Elsewhere, ceilings and walls interrupt the view.

4 **MGM GRAND** • *3799 S. Las Vegas Blvd. (at Tropicana); (800) 929-1111 or (702) 891-7777.*

The world's largest resort rivals Circus Circus as a family vacation spot. Although it doesn't have a kiddie theme like C-C, it has extensive facilities geared toward the younger set. Start with the MGM Grand Adventure, a 33-acre amusement park with thrill rides and shows. The wildest is the Sky Screamer, a 250-foot pendulum drop. The Grand also has a large swimming pool area. Inside the huge resort complex, kids can spend time and quarters in a large video arcade or follow the Yellow Brick Road to Emerald City, meeting robotics of Dorothy, the Tin Man and others of the "Over the Rainbow" cast. The MGM Grand Youth Center, near the entrance to the amusement park, has special lures for kids 3 to 16, with counselors who will look after the youngsters while the folks seek adult pursuits.

5 **THE MIRAGE** • *3400 S. Las Vegas Blvd. (adjacent to Caesars Palace); (800) 627-6667 or (702) 791-7111.*

Although the next-door Treasure Island is more of a family destination with its pirate ship battle, Buccaneer Bay video arcade and circus show, the Mirage has several youthful lures as well. The kids can't help liking the imposing indoor rainforest, and they'll be impressed by the white tiger enclosure. A new attraction, Siegfried and Roy's Secret Garden, is a small educational zoo in a jungle setting, with an adjacent dolphin habitat. And of course, the fire, brimstone and magic of the Siegfried and Roy show certainly will appeal to the younger set.

6 NEW YORK NEW YORK • *3790 S. Las Vegas Boulevard (Tropicana Avenue); (800) NY-FORME or (702) 740-6969.*

This new resort offers youthful lures such as a rollercoaster-entwined New York skyline façade, simulated motion rides and virtual reality games. An elaborately computerized Daytona 500 car race pitting eight "drivers" against one another will appeal to kids and their parents. Youngsters will like the look of the place inside and out, from the fireboats in the "harbor" at the base of the Statue of Liberty to the Manhattan Express rollercoaster and large Coney Island theme amusement center. At the food court, fashioned as a Greenwich Village street scene, youngsters can find plenty of hamburgers, fries, pizzas and designer ice cream.

7 SAM'S TOWN HOTEL & GAMBLING HALL • *5111 Boulder Highway; (800) 634-6371 or (702) 456-7777.*

Although this lively Western style resort out on the Boulder Strip isn't geared primarily for families, kids will like its Mystic Falls Park and Calamity Jane's Ice Cream Parlor. Mystic Falls is a large slice of the great outdoors brought inside, with a periodic laser and water show called the "Sunset Stampede." Calamity Jane's has a Coca-Cola theme, with old Coke advertising prints, bottles, signs and such. Sam's also has a swimming lagoon, volleyball court with real sand and a large bowling center, with an adjacent video game parlor and supervised children's playroom. (See "Kid-vid" listings below.)

8 THE STRATOSPHERE • *2000 S. Las Vegas Blvd. (upper end at Main Street junction); (800) 998-6937 or (702) 380-7777. Observation levels open daily 10 a.m. to 1 a.m.; various hours for rides. Tower admission $5 for visitors and $4 for Nevada residents; rollercoaster and free-fall rides are $5 each; less with a combination ticket. Tower admission included with reservations at the Top of the World Restaurant.*

The Stratosphere was designed with families in mind from the ground up, and we mean way up. The 1,149-foot observation tower, tallest in America, is capped with a rollercoaster and tummy-lurching free-fall ride—obvious lures for children and teens. Down closer to the ground, the facility has a large video arcade. A spiral corridor leading from the main casino to the tower elevators is lined with kiosks and shops, including many that appeal to families.

There is an irony to all of this. Bob Stupak, who conceived and built the Stratosphere, has been quoted as saying Las Vegas is an adult playground, not a family circus. However, he obviously recognized the family visitor potential as he designed his tower. He's no longer involved with the Stratosphere, which has nothing to do with his attitude regarding kids and Las Vegas.

9 *TREASURE ISLAND AT THE MIRAGE* • *3300 Las Vegas Blvd. (Spring Mountain Road); (800) 949-7444 or (702) 894-7111.*

Treasure Island is a family version of the Mirage. It has a similar tropical theme, although in this case, the pirates have taken over. Where the Mirage is lush and elegant, Treasure Island is more cheerful and lively—a kind of Las Vegas "Pirates of the Caribbean" with lots of treasure chests, sabres and deaths heads worked into the décor. Room prices are geared more toward families, and it offers a large combined video arcade and carnival midway called Mutiny Bay. Treasure Island's "Mystère" in a circus-style showroom rivals the Mirage's Siegfried and Roy as the best family show in town. And of course, the out-front Buccaneer Bay Show, in which a pirate ship battles *HMS Britannia*, is a popular family attraction. (See Chapter five, page 87.)

10 *TROPICANA RESORT & CASINO* • *3801 S. Las Vegas Blvd. (Tropicana Avenue, opposite the Excalibur); (800) 634-4000 or (702) 739-2222.*

This legendary resort, long known as a serious gaming venue, is gaining favor as a family destination with its lush tropical theme. It features a five-acre lagoon and swimming complex, where kids can rent water play equipment while the parents try the their luck at the world's only swim-up blackjack game. A deli inside the main building, just off the pool, will satisfy appetites without denting the family finances too seriously. Also inside is a "Wildlife Walk," a corridor busy with assorted chatty macaws, chattering marmosets, slithery anacondas and other critters. Don't worry kids; the snakes are under glass.

THE TEN BEST KIDS' ATTRACTIONS

1 *GAMEWORKS* • *In the basement of the Showcase, 3769 S. Las Vegas Blvd., adjacent to the MGM Grand, north of Tropicana Avenue; (702) 432-GAME. Daily 10 a.m. to 4 a.m.; free admission; charges for various games.*

Opened in mid-1997, Gameworks is the largest video arcade in Las Vegas, with hundreds of state-of-the-art electronic games, plus old fashioned carnival midway games such as skee-ball and basketball shoots. And there's more, both for kids and adults, including a 70-foot climbing wall, a fast food takeout, a Starbucks Coffee stall, a specialty French fry takeout and a bar and billiards room. This lively facility has an open beam, space age exposed-plumbing-modern look—perhaps resembling the engine room of the Starship *Enterprise*. (We have this vision of Scotty having so much fun with the video games that he forgets to beam Captain Kirk and Mister Spock back from the hostile planet Zorkon.)

The bar and pool parlor are for adults only—handy hangouts for mom and pop while the kids feed their electronically charged cards into the game machines. If the folks are computer nerds or just want a little quiet, they can retreat to a cozy lounge called "*theloft@gameworks.com*," with a computer terminal at each seat. We noted on our last visit that parents don't spend all of their time in the bar or billiards room, however. Many of them were right out there among the machines, riding the simulated Indianapolis Speedway Racers and the electronic Yamaha Waverunners, having the time of their lives. A few were even on that climbing wall, trying to make it to the top. (Don't worry, Dad; if you slip and fall, you're safely tethered. Of course, your kids will kid you about it all the way home.)

We were impressed by the fact that Gameworks is thoroughly chaperoned by helpful, friendly teenagers. Smoking isn't permitted, except by adults in the bar. Most of the electronic games, which are made by Sega, flash a message between rounds that says: "Winners don't use drugs." We can't think of a better place for your kids in Las Vegas.

2 **GRAND SLAM CANYON** ● *Circus Circus, 2880 S. Las Vegas Blvd. (upper Strip, south of the Sahara); (702) 794-3939. Daily 11 to 6. Free admission; all-day ride pass $13.95.*

While Grand Slam Canyon amusement park is considerably smaller than MGM Grand Adventures (below), it's covered and air conditioned, a good idea on a hot August school vacation day. It is in fact (Duck! Here comes a superlative!) America's largest canopied amusement park, housing the largest indoor rollercoaster. Other lures inside this pink canopy are a log flume ride, a very wet tubular water slide, animated dinosaurs, several virtual reality games and laser tag.

3 **GUINNESS WORLD OF RECORDS MUSEUM** ● *2780 S. Las Vegas Blvd. (between Stratosphere Tower and Circus Circus); (702) 792-3766. Daily 9 to 8. Adults $4.95; seniors, military and students $3.95; kids 5 to 12, $2.95.*

Plastic statues of the world's tallest and shortest people? Give us a break! However, after visiting the museum that's based on *The Guinness Book of World Records,* we were pleasantly surprised. The facility has been dressed up with computers, videos and interactive exhibits of the world's biggest this, longest that and most of those. You could spend a few hours here just watching the videos of record-breaking sports events, domino-toppling records and other momentous happenings. Of particular interest—and certainly appropriate for a Glitter City museum—is the "World of Las Vegas" exhibit, highlighting the history and superlatives of this city with the most. Speaking of the most, did you know that more Life Savers have been sold than any other kind of candy, and if they were stacked on end, their little holes would form a tunnel to the moon and back three times?

4 **LAS VEGAS NATURAL HISTORY MUSEUM** • *900 N. Las Vegas Blvd. (at Washington); (702) 384-3466. Daily 9 to 4; adults $5, students and seniors $4, kids $2.50.*

Although the natural history museum is an all-family attraction, it's particularly targeted to kids. In fact, one of its stated goals is to teach children a better understanding and appreciation of the natural environment. The museum's Young Scientist Center has "touch and feel" displays and educational interactive exhibits. Museum personnel conduct frequent teaching programs and tours specifically geared to youngsters. In the main exhibit area, placards are written to a grammar school level, to encourage kids to read and learn about the animal displays.

Kids will enjoy the realistic mounted mammal specimens, the giant sharks dangling from the ceiling in the Marine Room and real sharks and other fish in small aquariums. And they'll definitely make tracks for the Dinosaur Den to stare in awe at the realistic, life-sized models of *tyrannosaurus rex* and other primordial critters.

5 **LIED DISCOVERY CHILDREN'S MUSEUM** • *833 N. Las Blvd. (just north of the freeway underpass, opposite Cashman Field); (702) 382-5437. Wednesday-Saturday 10 to 5 and Sunday noon to 5, closed Monday-Tuesday. Adults $5; seniors and kids 12 to 16, $4; kids 3 to 11, $3.*

This outstanding children's museum and science center has more than a hundred hands-on kinetic and computer-operated exhibits. Even though your rug rats may lean more toward Glitter City's amusement parks, save some time for this discovery museum because of its great educational value. Youngsters can make lightning bolts, learn about fiber optics, study "live" weather maps beamed down by satellite and blow bubbles with dry ice. More pragmatic are inter-active exhibits that permit youngsters to choose a profession, deposit their paychecks, buy groceries and— Wait a minute! This is supposed to be a kids' museum, not future reality!

6 MGM GRAND ADVENTURES • *MGM Grand Hotel, 3799 S. Las Vegas Blvd. (at Tropicana); (702) 891-7979. Daily 10 to 6; hours may be later in summer. Park admission $3; various prices for rides and attractions; combination tickets available.*

You'd scream, too, if you were suspended as a pendulum on a cable, hurling through the air at near terminal velocity. The "Sky Screamer" is the best of several attractions at this mid-size outdoor amusement park and it's just possibly the wildest ride in Nevada. Riders are harnessed face down in a cable-suspended rig, pulled to the near vertical and then let go. Watching it (we were too chicken to ride), we could hear the wind whistling through the hair of the riders as they flew past in a stomach-churning arc. Other lures include a lively rollercoaster, a flume ride through rapids, bumper cars, live shows (geared mostly to kids), curio shops and, of course, plenty of places to eat.

7 SCANDIA FAMILY FUN CENTER • *2900 Sirius (off west-side I-15 frontage road, between Spring Mountain and Sahara); (702) 364-0070. Monday-Thursday 10 to 11 and Friday-Saturday 10 a.m to 1 a.m. Free admission; various fees for games.*

This is a good place to park the kids while you play adult games, or you can join them in a round of miniature golf. Facilities at this good-sized complex include two 18-hole mini-golf courses, mini-Indy racers, bumper boats, baseball and softball batting cages, a snack bar and a very large video arcade that rivals any in the casinos.

8 MANHATTAN EXPRESS & CONEY ISLAND MIDWAY • *At New York New York Hotel & Casino, 3790 S. Las Vegas Blvd. (Tropicana Avenue); (702) 740-6969. Manhattan Express ride $5; various prices for video and arcade games.*

The Manhattan Express rollercoaster is so wild—to ride or to watch—that it easily rates as one of the Ten Best kids' attractions in town. It's also as one of the best attractions for adults willing to take the plunge. And plunge it does. The rollercoaster ride begins in New York New York's city-within-a-city, then climbs with agonizing slowness toward the outdoor sky. After an initial hair-lifting plunge, it turns its riders every which way but loose, hurling in, under, around and through the scale model New York skyline. Having survived that— and everyone does—you can adjourn to the adjacent Coney Island midway and video arcade. It's one of the largest such facilities on the Strip and of course, it has a pleasing Coney Island theme, complete with Nathan's hotdogs. The Manhattan Express, in addition to being one of the wildest rides in town, is a visual treat. Where else but in Las Vegas can one stroll along a make-believe Brooklyn Bridge (the converted sidewalk in front of the casino hotel), look skyward and see a rollercoaster hurling its shrieking passengers past the Statue of Liberty and Empire State Building?

9 *THE SECRET GARDEN OF SIEGFRIED AND ROY* • *The Mirage, 3400 S. Las Vegas Blvd. (adjacent to Caesars Palace); (702) 791-7111. Daily except Wednesday 11 to 5:30; adults and teens $10, kids under 10 free; Dolphin Habitat open Wednesdays; adults and teens $5, kids free.*

The Mirage Dolphin Habitat with its impressive 2.5-million gallon sea water pool has been joined by a small, thickly vegetated animal sanctuary. Visitors can come in close yet safe contact with big cats, an Asian elephant and assorted other critters. ("When you breathe, they hear you," the announcer on the local radio commercial says breathlessly.) The "Secret Garden" is part a preservation program led by Siegfried and Roy, who perform with white tigers and lions in the Mirage main showroom. They are working to increase populations of rare white tigers and lions that no longer exist in the wild, and they've had considerable success with their breeding program. Among inhabitants of the garden are these albino cats, plus normal lions and tigers that carry the white genetic code, striped white tigers, a black panther and a snow leopard.

On Wednesdays when the main sanctuary is closed, you can still visit the Dolphin Habitat, where trainers work with these intelligent sea mammals.

10 *WET 'N WILD WATER PARK* • *2601 S. Las Vegas Blvd. (near the Sahara Hotel); (702) 737-3819. Open May through October, 10 to 8; adults and teens $22.95, kids to 6 to 10, $16.95.*

These three elements were made for each other—a 26-acre water park, the summer school holiday period and families on vacation. When the thermometer sizzles above a hundred and it's too hot for the exposed asphalt of MGM Grand Adventures, drop the kids at Wet 'n Wild for an afternoon of water slides, wading pools, wave pools and a water-powered rollercoaster. Drop them? If the sun is simmering and you're not doing so well in the casinos, you might want to join them!

THE TEN BEST CASINO KID-VID ARCADES

Most major casino resorts along the Strip and a few downtown have video arcades, although some are rather small. Here are the largest and the best. Our list includes all of those with carnival midways.

1 CIRCUS CIRCUS • 2880 S. Las Vegas Blvd. (upper Strip, south of the Sahara); (702) 734-0410.

The original Las Vegas family resort has the largest carnival midway in town, with a dozen or more toss 'n' shoot games circling the circus arena. It also has a fair sized video game parlor, and a rotating "Horse Around Bar" where adults can park with a drink while their kids play. The midway is on the second floor above the main casino, just inside the main entrance.

2 CAESARS PALACE • 3570 S. Las Vegas Blvd. (at Flamingo Road); (702) 731-7110.

This huge resort complex has two video parlors—Caesars Adventure Arcade above the Olympic Casino, near the entrance to the Omnimax Theater, and Cyberspace downstairs at the far end of the Forum Shops corridor. Both are in the north end of the resort. The Adventure Arcade is rather small; Cyberspace is larger, with more sophisticated electronic toys. Adjacent to the Adventure Arcade is the Cinema Ride, touted as the world's only 3-D motion simulator, with four different programs. Tickets may be purchased individually or as a package.

3 EXCALIBUR • 3850 S. Las Vegas Blvd. (Tropicana Avenue); (702) 597-7777.

Fantasy Faire is a large carnival midway second in size only to Circus Circus. It also has a midsize video game parlor, and a "Magic Motion Machine." The "Faire" is downstairs, just inside Excalibur's main entrance at Las Vegas Boulevard and Tropicana.

4 MGM GRAND • 3799 S. Las Vegas Blvd. (at Tropicana); (702) 891-7777.

The MGM Grand Arcade is down a stairway, just to the right of the MGM Grand Adventure park. It's a large and loud place with a virtual reality area, dozens of video games and a few midway games.

5 LUXOR HOTEL & CASINO • 3900 S. Las Vegas Blvd. (below Tropicana); (702) 262-4000.

Luxor has one of the largest kid complexes in town; it's on the Attractions Level above the main casino. To reach it from the main entrance (beneath the Sphinx tummy), go left and look for the escalator. It has a large video arcade on two levels called Virtua Land with dozens of video games, plus a simulator ride, a multi-media show, IMAX feature film and IMAX 3-D film.

6 *MONTE CARLO* • *3770 Las Vegas Blvd. (north of Tropicana Avenue); (702) 730-7777.*

Simply called the Arcade and Midway, this good sized setup is beyond the casino, off the Street of Dreams shopping arcade, opposite the Monte Carlo Pub and Brewery. It has the usual assortment of video machines and a few carnival midway games.

7 *NEW YORK NEW YORK* • 3790 S. Las Vegas Blvd. (Tropicana Avenue); (702) 740-6969.

The Coney Island midway is rather extensive, with lots of video games, several carnival games and a kid-oriented food court. It's reached by an escalator not far from the hotel check in desk. Games line a long corridor that leads to the Manhattan Express rollercoaster.

8 *SAM'S TOWN HOTEL & GAMBLING HALL* • *5111 Boulder Highway (at Nellis Boulevard); (702) 456-7777.*

Sam's kid-vid arcade isn't large, although we like its location, adjacent to the family oriented bowling alley, downstairs and well away from the casino action. A couple of ranks of video machines occupy the video room and a third rank stands against a wall outside. Another plus for those with mixed-age kids: There's a supervised children's playroom in the area. The video arcade is to the left at the base of the escalator to the bowling alley, and the playroom is to the right, upstairs beyond the bowling shop.

9 *STRATOSPHERE* • *2000 S. Las Vegas Blvd. (upper end at Main Street junction); (702) 380-7777.*

The Stratosphere's "Sky-Bound Aircade" is a midsize facility, with mostly video games, plus a couple of carney-type skee-ball and basketball tossing games. It's at the top of the escalator that leads to the Strat's other family lures—the sky tower with its viewing platform, rollercoaster and free-fall ride.

10 *TREASURE ISLAND* • *3300 Las Vegas Blvd. (Spring Mountain Road); (702) 894-7111.*

The kid-vid venue here is Mutiny Bay, located toward the rear of the casino, near the exit to the pool. Cleverly fashioned as a pirates village, it's a rather large complex, with a good selection of video games and several carnival arcade attractions.

"What is the use of a book," thought Alice, "without pictures?"
--Lewis Carroll, Alice's Adventures in Wonderland

Chapter eleven

POINTS OF VIEW
THE BEST VISTAS AND CAMERA ANGLES

Remember those "picture spots" at Disneyland? They helped aim amateur photographers in proper directions to get good photos. We present here the Ten Best vistas of Las Vegas and the Ten Best photo angles which—as any professional photographer can tell you—aren't always the same.

Our eyes provide us with near 180-degree vision and three-dimensional sight. Cameras, unless they're equipped with a fisheye lens, have a much narrower field of view and their products are two-dimensional. An awesome view doesn't always produce an awesome photo.

First, we offer the Ten Best views in and around Glitter City. We then follow with the Ten Best photo angles, accompanied by a quick course in scenic photography. Hopefully, you'll be able to take home some good photos of Glitter City, instead of just snapshots.

THE TEN BEST LAS VEGAS VISTAS

These selections are listed in no particular order, although number one is quite awesome:

1 THE BEST NIGHTTIME VIEW OF LAS VEGAS: *Mormon Temple* • *Upper Bonanza Road at Temple View Drive.*

From this vantage point high on the flanks of Sunrise Mountain, the grand carpet of Las Vegas lights shimmer like an upside down universe of colored stars. The Latter Day Saints (Mormon) temple also is an imposing sight at night, a modernistic spired white castle bathed in floodlights. To reach this aerie, drive north through downtown on Las Vegas Boulevard to Bonanza (the first major street after the freeway). Turn right (east) on Bonanza and drive about six miles until you see the temple gleaming before you.

2 THE BEST SUNSET VIEW: Stratosphere Tower • *2000 S. Las Vegas Blvd. (Main).*

The view down the Las Vegas Strip from this 1,149-foot tower is predictably impressive. It's much more awesome when the sinking sun casts crisp shadows on the Strip casinos. It then sinks behind the distant Black Mountains as the neon fairyland below you begins its nighttime glitter.

3 THE BEST VIEW OF THE STRIP: Rio Hotel parking garage roof • *3700 W. Flamingo Rd. (at Valley View Boulevard, opposite the Gold Coast).*

Actually, the best views are from the rooms on the east side of the sexy new Rio tower, although those cost around $100 or more a night. For a free—if lower level—view of the Strip, stroll across the upper level of the east parking structure—the one reached from Flamingo Road, with the catwalk entrance to the Masquerade Village Casino. From here, you can see the full sweep of the nearby Strip, from the Stratosphere tower to the Luxor Pyramid and beyond.

4 THE BEST FREMONT STREET EXPERIENCE VIEW: "Lucky Lookout" at Fitzgeralds Casino • *Fremont Street at Third, downtown.*

A small balcony hangs over Fremont street from Fitzgeralds' second-floor casino, providing a nice overhead view up and down the canopied pedestrian mall. This isn't the best place for viewing or photographing the "Fremont Street Experience" sound and light show, since you're tucked under the canopy and you're looking at it from an odd angle. However, it's a great place to lean on the rail and watch the human parade below.

5 THE BEST DOWNTOWN AND MOUNTAIN VIEW: Interstate 515 • *Northwest bound, nearing downtown.*

As you follow Interstate 515 northwest from Henderson, the elevated freeway offers a splendid view of Mount Charleston and the rest of the Spring Mountain range, with the Downtown Casino Center in the foreground. Watch for it as you sweep around a large curve just after you've passed the Charleston Boulevard interchange.

6 THE BEST STRIP AND MOUNTAIN VIEW: Boulder Highway • *Northwest bound from downtown Henderson.*

Personal prejudice shows here (as it does throughout this book), since this is a route we often take as we run errands from our Henderson home. Old Henderson—not the trendy new Green Valley area—sits on a slight rise, and the landscaped section of Boulder Highway as it passes through town provides a fine view of the distant Strip and the Spring Mountains. It's often hazy and even tainted with smog, but that's traffic-choked Glitter City's fault, not Henderson's. Check out the view at sunset, when sun-painted clouds may crown the mountains even as neon begins to paint the skyline of the Strip. Later, although the mountains are lost to the night sky, the lights of Glitter City present quite a show.

A closer Strip-and-mountain view is from Paradise Road between Harmon and Tropicana, and from the adjacent Thomas and Mack Center parking lot. However, it's rather cluttered with billboards, utility lines and other foreground distractions.

7 BEST VIEW OF MYSTIC FALLS PARK: From the capsule elevators at Sams Town • *5111 Boulder Highway (at Nellis Boulevard).*

Mystic Falls is a "park under glass," a 25,000-square foot oasis of trees, plants and waterfalls on an inner courtyard formed by the hotel towers of Sam's Town. It's covered by a giant greenhouse roof, so this refuge is climate-controlled. A laser and water show called the "Sunset Stampede" is presented here periodically; see Chapter five, page 88. Windowed elevators scale the inner walls of the hotel tower, providing a fine view down to the park. Since the ride and thus the view are brief, get off on the ninth floor and you'll find several corridor windows looking down to Mystic Falls.

8 THE BEST VIEW OF HOOVER DAM: Small turnout on the Nevada side • *About a third of a mile from the visitor center parking structure.*

So all right, Hoover Dam isn't in Las Vegas, although it's an integral part. Without that darned dam, there would be no water and power and therefore no Glitter City. Our favorite vista point is from a narrow turnout on the Nevada side. From here, you get the complete panorama—a slice of Lake Mead, the curving crest and great concrete wedge of the dam and a stretch of the Colorado River burbling through Black Canyon below the dam site.

The viewpoint is on the north side of the highway, so it's best to catch it as you leave the dam. On the approach route, you'd have to cross traffic on this narrow, curving road. Although the turnout is small, it's rarely crowded since most visitors overlook it. The best vantage point is from the extreme lower end of the turnout; otherwise, your view is obstructed by a large gantry crane. Although this is a grand view, it doesn't make a good photo, because that crane and high tension wires clutter the foreground. For pictures, we prefer the Arizona side; see below, under "The Ten Best picture spots" on page 178.

9 THE BEST VIEW OF LAKE MEAD: Lake Mead Vista Point. • One and a third miles uphill from Hoover Dam, off U.S. 93 on the Nevada side.

As you're approaching or leaving Hoover Dam, watch for a Lake Mead vista point sign on the north side of the highway. A short road leads to an overlook where you'll catch a pleasing panorama of the blue-green lake, with its rugged shoreline and a couple of small offshore islands. You won't see the dam itself; a rocky outcropping to your right blocks that part of the view.

10 BEST PLACE TO WATCH PLANES LAND: Park 2000 Mall • East of McCarran International Airport, at Eastern Avenue near Sunset Road.

Calling this a "view" is stretching a point, which is why we saved it for last. The views are of the underbellies of jet airplanes. Although we've flown only a few hundred times while traveling to seventy countries, islands and other landfalls, we still enjoy watching those big aluminum monsters take off and land. A shopping and office complex called Park 2000 on the east side of Eastern Avenue provides views of the big birds passing a few hundred feet overhead, sweeping gracefully earthward.

Plane watchers also can drive to a turnout beside the south fence on Sunset Road, midway between Las Vegas Boulevard and Eastern Avenue. From either vantage point, you'll see planes land and take off every few minutes since McCarran is one of the nation's busiest airports. Kinda makes a fellah want to hum the theme from *The High and the Mighty*. And if you miss the significance of that, you haven't been flying for as long as we have.

Shooting Las Vegas

Because photographs are two-dimensional, good photographers apply several techniques to give them depth. You can suggest dimension in a scenic by placing a tree limb or interesting street lamp in the foreground, and perhaps something in the middleground. On the other hand, if you're focusing on a particularly interesting object, don't clutter your photo with framing; let the viewer see nothing but that object.

Most outdoor photos are predominately blue, green and brown, the colors of the sky and the earth. To brighten them, add colors from the warm side of the spectrum—reds, yellows and oranges. Dress Aunt Maud in a bright yellow dress or place a brilliant flower in the foreground, off to the side where it won't interfere with the main subject of the photo.

When you photograph people, don't force them to squint into the sun. Position them with the sun behind you but to the right or left so it strikes them at an angle, accenting their features. (*"My, what a big nose you have, Uncle Charlie!"*) Also, have your subjects interact with the setting instead of just staring morosely at the camera or—worse—wearing a silly grin.

Light and shadows are key elements in photography, giving two-dimensional photos a feeling of depth. Early morning and late afternoon are the best times to shoot, when shadows are stronger, bringing out detail in your subject. This is particularly true for structural photos—the kind of pictures you'll be taking along the Las Vegas Strip. Further, in the late afternoon, the atmosphere attains a subtle golden quality, giving warm tones to your pictures. If clouds are drifting overhead, watch for the likelihood of a spectacular desert sunset. At midday when the sun is shining straight down, objects appear flat, washed out and uninteresting.

Do it at night

Since Las Vegas is indeed Glitter City, some of the best pictures will be of the nighttime neon jungle. However, don't just take long shots of the Las Vegas Strip and downtown Fremont Street. Move in on these bright lights; detailed photos can be quite fascinating. For night photography, take a normal exposure as dictated by your light meter, and then go half a stop and a full stop in either direction. Some sophisticated cameras will do this automatically.

It's best to have a tripod for shooting night lights, However, you can capture a lot of Vegas glitter with a hand held camera if you have a fast lens (2.8 or 3.5) and fast film (200 speed). We never use anything faster than 200 ASA because the results are too grainy. With camera in hand, we've gotten good shots of the Fremont Street Experience by waiting for a bright moment during the show and then firing away.

AIMING YOUR CANON:
THE TEN BEST PICTURE SPOTS

You can get good results with our suggested picture spots with an adjustable camera (we're partial to Canons) or a simple point and shoot. If you have an adjustable camera, a 28mm to 80mm zoom lens will greatly enhance these photo opportunities.

1 THE BEST AERIAL SHOT OF THE STRIP: *From the Stratosphere Tower* • *2000 S. Las Vegas Blvd. (upper end of the Strip, near Main).*

The south side viewing terrace of the Stratosphere Tower provides a fine vista down Las Vegas Boulevard. Like most aerials, it looks rather flat and uninteresting during the daytime, so get up there just before sunset and start shooting as the sky dims and the glitter of Glitter City begins to bloom. Take a variety of shots, capturing the changing light. When you get your roll of film back, some of the pictures should be spectacular, particularly if you were fortunate enough to catch a few clouds on the horizon. This is best as a vertical, using a medium length lens.

2 THE BEST LOW LEVEL SHOT OF THE STRIP: *Mirage Garage rooftop* • *Aisle 8-B or 7-D, at the southeast corner.*

Two levels of the Mirage parking garage are exposed to the sky and they provide impressive views of Las Vegas Boulevard. By standing in the far southeast corner of either level 7 or 8, you can get nice close-ups of the Strip—either day or night. The 7-D corner offers better night shots since more lights are in view.

In shooting, you'll want to crop out the Mirage rooftops in the foreground, so this will be a shallow horizontal. Your pictorial panorama will include, reading from left to right, the beaded New England seaport style façade of Casino Royale, Harrah's with its bright new Mardi Gras marquee, the Imperial Palace, the bronze-windowed Flamingo Hilton Tower, the Mirage marquee, Caesars Palace, the faraway skyline of New York New York, the marquee of Monte Carlo, the revolving Planet Hollywood globe of Caesars and finally, a slice of the glass dome housing the Mirage rainforest, with the waterfalls, palm trees and beaded entrance of the Mirage in the foreground.

3 THE BEST CLOSEUP OF STRIP NEON: *Las Vegas Boulevard and Flamingo Road* • *From the southwest corner of the intersection.*

If you stand on the southwest corner of this intersection and point your Pentax across the boulevard to the northeast, you'll get a dazzling shot of the brilliant red and orange neon piping of the Barbary Coast Casino, with the huge pink and red neon torch of the Flamingo Hilton just behind. This fairly tight shot can be either a horizontal or vertical.

4 THE BEST OVERALL SHOT OF THE CITY: Las Vegas Mormon Temple at sunset ● *Upper Bonanza Road at Temple View Drive.*

Face it, folks. Other than the glitter of the Strip and downtown, Las Vegas is a rather flat and uninteresting city for overall photographs. Even the area's two best vista points, the Mormon Temple and Stratosphere Tower, produce rather uninteresting photos unless you capture some of that glitter. To accomplish this from the temple, which sits high in the flanks of Sunrise Mountain (see "The best nighttime view" above), plan on arriving around sunset. Find a spot with no foreground obstructions, set your camera on a tripod if you have one, and take a series of shots as the sky darkens and the lights of Glitter City begin to glimmer. We'd recommend shooting about every ten to fifteen minutes—what the heck, blow a whole roll! You'll be pleased with some of the results when your pictures come back from the lab.

5 THE BEST SHOT OF VEGAS VIC AND CANOPIED FREMONT STREET: Outside the Golden Nugget ● *First and Fremont streets downtown.*

The 60-foot Vegas Vic sign has been the enduring symbol of Las Vegas since 1951. Happily, he survived the installation of the Fremont Experience arch, which just clears his Stetson. He's been joined in recent years by a neon cowgirl, Vegas Vickie, perched above the Girls of Glitter Gulch sign just down Fremont. For a nice shot of this pair, with the Fremont Street Experience canopy arching overhead, stand in an alcove against the wall of the Golden Nugget, just to the left of the northwest exit, opposite the Fremont Street Experience souvenir shop. With a medium wide angle, you can get Vic in the foreground and Vickie beyond, with the barrel arch canopy above them.

This is a vertical, and it's best at night between Fremont Street Experience shows since the neon is turned off during these electronic performances. We like this angle so well that we shot it for the cover of our other guidebook, *Nevada Discovery Guide.*

6 THE BEST SHOT OF THE SPHINX: Just south of the obelisk ● *Luxor Hotel, 3900 S. Las Vegas Boulevard, south of Tropicana Avenue.*

The Luxor sphinx, wearing that silly melancholy expression, is probably the most photographed new object in Las Vegas. For a particularly effective angle, stand just south of the obelisk and shoot through the fountain with its "ruined" temple columns. You'll get the sphinx, a nice foreground of the toppling temple, lagoon and palm trees, and the great peak of the black glass pyramid behind. This is a horizontal, and you can choose to widen your view to include the new stepped, black box Luxor hotel towers to the far right. Try this shot early to mid-afternoon, when you get some nice shadow highlights on the face of the sphinx.

7 *THE BEST SHOT OF KING ARTHUR'S TOWERS: Through a New York Harbor fireboat* ● *Corner of Las Vegas Boulevard and Tropicana Avenue.*

Through a fireboat? Among the grand visual gimmicks at New York New York casino are two fireboats sitting in a miniature harbor and squirting water through their hoses. For an interesting photo of the brightly colored Arthurian towers of the Excalibur across the street, shoot through the arching water jets of the fireboat on the Las Vegas Boulevard side of the harbor. This is a vertical shot and it should be taken early in the morning before sun gets in your face, since you're looking southwest.

8 *THE BEST SHOT OF THE PRETEND NEW YORK SKYLINE: Near the Statue of Liberty* ● *Southwest corner of Tropicana Avenue and Las Vegas Boulevard.*

If you stand a little to the left of the Statue of Liberty in front of New York New York Casino, you'll get a great shot of the statue, and the skyline behind it, with the Chrysler Building and Empire State Building. With a wide angle lens, you can capture one of the New York Harbor fireboats in the middleground and a bright flower bed in the foreground.

The Manhattan Express track runs through the middle of this set-up, so wait for a rollercoaster to appear before you shoot. This is a wide-angle vertical. Shoot it from middle to late afternoon, when the Statue of Liberty is side-lit and shadows accent the skyline buildings.

9 *BEST CITY-MOUNT CHARLESTON PHOTO: Park 2000 Mall* ● *East of McCarran International Airport at Eastern Avenue near Sunset Road.*

Mount Charleston often is dusted with snow in the winter and spring, presenting a pleasing backdrop to the Las Vegas Strip. However, it's difficult to combine these two elements in a single photo because the terrain is flat and the high rises of Strip hotels and other structures block the mountain view. One of the few places where you can get a clear shot is across the landing field of McCarran International Airport, since this obviously contains no obstructions. This requires a good telephoto lens and a clear day, and you can add a bit of drama by getting a jet in the foreground as it touches down. Planes pass overhead every few minutes on their final approach.

From a landscaped berm along the Park 2000 mall on Eastern Avenue, you can clear the airport's fence with your lens and get a wide panorama of the lower Strip, with Mount Charleston and the Spring Mountain range beyond. You may be tempted to cross Eastern Avenue and press your lens against the wire mesh of the fence, although we don't recommend it. There's no pedestrian crossing here and no sidewalk on the airport side of the street. Passing traffic may dust off your fanny.

This is a horizontal shot, best attempted in the early morning, since you're facing due west.

10 THE BEST HOOVER DAM SHOT: East side parking lots ● *Arizona side of the dam, off U.S. Highway 93.*

The 726-foot-high dam is an awesome spectacle, particularly when you look down its dizzying slope from the sidewalk along the highway that crosses it. However, that great wedge of gray concrete doesn't make a very interesting photo. Our favorite angles are from the parking lots terraced in the canyon walls on the Arizona side. There, you can see the curving crest of the dam, the rugged canyon, the handsome new russet-colored visitor center and the dam's attractive art deco intake towers rising from turquoise-colored Lake Mead in the foreground.

Parking Lot 13 offers a good view of all of this if you have a wide angle lens, preferably a 28 millimeter. If you don't, try the higher lots which are farther away. The last lot with a view, before the road disappears over the canyon crest, is opposite a milepost one highway marker.

Whoever said money can't buy happiness didn't know where to shop.
— **Author unknown**

Chapter twelve

CREDIT CARD CORRUPTION

SHOPPING UNTIL YOU'RE DROPPING

Since the greater Las Vegas population now tops a million, it is no surprise that the area provides ample shopping opportunities. The influx of thirty million annual visitors inflates these opportunities considerably, and we aren't just referring to souvenir shops. Some of the larger casinos have shopping arcades with selections—and prices—that rival those Beverly Hills' Rodeo Drive.

What Las Vegas does not have is a central shopping district or downtown commercial center, since downtown is given over mostly to casinos. Most shopping facilities have gone in two directions—to the suburbs or under the protective canopies of major casino resorts.

THE TEN BEST SHOPPING MALLS AND CASINO SHOPPING ARCADES

Although Las Vegas and adjoining Henderson have many shopping malls, only a few are worthy of a special trip. Further, few of the resorts have significantly large shopping arcades. We have thus grouped them together in our Ten Best list. We begin with the best mall and best casino shopping arcade, and then follow with the rest of the best in alphabetical order.

1 THE BEST SHOPPING MALL: Fashion Show Mall •

South Las Vegas Boulevard and Spring Mountain Road; (702) 369-8382. Most stores open Monday-Wednesday 10 to 8, Thursday-Friday 10 to 9, Saturday 10 to 7 and Sunday noon to 6; various restaurant hours.

Except for the silly Steven Spielberg submarine-theme restaurant called Dive!, which pokes its snout through the outer wall, this is the town's most fashionable shopping mall. It's located right on the Strip, luring high rollers with Saks Fifth Avenue, Abercrombie and Fitch, Neiman Marcus and Williams-Sonoma, plus more than fifty specialty shops and boutiques. We generally make a beeline for the Ethel M chocolate outlet. The mall has four restaurants—Dive!, the highly regarded Chins Chinese restaurant, Mortons of Chicago and a trendy Italian café called Sfuzzi. The mall also has a large food court.

1 THE BEST CASINO SHOPPING ARCADE: The Forum

Shops at Caesars • 3500 S. Las Vegas Blvd. (at Flamingo Road); (702) 893-4800. Most shops open Sunday-Thursday 10 to 11 and Friday-Saturday 10 to midnight.

Nearly a hundred stores line a curving courtyard of marble floors and columns in the Forum Shops at Caesars, with a pretend sky overhead that keeps pace with the real sky outside. Two Roman fountains—one serious and one comedic—anchor each end. This is the world's largest casino shopping complex, offering everything from kids shops and candy shops to restaurants and boutiques. The selection includes such upscale outlets as Christian Dior and Gucci, plus Wolfgang Puck's trendy café, Spago. If you can't find what you seek in the Forum Shops, try the Appian Way, an even more upscale shopping corridor elsewhere in Caesars.

The next best shopping malls

3 BELZ FACTORY OUTLET WORLD • 7400 S. Las Vegas

Blvd. (Warm Springs Road, south of the Strip); (702) 896-5599. Monday-Saturday 10 a.m. to 9 p.m. and Sunday 10 to 6.

Naturally, a town overflowing with superlatives has to have the country's largest covered factory outlet mall. This place is *huge,* stretching for more than a third of a mile along the far southern end of the Las Vegas Strip. Belz recently added several new shops to bring its total count to 140, so grab your credit card and pull on your hiking shoes. Fortunately, you can seek respite between shopping bouts at two large food courts and several snack stands in this massive mall. The facility hosts a variety of fairs, shows and special promotions during the year.

4 **BOULEVARD MALL** • *3520 S. Maryland Parkway (between Desert Inn Road and Sierra Vista); (702) 732-8949. Most shops open weekdays 10 to 9, Saturdays 10 to 8 and Sun day 11 to 6.*

Nevada's largest shopping mall, this 140-store complex is anchored by four major department stores—Macy's, Sears, Dillards and JCPenney. It's a very attractive facility, with indoor palms and a towering barrel-arched roof with glass insets. If hiking from shop to shop within this massive single-level complex works up a thirst or an appetite, you can take a break at the Panorama Food Court's cafés and food stalls. This extensive shopping venue even has a foreign currency exchange for overseas visitors.

5 **GALLERIA AT SUNSET** • *1300 W. Sunset Rd. (opposite Sunset Station Casino), Henderson; (702) 434-0202. Most stores open Monday-Saturday 10 to 9 and Sunday 11 to 6.*

Southern Nevada's newest shopping mall, in next-door Henderson, also is one of its most attractive. This large two-level complex is bright and airy, topped by a massive greenhouse roof. Its anchors are Robinsons-May, JCPenney, Mervyn's California and Dillards. More than 120 smaller boutiques and stores are tucked between them. Shoppers can take a break at a large second-floor food court, which is decorated with giant topiaries. Some of the seating offers a view of the surrounding valley and mountains. Although the Galleria at Sunset is out of town, it's easy to reach. Simply head southeast on I-515, take the Sunset Road exit in Henderson and go west less than a mile. It's opposite the new Sunset Station Casino-Hotel.

6 **MEADOWS MALL** • *4300 Meadows Lane (at Valley View, just south of Freeway 95 interchange); (702) 878-4849. Most shops open weekdays 10 to 9 and weekends 10 to 6.*

Nevada's second largest covered mall, the Meadows is just south of I-95 in North Las Vegas. It has 140 shops, with Macy's, Dillard's, JCPenney and Sears as the anchors. Shoppers can take a break at a large food court, or park themselves and their packages at balcony seating along the mezzanine. They can park their kids at a carousel that swirls on the main floor. To reach the Meadows Mall, head north on the U.S. 95 freeway, take the Valley View exit, drive less than a mile south and turn right into the mall.

The next best casino shopping arcades

7 **MGM GRAND** • *3799 S. Las Vegas Blvd. (at Tropicana); (702) 891-7777.*

As befitting the world's largest resort, the Grand has two shopping areas. Several rather upscale shops share the newly designed Studio Walk with its restaurant row. Among them are the Art of Entertainment Gallery featuring art work either by or about Hollywood personalities, Collezioni and Marshall Rousso clothing shops, an athletic logo shop, jewelry store and a new upscale department store. Downstairs, beyond the hotel lobby, are several Star Lane Shops. These are primarily curio and gift shops, including a "pearl factory," luggage store, ice cream parlor and one of those computer-video photo shops where your ordinary face can be placed upon an extraordinary body.

8 **MONTE CARLO** • *3770 Las Vegas Blvd. (north of Tropicana); (702) 730-7777.*

Although small, this is one of the most attractive of the town's casino shopping malls, fashioned like a back street in old Monaco. Squared cobble paving, old stone storefronts and a high, black ceiling create an effective illusion for this arcade, called the Street of Dreams. It has a jewelry store, Bon Vivant apparel shop, a couple of boutiques and a Monte Carlo logo booth. Several old European style storefront façades suggest that more shops may be added later. The Street of Dreams also is home to the Monte Carlo Pub & Brewery, which doesn't look at all like old Monaco.

9 **RIO SUITE HOTEL & CASINO** • *3700 W. Flamingo Rd. (at Valley View Boulevard, opposite the Gold Coast); (702) 252-7777.*

The Rio has twenty shops and boutiques and many are conveniently arrayed along a balcony above the new Masquerade Village Casino. Browsers can explore the shops and lean over the balcony railing to watch the action below. They also can watch the action above, when floats of the "Masquerade Show in the Sky" parade past, suspended from ceiling tracks. Hours of the show are posted in the casino below. The store collection includes men's and women's shops, tropical wear and sporting garb, a *faux* jewelry shop, a smoke shop, shoe shop, and a voodoo magic and souvenir store (listed below, under "The Best specialty stores"). An ice cream parlor, restaurant, bar and margarita takeout also occupy the balcony.

10 **STRATOSPHERE SHOPPING ARCADE** • *2000 S. Las Vegas Blvd. (Main); (702) 380-7777.*

This isn't a collection elegant boutiques or designer shops. The walkway leading to the Stratosphere's tower elevator is lined with more than a score of curio shops, including some of the most specialized you'll find anywhere on the planet. This is where you go for a kiosk that sells only key tags of various states, personalized with your name; another selling ethnic T-shirts and caps from Puerto Rican to Croatian; a kiosk marketing personalized heraldic certificates that trace your family name; yet another mart that sells only silly ties; and finally, a create-your-own-hat shop.

THE TEN BEST SPECIALTY STORES

What's your choice? A store with thousands of cowboy boots? A curio shop that sells only magnets or a kiosk that sells only personalized state key tags? Glitter City has an amazing number of specialty shops. Here are the ten that we felt were the most interesting. These stores and shops, found both within and outside of casino complexes, are listed in no particular order.

1 THE BEST PLACE TO BUY LAS VEGAS SOUVENIRS: Bonanza Gift and Souvenir Shop • 2460 S. Las Vegas Boulevard (Sahara Boulevard); (702) 384-0005 and (702) 385-7359.

Claiming to be the world's largest, this is more of a souvenir shopping center than a souvenir shop. Several curio shops and a convenience store and liquor mart occupy this large facility. The liquor prices here are among the better on the Strip. A close runner-up to the best place to buy Las Vegas souvenirs is good old Woolworth's, downtown at the corner of Las Vegas Boulevard and Fremont. The selection isn't quite as extensive, although some of the prices are better.

2 THE BEST PLACE FOR ENTERTAINMENT MEMORABILIA: Rock 'N' Roll Hollywood Sports Legends Gallery • Fashion Show Mall, Las Vegas Boulevard (Spring Mountain); 731-1292.

This store offers just what its elongated name says—a mix of sports, rock star and Hollywood collectibles. Here, you buy a simulated platinum record autographed by the star, signed posters and pictures of sports, music and movie celebrities and movie props. The collection includes such goodies as the room key to a motel where Elvis Presley stayed in Cedar Rapids, Iowa; and an autographed photo of Whitney Houston accepting a Grammy.

3 THE BEST MONEY STORE: The Money Company • The Stratosphere tower shopping arcade, 2000 S. Las Vegas Blvd.; (702) 385-4736.

No, this isn't a bank or a loan office. It's a specialty shop that sells only items with money themes. You can buy a "money belt," which is a plastic belt of pretend hundred dollar bills; plus money candy, money pillows stuffed with genuine shredded U.S. currency, all kinds of money logo wearing apparel and hundred dollar bill imprinted toilet paper. The most appealing thing about this place is its main decorator piece—larger than life mannequins of bad guys and cops in a tug-of-war over a safe filled with pretend gold bars. In the back of the store, a giant Uncle Sam clutches fists full of currency. (It must be tax time.)

4 **THE BEST COWBOY STORE: Cowtown Boots & Western Wear** • *2989 W. Paradise Rd. (Riviera Boulevard, across from the Las Vegas Hilton); (702) 737-8469. Monday-Saturday 9 to 6, Sunday 10 to 5.*

Since Las Vegas is—among many other things—a kind of rhinestone cowboy town, it's not surprising that one of the country's largest Western clothing stores would be located here. In this big barn of a place, cowboys and wanna-be cowboys can find thousands of boots ranging in prices from less than a hundred dollars to several hundred, lots of Stetsons and Resistols, embroidered and beaded cowboy shirts and stacks of pairs of Wranglers. That's right, Wranglers. They, not Levi's, are the official pants of rodeo cowboys and many pretend cowboys.

5 **THE BEST GAMBLERS' STORE: Gamblers General Store** • *800 S. Main St. (at Gass), (800) 322-CHIP or (702) 382-9903. Daily 9 to 5.*

If you're serious about learning the gambling game or you want a *real* gambling souvenir, stop in at the world's largest store devoted to the trade. It has an extensive selection of books on gambling plus every gaming device imaginable. Want a handful of used casino dice, a craps stick, complete *pai gow* set, roulette wheel or baccarat layout? It's all here, plus a selection of used slot machines, priced from $1,000.

6 **THE BEST PLACE TO CLOWN AROUND: Ron Lee's World of Clowns** • *330 Carousel Parkway; (702) 434-3920. Daily 8 to 5.*

Actually, it's the exhibits that do the clowning. This combined store and museum has a good selection of clown, puppet and animated character collectibles. You can take self-guided tours and learn how clown puppets and other animated characters are made, or catch a ride on a large indoor carousel. Clowns through the ages are displayed in a small museum. You can finish your visit with lunch at a cute café decorated with puppet and clown figurines and international flags.

7 *THE BEST PLACE TO SHOP FOR YOUR REALLY STRANGE FRIENDS: Spencer Gifts • Galleria at Sunset Mall, Sunset Road west of I-515 interchange in Henderson, (702) 436-5514; and Meadows Mall, Valley View south of I-95 interchange, 870-8770.*

This specialty shop walks a fine line between novelty and raunchy gifts. Its curious offerings include Elvis clocks, Liz Taylor pop-up cards, highly suggestive gift cards and T-shirts, lava lamps, cat and pig telephones, *The Three Stooges Book of Party Games* and an interesting assortment of kinetic toys.

8 *THE BEST HEX SHOP: Nawlins Vu-Du Shop • Rio Suite Hotel, 3700 W. Flamingo Rd.; (702) 252-7777.*

Mad at your mate or sore at your supervisor? You can buy a authentic voodoo doll or other hexing device at this Creole/Cajun shop on the balcony above the Rio's Masquerade Village. Other offerings include beaded voodoo bottles, tarot cards, dried alligator heads (good grief!), voodoo potions, "throw beads" from Mardi Gras parades and Mardi Gras masks and figurines.

9 *THE BEST PLACE TO FRY YOUR TONGUE: Calido Chile Traders • In the Boulevard Mall, Maryland Parkway at Desert Inn Road; (702) 894-9691.*

If you want to add a bit of spice to your life, step into this little shop devoted to chili peppers and other peppy products. You can purchase an assortment of hot and lively sauces, canned peppers, garlic and jalapeno catsups, tabasco sauces and sizzling dips. Serious chili pepper devotées can dress up their lives with chili pepper neckties, shirts, belts, undershorts, fanny packs and T-shirts.

10 *THE BEST PLACE TO BUY ADULT CHOCOLATES: Ethel M Chocolate Factory • Two Cactus Garden Drive (off Sunset Way), Henderson; (702) 433-2500. Free tours daily 8:30 to 7.*

We aren't talking about chocolates in naughty shapes. These "adult" goodies are delicious liquor-filled chocolates, which are made here and sold in a large gift shop adjacent to the factory. Nevada is one of the few states where liquor-laced chocolates can be produced and marketed. Ethel M also produces conventional chocolates, plus such candies as Mars Bars, M&Ms and Three Muscateers. Only chocolates are produced at this facility. Visitors can watch them being made through large view windows or on video monitors, and then receive a free chocolate at the end of the tour. The best time to see chocolates in production is on weekday mornings.

Chapter thirteen
THERE ISN'T ONE

Out of consideration for supersticious gamblers, we have eliminated Chapter thirteen from this book.

True enjoyment comes from activity of the mind and exercise of the body: the two are ever united.
— **Humboldt**

Chapter fourteen

GETTING PHYSICAL
WORKING OFF THOSE BUFFETS

One gets the impression after exploring Las Vegas that the word "park" is used only as a verb—the act of leaving your car somewhere while you gamble, party or dine. The Strip and downtown area suffer a paucity of public parks, which normally are popular places for walking, running and biking. Bike lanes on streets are rare, and there are no serious walking-running-biking paths in the metropolitan area.

However, there are many opportunities for getting physical, and we aren't referring to hotel room call girls. Outlying areas have some fine public parks and the Las Vegas Valley is surrounded by a grand wilderness of desert and mountain. Valley of Fire State Park and Red Rock Canyon National Conservation Area offer wonderful hiking and biking opportunities. Mount Charleston has several trails for serious hikers and backpackers.

Back in town, serious walkers who want to crank off a few miles will find plenty of level sidewalks, in case they need to shed their newly acquired buffet paunches. The Strip is popular with walkers and striders, although traffic signals will interrupt your pace. We advise against biking along the Strip or anywhere downtown. With heavy traffic and no bike lanes, it's downright foolhardy. Several bike fatalities and injuries occur each year.

Although suburban areas have a few good walking and biking areas, most of the best are out of town. We hope you cyclists brought your bike racks.

THE TEN BEST WALKS AND HIKES

This category is divided into flatlander walking and uphill hiking, with our number one choices in each division, followed by the rest in no particular order.

1 THE BEST WALK: The Strip ● *South Las Vegas Boulevard; various lengths; easy (unless it's a hot August afternoon).*

Dave Bonnot of Sonora, California, a good friend and the designer of this book's cover, visited Las Vegas shortly after the Stratosphere opened. Emerging from the Mirage, he and his wife Dianne glanced up Las Vegas Boulevard and saw the new tower. "Hey, let's walk up there and check it out!" The tower seemed to retreat—like another mirage—as they advanced and they were foot-weary by the time they arrived.

Because of the high visibility of many of the Strip hotels, distances along Las Vegas Boulevard seem compressed. However, it's still a fun place for walking; you'll see a constant parade of visitors moving between the resorts. Where else on the globe can you take a stroll past a pyramid, a Technicolor medieval castle, a pretend New York skyline, an Italian-Swiss lake, Roman statuary, a volcano and a pirate ship? When your feet start complaining, you can find places to park and watch the rest of the crowd walk past. (See "The Ten Best places to people watch" in the next chapter.) We prefer to do our walking at night when the Strip is ablaze with neon—and the sun is no longer blazing.

Incidentally, that short stroll between the Mirage and the Stratosphere is more than two miles, as footsore Dave and Dianne learned. If you hike from the Stratosphere to the Luxor—southernmost of the major casino resorts—you'll cover about four miles.

1 THE BEST HIKE: White Domes area, Valley of Fire State Park ● *Moderate; various lengths.*

Our favorite southern Nevada hike used to be from the Valley of Fire's Rainbow Vista trailhead to the White Domes area. Then park officials spoiled it by running a paved road out there. Sulking, we drove to the end of the road recently, parked and began exploring what used to be the end of our hike. We spent the better part of that day investigating the myriad of multicolored rock formations, probing areas we hadn't seen before, and decided this wasn't so bad after all.

For your first leg, after checking out those curious sandstone domes, follow a short trail past them. It goes briefly uphill and then down into a rocky canyon. There, you'll soon encounter what appears to be an abandoned prospector's cabin. It's actually the remnant of a set for a Western movie shot here several years ago.

This is a good place to begin a random exploration of the area. Off-trail hiking is permitted in the Valley of Fire and the best routes are the dry washes rimmed by fantastically eroded formations. Several extend out from this canyon, so pick one and begin enjoying the landscape. Get down on your knees and study the marbling of cross-bedded deposits left by ancient sandstorms. Note the subtle burgundies, pinks, magentas and rosés swirled together in a petrified confection.

Dry washes also are useful for finding your way back. Make note of landmarks as you hike, since it's easy to become confused and lost in this area. That old fake cabin is a handy beacon. It's a good idea to take a compass with you. If you do become disoriented, you can pick a proper direction and—with the help of a park map—find your way to a road. And don't forget plenty of water; this is desert country.

The next best walks

3 BELZ FACTORY OUTLET WORLD • 7400 S. Las Vegas Boulevard at Warm Springs Road. Any length; easy walking, and it's air conditioned!

What? A power walk through a shopping mall? The notion may seem silly at first, although it makes perfect sense, particularly on a summer day. The world's largest enclosed factory outlet mall, Belz is a third of a mile long. The main corridor is straight, uncrowded and air conditioned, and the entire mall is smoke-free. You can move right along without running into too many shoppers. (Have you ever tried to hurry through a casino, with its crowds and rows of slot machines?)

By striding from one end to the other and back, and diverting into the side corridors, you'll cover about a mile. Belz offers advantages in addition to air conditioning—you can window shop as you walk, and you can refuel at one of several food courts and refreshment stands.

4 UNIVERSITY OF NEVADA AT LAS VEGAS • Various campus paths and roadways; all level. Campus maps available at the visitor center off Maryland Parkway and Harmon Avenue, the Student Union just to the south, and Barrick Museum of Natural History near the eastern end of Harmon Avenue. Metered visitor parking near all of these areas, twenty-five cents for thirty minutes.

An extensive webwork of roads and paths winds throughout the large, attractively landscaped campus of UNLV. It's a particularly inviting place for serious walkers. Further, you can pause to visit its many attractions, such as the Marjorie Barrick Museum of Natural History, Great Hall of Engineering with a replica of a Howard Hughes racing plane suspended from the ceiling, and several galleries in the Alta Ham Fine Arts Building. The entire campus has been designated as an arboretum and you'll see a wide variety of shrubs, flowers and trees—some native and some imported. The most attractive landscaping is adjacent to the Barrick Museum.

You can pause for refreshment at the Student Union, which is open weekdays 7 a.m. to 6 p.m. The Union Café here is open 7:30 to 2:30; an adjacent TCBY yogurt and light snacks is open Monday-Thursday 7:30 to 8 p.m. and Friday 7 to 4.

UNLV is an easy reach from downtown Las Vegas or the Strip. If you head east from Las Vegas Boulevard on Harmon Avenue, you'll enter the western side of the campus, near the Barrick Museum. For another approach, follow Maryland Parkway south from downtown, cross Flamingo and the campus appears shortly on your right. At a stop light at Maryland and Harmon, turn right into a parking area. The campus visitor center is in Maude Frazier Hall just beyond the parking area; look for the large red "UNLV" letters on the side of this low structure. The Student Union, with its café and takeouts, is two buildings south. Visitor parking is limited to thirty minutes at the Maryland and Harmon lot. It's not restricted at the Student Union lot, as long as you keep feeding quarters into the meters.

5 *LORENZI PARK* • *Washington Avenue between Valley View Boulevard and Rancho Drive. Lorenzi Park Lake path; half a mile; easy.*

Lorenzi is the largest park in Las Vegas proper, spread over several acres north of the U.S. 95 freeway. Its facilities include a fake lake, art museum and historical museum, plus the usual picnic areas, lawns and kiddie playgrounds. A gravel path rimming Lorenzi Park Lake offers the opportunity for an easy, leisurely stroll. As you walk around the pond, you can peel off to investigate the formal "Garden of Four Seasons," consisting mostly of rose bushes and a few trees. At the lake's upper end, you'll encounter the Nevada State Museum, well worth a pause. (See Chapter nine, page 154.) For longer walks, stride about the grassy lawns of this large park.

To get to your starting point, take Freeway 95 north from downtown, exit at Rancho Drive, follow it northwest about half a mile and turn left onto Washington Avenue. The park appears shortly on your left. Drive along the park's upper edge and turn in at the sign indicating the Senior Center (opposite Baker Street). You'll find the lake behind a cluster of park buildings.

6 *SUNSET PARK* • *Sunset Road and Eastern Avenue. Sunset Lake walking/jogging path; one mile loop; easy.*

This large Clark County park offers the most serious walking and jogging trail in southern Nevada. It's a especially prepared red clay path that covers a precise measured mile, rimming a pleasant artificial lake. It also has a "World Course," similar to a par course, with exercise stations along the route.

This is one of the largest landscaped parks in the county, covering 309 acres, with a swimming pool, tennis and volleyball courts, playgrounds, game fields and that fake lake. The circumference of the lake is less than a mile, so the walking/jogging path has a large kink in it to create the required distance. There's also a shorter concrete path that follows the lip of the lake. To get to Sunset Park, head far south on Las Vegas Boulevard, turn left (east) onto Sunset Road just below the airport and follow it a mile to Eastern Avenue. The park is at the southeast corner, with access either from Eastern or Sunset.

The next best hikes

7 MOUNT CHARLESTON SUMMIT • North Loop Trail; twenty-mile round trip; very strenuous.

Get a very early start for this tough hike, or plan on two days for the trip unless you're in excellent shape. It's not a technical climb, just an extremely steep grunt up the rocky ramparts of southern Nevada's tallest peak. There are some steep dropoffs along part of the trail so those with vertigo problems shouldn't try it.

To get to the Mount Charleston hiking area, drive north on U.S. 95 and then take State Route 157 west up the mountain, into Kyle Canyon. Check at the ranger station below Mount Charleston village for a map, and get a weather and trail condition report, since you wouldn't want to be caught in a mountain storm.

This is an early summer through fall hike; Charleston is usually snowcapped from winter into late spring. The hike begins on Little Falls Trail near the end of State Highway 157 above Mount Charleston Lodge. The first few hundred yards is deceptively gentle, then you switch to the Cathedral Rock Trail—nearly a mile of a moderate upgrade, with some rather scary exposure. From there, it's a tough nine-mile uphill trudge to the summit on the North Loop Trail. From the top of Charleston, you can see—well—almost forever. You'll take in the entire sweep of southern Nevada and pieces of California and Arizona. Sit down, catch your breath and enjoy the view. You've earned it!

8 BRISTLECONE PINES TRAIL: Mount Charleston • Six miles round trip; moderate.

So all right, you aren't ready to tackle the Charleston summit, particularly after last night's buffet followed by four strawberry daiquiris at the "Folies Bergere" show. The Bristlecone Pines Trail is considerably less strenuous and it offers some fine alpine scenery. This is one of the most popular trails in the area and it's open to mountain bikes, so you might want to plan a weekday hike, when it's less crowded.

To get here, head north on U.S. 95 and take State Route 156 west up the mountain toward the Lee Canyon Ski Area. If you want to pick up a hiking map, drive up State Route 157 (which comes first) and follow it to a ranger station in Kyle Canyon, just below Mount Charleston Village. Then take the Highway 158 crossroad over to Route 156 and continue up to Lee Canyon.

The Bristlecone Trail is a semi-loop with two trailheads—a lower one near McWilliams Campground on Route 156 below the ski area, and an upper one at the far end of the ski area's highest parking lot. We'd recommend starting at the lower trailhead, since you'll be walking downhill at the end of your hike. If you begin at the upper trail, you must finish our hike by trudging a mile up hot highway asphalt to get back to your car. To find the lower trailhead, look on your right for an unmarked dirt road just below McWilliams Campground; it leads to a trailhead parking area.

The first three miles of the hike take you up an abandoned forestry road that isn't very interesting, although views of the rugged ramparts of Mount Charleston are nice. At the junction with the Bonanza Trail, the Bristlecone Trail leaves the old road and becomes a proper hiking path, winding through scenically rugged high country. The vegetation thins out as you enter the rocky realm of the bristlecone pine.

What's a bristlecone?

These hardy trees, especially adapted to high, windy and rocky regions, are the oldest living things on earth. Some—although not those on Mount Charleston—have survived nearly five thousand years, much longer than California's famed redwoods. Bristlecones can be identified by their short, closely compacted needles, which hang in clusters like green bottle brushes or raccoon tails. Since the Mount Charleston area isn't particularly harsh, many of the bristlecones are large and upright, like conventional evergreens. Look in dry, rocky niches along the trail and you'll find the more classic variety—stunted and gnarled, huddled near the ground, with weather-bleached bark and just a few fronds to give them life.

The trail snakes through this rocky area and then winds down into an attractive forest of white fir, ponderosa pines and quaking aspen. It emerges onto a ridge above the upper Lee Canyon Ski Area parking lot and ends near an emergency helicopter landing pad. Walk down the parking lot and follow the winding road about a mile back down to McWilliams Campground to complete your circuit. An ideal time to take this hike is during an autumn afternoon, when the aspens are splashed with yellow and the late sun's rays play a light and shadow show on the steep, terraced crests of Mount Charleston.

9 ICE BOX CANYON: Red Rock Canyon National Conservation Area • *Two to three miles round trip; moderate to moderately strenuous.*

Ice Box Canyon is one of several marked hiking trails radiating out from Red Rock Canyon's scenic drive. You can pick up a hiking map indicating the various trails at the visitor center. The Ice Box trail starts at the road's edge and follows the convoluted rim of the canyon for about a mile. It then drops down into the chasm floor, where the marked trail ends. Walls blackened by desert varnish rise above you, offering both visual splendor and shade. Rock cairns help guide your progress through this wonderland of geological shapes.

You can set your own pace and distance here, traveling farther up the canyon by following its dry bed, although the hike becomes more challenging. You'll have to clamber up some rocky slopes where seasonal streams cut narrow gorges as they cascaded down steep cataracts. An advantage of this hike is that you can't get lost, since you're always following the stream bed. However, make sure you note the point where the trail leaves the rim and enters the chasm, so you won't accidentally bypass it on the return leg.

10 BOULDER CITY HIKING TRAILS • *Various lengths and difficulties. Get a trail map at the River Mountain trailhead or from the Boulder City Parks and Recreation Department, 900 Arizona St., (702) 293-9256.*

Boulder City's location on a bluff above the rugged Black Mountains and Lake Mead provides an ideal setting for hiking trails. The city has joined with the National Park Service and UNLV to create an interesting and challenging trail network.

The main complex is called the River Mountain Trail system. It begins at a trailhead parking area to the left as you travel downhill toward the lake from Boulder City on the Highway 93 bypass. Watch for the trailhead sign less than a mile after you turn left off the Nevada Highway onto Buchanan Boulevard to take the bypass. If you pass St. Jude's Ranch for Children, you've gone too far.

From the trailhead, the River Mountain Trail leads about two miles uphill, connecting to three other trails called Black Mountain (half a mile), Red Mountain (one-third mile) and Bootleg Wash (just over half a mile). The Black and Red mountain trails are tough uphill trudges to rocky peaks that provide fine views of Lake Mead and the surrounding rough-hewn terrain. Elevation gain on the trail system is 1,185 feet, so pick a cool day and carry plenty of water. Part of this trail system was built in the 1930s by the Civilian Conservation Corps.

Another trail heads downhill from the trailhead, passing through housing developments and cleverly utilizing concrete drainage channels for the first two miles. Linking trails travel all the way to the Lake Mead shoreline, about nine miles below. If you want to try a portion of this trail, we'd recommend hiking uphill first so you can cruise the downslope at the finish. For an interesting six-mile round trip, drive down to a parking area off Lakeshore Drive above Lake Mead and hike up to the River Mountain trail parking area and back.

To get there, head downhill on Highway 93 and take the Lakeshore Drive turnoff to the left, at a sign indicating the Alan Bible Visitor Center of Lake Mead National Recreation Area. Drive a short distance past the visitor center parking area to a second parking lot. (Both are on your right.) Park and walk slightly uphill to a concrete strip called the Railroad Trail. Go right, follow it through a tunnel under Lakeshore Drive and begin climbing uphill toward Boulder City. The trail turns to gravel and then to concrete again as it enters Boulder City's open storm drainage system.

THE TEN BEST BIKE ROUTES

As we indicated in the beginning, biking is not recommended in downtown Las Vegas or along the Strip because of heavy traffic. We have found several biking areas in the suburbs, although many of our favorites are out of town. Incidentally, all Citizens Area Transit (CAT) buses are equipped with bike racks, so you can shuttle to your starting point. Call (702) 228-7433, or pick up a bus schedule at the Downtown Transportation Center, 300 N. Casino Drive at Stewart Street.

The Red Rock Canyon area offers some of the best bike riding, so we begin there:

1 RED ROCK CANYON NATIONAL CONSERVATION

AREA • *Scenic Loop drive; 14.7 miles including a short highway portion. Pick up a route map at the visitor center, open daily 9 to 4. Moderate to strenuous; some hills, with an elevation gain of a thousand feet.*

Red Rock Canyon National Conservation Area preserves a rocky wonderland created by weathering of the Keystone Fault in the foothills of the Spring Mountains. More than a thousand feet higher than Las Vegas and less than an hour's drive away, it's a favorite retreat of locals, including bike riders. The main drive is a one-way loop, starting at the visitor center and traveling along the base of these fantastic rock formations. Although there is no separate bicycle lane, the road is wide and traffic is slow, since there is a 35-mile-an-hour speed limit.

The first five miles of this route is a tough, gently winding climb with a 1,000-foot elevation gain. Once at the crest, which is at 4,771 feet, put your bike in high gear and glide effortlessly downhill to the end of the scenic route at Highway 159. Here, you can turn left and pedal back to the visitor center to complete a 14.7-mile loop, or turn right for a ride to Blue Diamond, described in our bicycle route number three below.

2 RED ROCK CANYON APPROACH • *Along upper Charleston Boulevard. Just under eleven miles from Rainbow Boulevard to the Red Rock Canyon visitor center; moderate with a gradual uphill climb.*

Most people drive to the Red Rock Canyon area to begin their biking, but why not pedal to it? Charleston Boulevard, which leads directly from Las Vegas into the canyon area, is straight and wide, and most of the stretch between Rainbow Boulevard and the visitor center is marked with bike lanes. We recommend starting at Rainbow since it's nearly clear of the suburbs and traffic begins to thin as you continue westward. Starting at this intersection, you'll pick up shoulder bike lanes on Charleston Boulevard after about half a mile.

This isn't a particularly inspiring route through suburbs and then open desert, although it's a good workout with its gradual uphill climb. The ruby red ramparts of Red Rock Canyon will dance invitingly before your eyes as you pedal. When you reach the sign indicating the visitor center and scenic drive, turn right. The center appears shortly and you can take a break before continuing your day's outing.

3 RED ROCK CANYON TO BLUE DIAMOND • *State Highway 159. Twelve-mile round trip from the end of the Scenic Drive (above) or sixteen-mile round trip from the Red Rock Canyon visitor center. Moderate to moderately strenuous; some low hills.*

This route is an extension of the Red Rock Canyon loop, continuing south on State Route 159 to the prim little town of Blue Diamond. It's best traveled on a weekday since weekend traffic can get thick. The highway is fairly wide with broad shoulders, although they aren't designated as a bike lanes here. With only a few rolling hills, this is not a tough ride.

You'll see dramatic red rock slices of the Keystone Fault at the base of the Spring Mountains as you ride. You might want to pause at Spring Mountain Ranch State Park and Bonnie Springs/Old Nevada along the route. Both are described in Chapter seventeen. Your turnaround point is Blue Diamond, a former company town and now a cute little residential enclave in the desert. Pedal up to the Village Market for a snack and cool drink before beginning the return leg.

4 MOUNT CHARLESTON "ESCAPE" • *State Route 156, from Lee Canyon Ski Area to U.S. 95. About 17 miles; all downhill.*

The two approach routes to Mount Charleston, highways 156 and 157, are fairly straight and the views of desert and mountain are quite impressive. However, unless you're an iron man or woman, you won't want to pedal *up* these highways; you would suffer an elevation gain of a mile or more. However, if you can arrange a shuttle, a trip down either route becomes glorious free flight—which is why we call this an escape. There is no bike lane and the roads aren't very wide, although they're relatively straight. We suggest doing this ride on a weekday when traffic is light. The roads can get very busy on summer weekends.

Important: Make sure your bike brakes are in good order; this is a long downhill roll!

Start at the parking area for Lee Canyon Ski Area at the end of State Route 156 and head downhill. After a few spirals, the road straightens out, so you won't have to fret about blind curves. As you glide along, look to your right (carefully, of course) and you'll see imposing rocky ramparts of Mummy Mountain and Mount Charleston. After you pass the intersection of routes 156 and 158 (a crossroad that links to Highway 157 and Kyle Canyon), the surrounding pine forest begins to thin out, fading to a piñon juniper zone. As you sail farther toward the beige desert below, Joshua trees appear among the junipers, then they surrender to greasewood desert. In about seventeen miles, you have traveled through four of the earth's life climate zones!

5 BOULDER HIGHWAY • *From Boulder Station (near the I-515 Boulder Highway interchange) in Las Vegas to the Clark County Heritage Museum in Henderson. About fourteen miles one way; easy to moderate.*

Although Boulder Highway is busy with vehicles and the scenery isn't exactly awesome, this is a good bike riding stretch if you just want to crank off a few miles. The long, gentle incline toward Henderson will give you a good workout. Most of the highway is divided and it has wide shoulder lanes to keep peddlers out of traffic and visa versa. (However, they aren't marked as bike lanes.) You'll have to veer around a few parked cars along the way, although most of the shoulder lanes are open.

To haul your bikes to the starting point, drive east from downtown on Fremont Street; it becomes Boulder Highway. Begin your pedal power near the Boulder Station Casino, or you can backtrack to the Showboat at Charleston and add another mile to your ride. However, you'll encounter more parked cars in the shoulder lane along this stretch. Pedal southeast through the eastern edge of Las Vegas, past Sam's Town, the Silver Bowl Sports Complex and into the desert countryside. As you enter Henderson, the highway becomes a handsomely landscaped boulevard.

You can use the Clark County Heritage Museum as your turnaround point, or continue another half mile before Boulder Highway blends into the freeway, where bikes are forbidden. (Stay to the left at the Wagon Wheel Drive/Car Country Road sign; the bike lane ends just beyond here, at Roberts Road). On your return, you can enjoy the distant and often hazy Las Vegas skyline, with Mount Charleston and the Spring Mountain Range beyond.

6 UPPER BONANZA ROAD • *Between Nellis Boulevard and the Mormon Temple. About five miles round trip; easy to moderately strenuous.*

Bonanza is a street of many personalities, running through some of the town's poorest neighborhoods in northwest Las Vegas and some of its most expensive view mansions in the northeast. It is to the latter area that this route extends, in a gentle and persistent climb toward rugged Sunrise Mountain and the glistening white spires of the Las Vegas Mormon Temple. This area tops our list as the best nighttime view of Las Vegas (Chapter eleven, page 171).

Start your ride at Bonanza and Nellis; there's plenty of parking in nearby strip malls. Bonanza has no marked bike lanes, although the curb lane is quite wide and parked cars are few. The scenery and quality of homes improve dramatically as you pedal resolutely toward Sunrise Mountain and those temple spires. You may want to pause and explore the beautifully landscaped temple grounds. Then continue to the end of Bonanza and turn right onto Los Feliz, which takes you past pricey view homes. The entirety of Las Vegas spreads below. It's an awesome view at night—but do your riding in the daylight, please.

After a few blocks, turn right again onto Stewart, start downhill with that view before you, then go right at a stop sign onto Hollywood Boulevard which takes you—not to Hollywood—but back to Bonanza Road.

7 WEST CHEYENNE AVENUE • *City View Park in North Las Vegas to Rancho Drive. Nine-mile round trip; easy to moderate.*

This mostly level stretch offers some fine views of downtown Las Vegas and the Strip, as well as vistas of the Spring Mountains on the west-bound leg. To begin, park your bike-toting car in the lot at City View Park in North Las Vegas. To reach the park from downtown or the Strip, head north on I-15 to the Cheyenne Avenue exit and drive west for just over half a mile. Look for the turn-in to the park on your left; it occupies a low knoll.

From the parking lot, pedal west on Cheyenne Avenue toward the Spring Mountains. You'll encounter a slight upgrade initially, and then the route becomes quite level. Although there are no designated bike lanes, the shoulder lane is very wide. The scenery here isn't awesome, although distant views of the mountains and Las Vegas are appealing. You'll be peddling mostly through an industrial area, although it's not an *ugly* industrial area. You'll pass a big FedEx facility, warehousing complexes and the Hughes Cheyenne Center.

Turn around at Rancho Drive, since the route becomes rather congested as it enters the west Las Vegas commercial and residential area. There's a mini-mart and McDonald's at the intersection, in case you need refreshment.

8 **SUNRISE MOUNTAIN AREA RUN** • *Lake Mead Boulevard, from Christy Lane through a pass in Frenchman Mountain in the Sunrise area. Seven-mile round trip; strenuous climb followed by an easy return.*

This route, offering rugged desert scenery and fine Las Vegas panoramas on the return, should be attempted only if you're in good shape and have a low-geared bike, since it begins with a long uphill pull. Start at the intersection of Christy Lane and begin pedaling uphill on Lake Mead Boulevard through a commercial and residential area. Lake Mead has four lanes through here, with a wide shoulder lane to keep you out of traffic. Initially, the grade is rather gentle and then it steepens as you pass through an area of new hillside homes and condos.

By the time you clear the last of the homes, you'll be in low gear and panting. The highway narrows, although it's gently curving with no blind corners. The traffic is much lighter above the developed area. The route takes you through a narrow cleft of Frenchman Mountain, marked by wildly rugged desert hills on both sides.

As you pedal uphill, look to your right for a concrete monument marking an interesting geological phenomena called the "Great Unconformity." You may be ready to take a break by this time, so park your bike follow a short trail across a dry wash. It takes you to an exhibit describing a dramatic faulting action that turned Frenchman Mountain on its side. The resultant upheaval placed layers of 1.7 billion-year-old Precambrian schist next to 500 million-year-old Cambrian Tapeats sandstone. It's called an "unconformity" because 1.2 billion years of geological deposits between them are missing. A detailed sign at the site explains all of this.

About a mile above this exhibit, the route levels out as it crosses a shallow pass through the hills. Look for an area with wide gravelly shoulders on both sides of the highway, with dirt roads leading into the desert. This is our suggested turn-around point, since the descent down the other side of Frenchman Mountain involves some blind curves.

Coasting back down Lake Mead Boulevard, you'll enjoy an ever widening panorama of the Las Vegas Valley as the desert hills part before you. You'll pick up the wide highway shoulder again as you sail past the new homes and condos on your quick downhill run back to Christy Lane.

9 **SUNSET PARK** • *Sunset Road and Eastern Avenue, below McCarran International Airport. Varying distances, all level.*

There are no designated bike routes in this 309-acre county park (see "The Ten Best walks" on page 190), although it has about two miles of vehicle roads. The speed limit is fifteen miles and hour and traffic is light, so cyclists should have no problem peddling over this flat chunk of reclaimed, landscaped desert. The only obstacles are occasional speed bumps.

The park is at the southeast corner of Sunset and Eastern, with entrances off both roads. Pick any of several parking areas, unload your bikes and begin peddling randomly past this huge park's cool green lawns, trees and recreational facilities. If you head south past the Clark County Park Ranger Office, a paved road will take you into a swatch of undeveloped desert that's still within park boundaries.

10 UNIVERSITY OF NEVADA AT LAS VEGAS • Road

network within the campus; varying distances, all level. Campus maps available at the visitor center off Maryland Parkway and Harmon Avenue, the Student Union just to the south and Barrick Museum of Natural History near the eastern end of Harmon Avenue. Metered visitor parking near all of these areas; twenty-five cents for thirty minutes.

A network of narrow roads on the UNLV campus is used only by pedestrians, bikes and a few golf cart type service vehicles. Although they're busy with students during school days, they're relatively empty on weekends and during university holidays—a great time to pedal about this large, handsomely landscaped complex.

As we indicated in our UNLV walk above, you can stop and visit and assortment of attractions. Since many students get about on bikes, you'll find bike racks in front of most of the buildings. The Student Union on Maryland Parkway just south of Harmon offers refreshments and a cool retreat from the heat, although its closed on weekends. (For details on getting to the campus, and Student Union Hours, see "The Ten Best walks and hikes" above, page 189.)

Chapter fifteen

ASSORTED LISTS
...THAT DON'T FIT INTO OTHER LISTS

Twenty years ago, with the help of the Las Vegas News Bureau, we put together a 24-hour marathon, staying up all night to prove that visitors can party around the clock in this town. We called it "Around the Clock in Glitter City," and it made a great story for a travel magazine. Later, we repeated the process for our travel guide, *The Best of Nevada* and then we foolishly did it again for a recent revision, re-titled *Nevada Discovery Guide.*

Could we party around the clock a fourth time, two decades after the original marathon, even as we push Social Security age? Good grief, no! We've updated and edited the version from our *Nevada Discovery Guide*, using a fictitious person in order to conceal our identity.

TEN STEPS TO INSOMNIA — PARTYING AROUND THE CLOCK

You have to catch that damned plane first thing tomorrow. You're going back to that lousy job, back to back taxes, back to a wife that snores and a dog that sheds—or is it the other way around? But there's still so much to do; so much to see; so little time! That boring convention kept you so busy, you hardly got to explore Las Vegas. Twenty-four hours left; you've got to do it all!

1 — *8 to 8:59 a.m.* • You stuff yourself at the Excalibur breakfast buffet. Apple pancakes, waffles, bacon, sausage, ham, fruit, sweet rolls, bagels, more sweet rolls. This is going to be a long day so it's essential to carbo-load.

You waddle downstairs to the Magic Motion Machine for a simulated rollercoaster ride to settle your stomach. It doesn't. Maybe a *real* rollercoaster ride? You cross the pedestrian walk to New York New York and hop on the Manhattan Express. Your entire life and the Manhattan skyline flashes past and minutes later, you stagger through the Cony Island midway, trying to recover your equilibrium. Has your stomach settled? You aren't sure; it's still back there on the rollercoaster.

2 — *9 to 11:59* • Needing to experience the cultural side of Las Vegas, you take a taxi to the Liberace Museum out Tropicana Avenue. You check out the glittering wares of the wonderfully outrageous showman, wondering how you'd look in a gold lamé jacket, sequined boxer shorts and ostrich plume cap.

You return to the Strip and tell the driver just to cruise until something catches your fancy. A giant clown with a lollipop beckons, so you get out at Circus Circus. Feeling like a kid, you invest two dollars in a coin toss game, win a medium-sized panda and—on an impulse—hand it to a passing child.

3 — *Noon to 3:59 p.m.* • You catch another cab to the Imperial Palace, where you simmer with harmless envy, admiring the $50 million Duesenberg collection at the auto exhibit. But you're not rich. You're an ordinary guy with an ordinary job and a wife and a dog that shed. The spicy bloody Mary at the auto collection bar finally calms your stomach. You invest a few quarters in the Imperial Palace casino, then you step blinking into the bright afternoon sunshine. The Stratosphere Tower, just up the Strip, catches your eye. You decide to walk to clear your head. Two weary miles later, you finally arrive. You catch the elevator to the observation deck and decide to ride the rollercoaster that twists around the top. There goes the stomach again.

From the Stratosphere, you catch a cab to the downtown area, walking beneath the filigreed shade of the Fremont Street Experience canopy, and then you step into Jackie Gaughan's Plaza. After failing to win the $402,639.95 progressive jackpot at the video poker carousel, you retire to the lounge. You order a drink and listen to the husky sounds of a fine male vocalist.

4 — *4 to 6:59 p.m.* • Your fussy stomach has finally dispatched that last breakfast sweet roll and recovered from the roller-coaster rides. You gulp down a 99-cent shrimp cocktail at the Golden Gate, chased by a $1.50 chili dog at Fitzgeralds and a $1.50 piña colada at the Nevada Club. Who has time for normal food? The plane leaves tomorrow morning. The plane, boss, the plane!

5 — *7 to 9:59 p.m.* • Omygawd, what happened to the time! You grab a cab and the driver, apparently bent on suicide, lurches crazily through the Saturday night traffic. He delivers you barely in time for the Siegfried and Roy Show at the Mirage. Maybe it was the shrimp cocktail and chili dog, but you'd swear you saw an entire elephant disappear. After the show, you pause at the Lagoon Saloon and order a piña colada to clear your head. Later, as you step into the cool night air, the volcano in front of the Mirage erupts. What a town!

6 — *10 to 11:59 p.m.* • Another *kamikaze* cab ride delivers you to the Comedy Stop at the Tropicana. You're early so you grab a margarita and a burrito to go from Papagayo's Mexican Restaurant. Your stomach wants to go to bed but you're just getting started. One of the comics tells a gag about a guy in a sawmill who accidentally cut off all of his fingers. He couldn't have them re-attached because he was unable to pick them up. That's really sick, so why are you laughing?

7 — *Midnight to 4:59 a.m.* • You take the pedestrian overpass across Tropicana Avenue to the MGM Grand; the night air helps clear your head. Inside, you settle at the Flying Monkey Bar to listen to a fine reggae group. A mai tai seems appropriate here, accompanied by bar peanuts. A leisurely two hours slip past; so do several more mai tais. Yet another cab delivers you to Caesars Palace, and adjourn to Cleopatra's Barge, where you listen to rock music and watch other couples dance. You wish you'd brought your wife. It occurs to you that bars are closing in the rest of the world, but Las Vegas seems to be catching its second wind. So are you.

8 — *5 to 6:59 a.m.* • After the Barge closes, you hit The Beach, a sports bar and night club just off the Strip on Convention Center Drive; it stays open 24 hours. You hope your eyes can do the same. A particularly sexy young singer wriggles sensuously, almost squirming out of her tiny dress as she belts out a good blues number. Her sultry performance arouses your tired eyes and other parts.

Feeling wonderfully nocturnal, you return downtown settle into the Omaha Lounge at Jackie Gaughan's Plaza, where a sultry soloist is caressing the microphone and the audience with her voice. You listen to several numbers then, growing restless, you walk outside and drift from casino to casino. Images of Frank Sinatra singing *My Time of Day* flicker through your mind. Fremont Street and its canopy are bathed in glitter brighter than the sun, which still sleeps somewhere beyond Sunrise Mountain. You like the gentle laughter of the few pre-dawn gamblers in the casinos, replacing the raucous noise of earlier crowds. You can hear the brittle rattle of the dice, the click of a roulette wheel. Sinatra was right; it's a nice time of day.

9 — *7 to 7:59 a.m.* • Suddenly famished, you walk to the Fremont Casino café and order steak, two eggs, hash browns and toast. Awaiting its arrival, you mark a $7 keno ticket, with the promise of winning $100,000. The promise is not kept, but the breakfast isn't bad for under three bucks.

10 — *8 a.m.* • You glance at your watch. Omygawd, the plane! You hail a final cab and doze in the back seat with visions of $402,639.95 jackpots, Duesenbergs, volcanoes, lamé jackets, filmy dresses covering tender young breasts and piña coladas dancing in your head. The cab lurches to a stop in front of the Excalibur, jerking you back to reality. You ask the driver to wait while you dash upstairs. You've got just enough time to stuff your things into your suitcase and catch that plane. You're remarkably alert, pleased that you have seen the elephant.

Even if the damned thing disappeared on you.

THE TEN BEST PLACES TO PEOPLE WATCH

Tired of pulling slot machine handles? Weary of rolling them bones? Did you attempt the marathon we described above, or did you overdo it at the buffet? Sometimes, you just want to sit and watch the rest of us. Here's where:

1 BENEATH THE FREMONT STREET CANOPY • *Fremont Street between Fourth and Main downtown.*

The Fremont Street Experience is popular for its nightly sound and light show. It's also a great place just to hang out, day or night. The canopy offers a little shelter from the sun and misters cool things down on hot summer days. The pedestrian mall has become something of a local happening, with coffee and cappuccino stands, curio kiosks and street musicians. To enjoy the action, fetch a tub of suds from a nearby casino bar, find a bench or umbrella table and just sit. Watch the tide of human traffic pass and listen to the sounds of jackpots issuing from adjacent casinos. If you sit and watch long enough, you'll see most of the thirty million people who visit Las Vegas each year, since most of them wind up downtown. You'll probably want to go get another tub of beer.

2 **THE BOARDWALK'S SIDEWALK: Holiday Inn Board-walk ●** *3570 S. Las Vegas Blvd. (at Flamingo Road); (702) 731-7110.*

A raised terrace in front of the Boardwalk Casino on Las Vegas Boulevard provides a fine perch for watching the world go by. Step inside this cheerful little casino for a snack or drink from The Deli, and then step outside and settle onto one of the benches. Actually, the Boardwalk folks won't really object if you don't buy anything at all.

3 **FORUM SHOPS FOUNTAINS: Caesars Palace ●** *3500 S. Las Vegas Blvd. (at Flamingo Road); (702) 731-7110.*

The Forum Shops at Caesars comprise the world's largest casino shopping complex, anchored on either end by Roman style fountains. You'll find several wrought iron benches near both, where you can sit back and watch a constant parade of shoppers and browsers. At the Festival Fountain, "statues" of Bacchus and other Roman deities become animated and present a brief laser show. It's rather corny, but it's something to watch while you rest your feet.

4 **MYSTIC FALLS PARK: Sam's Town Hotel & Gambling Hall ●** *5111 Boulder Highway (at Nellis Boulevard); (702) 456-7777.*

Mystic Falls is a climate-controlled water park and garden under glass, rimmed by Sam's Town hotel towers. This is a very inviting place for people watching, with its meandering paths, benches, tables and chairs and a couple of gazebos. If you'd like to dine while you people-watch, ask for a patio table at the adjacent Papamio's Italian restaurant.

5 **SANTA FE WAITING ROOM: Santa Fe Hotel & Casino ●** *4949 N. Rancho Dr. (at Highway 95 north); (702) 658-4900.*

Although it's seven miles north of town and missed by most visitors, this atrium-ceiling foyer is one of the area's more pleasant inner spaces. It's fashioned after the waiting room of an old Santa Fe depot, with a circular bar in the center, tables and chairs for relaxing and even a library style newspaper rack. Two restaurants, two takeouts and an ice cream parlor occupy the fringes of this appealing space. Another interesting place to people watch is in the adjacent Santa Fe ice rink. You might catch the pro hockey Las Vegas Thunder in action, since this is the team's practice arena.

6 **TROPICANA CORNER PEDESTRIAN BRIDGES** • *South Las Vegas Boulevard and Tropicana Avenue.*

Six of the world's largest casino resorts are gathered near the busy corner of Las Vegas Boulevard and Tropicana Avenue, which is spanned by a four-way pedestrian overpass. The Tropicana, Excalibur, MGM Grand and New York New York share the corner, while the Luxor and Monte Carlo are short walks away. Catch an escalator to any of the four overpasses, find a place to lean and watch the people and the traffic flow past. From here, you can admire the clever skyline of New York New York, the multi-colored castle towers of Excalibur, the palm-trimmed Tropicana "Island of Las Vegas" and grand mass of the MGM Grand—the world's largest resort hotel. A balcony adjacent to the second floor entrance to New York New York is a good spot for people watching.

7 **FLAMINGO-BARBARY COAST CORNER** • *The intersection of Las Vegas Boulevard and Flamingo Road.*

This is the second busiest corner on the Strip, after the Tropicana Avenue intersection above. An attractive brick decorator wall, raised planters and several park benches occupy the sidewalk in front of the Barbary Coast casino. It's a particularly appealing place to perch at night, all a-glitter with the elaborate neon of the Barbary Coast and the giant "torches" of the next door Flamingo Hilton. From here, you can see the colors and contours of Balley's across Flamingo Road, and Caesars Palace and the new Bellagio across Las Vegas Boulevard.

8 **FASHION SHOW MALL PLAZA** • *Las Vegas Boulevard at Spring Mountain Road. Sfuzzi Restaurant open for lunch and dinner; (702) 699-5777.*

The boulevard entrance to Fashion Show Mall has been fashioned into an attractive patio, with brick planters, retaining walls and fountains. Although there are no benches, many of the planters and terraced retaining walls are at seat-level. You can perch and watch the pedestrian parade, while listening to the whump-whump of stereo speakers from Steven Speilberg's submarine-theme Dive! restaurant. Mist sprayers keep passersby and lingerers cool on hot summer days. If you prefer wine and/or pasta with your people watching, you can adjourn to Sfuzzi, across the mall entrance from Dive! This trendy Italian restaurant with a funny name has a patio just off the plaza.

9 **STREET OF DREAMS: Monte Carlo** • *3770 Las Vegas Blvd. (north of Tropicana Avenue); (702) 730-7777. Monte Carlo Pub and Brewery open for lunch and dinner.*

You can just sit and daydream along this corridor while watching people pass. The Street of Dreams is fashioned as an old Monaco village lane, with cobbled pavers and stone shop fronts. Find a seat on one of the park benches along the "street" for your people watching. Or step inside the lively Monte Carlo Pub and Brewery and ask for one of the alcove tables on the outer edge, adjacent to "Dream Street." A busy American style brewpub on a back street in Monaco? Of course. Why do we have to keep reminding you that this is Las Vegas?

10 VILLAGE EATERIES: New York New York ● 3790 S. Las Vegas Boulevard (Tropicana Avenue); (702) 740-6969.

The best food court in town is fashioned as a Greenwich Village street scene, complete with plastic trees and storefront façades. Tables are set along the edges of the brick and cobblestone "streets." Pick up a pizza or beer or hot dog or whatever from one of several take-outs and settle down at one of the tables for a pleasant bout of people watching

THE TEN BEST DESIGNER COLLISIONS

Casino resort designers love themes—South Seas (Mirage and Tropicana), pirates (Treasure Island), Arthurian castle (Excalibur) and old Manhattan (New York New York). However, they sometimes just can't seem to leave them be. The results often are harmless yet visually jarring thematic collisions. On the other hand, some of these sudden architectural transitions are rather eye-appealing.

1 I'LL TAKE MANHATTAN AND CLEOPATRA, TOO: Luxor Hotel and Casino ● 3900 S. Las Vegas Blvd. (south of Tropicana Avenue).

Standing inside the cavernous pyramid of the Luxor, you look up and see—the Manhattan skyline? For some curious reason, designers of the Luxor decided to give a New York theme to the buffet. However, by the time you arrive, Manhattan may have been moved to the basement and a new King Tut museum will be in this site.

2 KING ARTHUR TO KING TUT—A BRIDGE TOO FAR? Excalibur and Luxor ● South Las Vegas Boulevard at Tropicana.

The turreted Technicolor castles of the Excalibur are linked by a pedestrian walkway to the new hotel tower of the Luxor. Both are properties of Circus Circus Enterprises. There is no architectural transition between the two; enter the walkway and zap! You've left King Arthur behind and arrived in Ancient Egypt. Ancient Egypt? Well, sort of. The façade of the new Luxor hotel tower suggests Isis Temple, then it changes abruptly into a black glass tower.

3 HUDSON RIVER TO THE RIVIERA—A BRIDGE TOO STRANGE? New York New York and Monte Carlo • South Las Vegas Boulevard, north of Tropicana Avenue.

You can walk north from the Manhattan-theme New York New York casino on a mockup of the Brooklyn Bridge and wind up at the Monte Carlo, whose marble entry with its bronze fountains and nubile statuary is right out of the Riviera's Monaco. En route, you pass the Motown Café honoring "motor town" rock music or the Detroit sound. From New York to the Riviera via Detroit? Only in Las Vegas, kids.

4 BACCARAT GONE BANANAS: Monte Carlo Hotel & Casino • 3770 S. Las Vegas Blvd. (north of Tropicana Avenue).

Step inside the elegant Monte Carlo casino with its marbled entry, plush carpeted floors and beaded chandeliers. Look immediately to your left and you see—the Hyper Market Deli? It's a combined mini-mart and curio shop, where you can buy bottled drinks, snacks and even fresh fruit. Gosh, guys, why didn't you make it an old French or Italian market stall instead of a modern mini-mart? And what's hyper about a banana?

5 DAMN THE DESIGN AND FULL SPEED AHEAD: Fashion Show Mall • South Las Vegas Boulevard and Spring Mountain Road.

Fashion Show Mall is the most elegant in town, with such upscale stores as Neiman Marcus and Saks Fifth Avenue. The architecture is of course quite tasteful. But, what's with that submarine snout and conning tower sticking out of the mall's front wall? It's Steven Speilberg's theme restaurant and pub called Dive! (That's his exclamation mark, not ours.) To add further architectural contradiction, a trendy Italian restaurant called Sfuzzi has a Florentine façade with the Mona Lisa portrait which, with the use of clever brush strokes, is peeling away from the wall.

6 SKATING ALL THE WAY TO SANTA FE: Santa Fe Hotel & Casino • 4949 N. Rancho Dr. (at Highway 95 north); (702) 658-4900.

This architectural conflict is really cool. The Santa Fe Casino has a Southwestern railroad theme and a skating rink. Enter through the handsome high ceiling Santa Fe railroad station style lobby, proceed through the casino and step into a full blown ice arena. It's a great place to cool off on a hot day, or to watch the Las Vegas Thunder hockey team at play. This is their practice arena.

7 *NOW, THAT'S ITALIAN? Bugsy's Deli at the Flamingo Hilton* • *3555 S. Las Vegas Blvd. (Flamingo Road); (702) 733-3111.*

Although rather simply decorated, this small deli named in honor of the Flamingo's founder is quite cute. Olive oil cans and bottles, sausages and garlic strands decorate a plate rail above the service counter. One of the seating areas is adorned with a vineyard mural right out of the Italian countryside. But, wait a minute... Wasn't Bugsy Siegel Jewish?

8 *EAST MEETS WEST—AND SOUTH AND NORTH: Studio Walk, MGM Grand* • *3799 S. Las Vegas Blvd. (at Tropicana Avenue).*

The architectural mix is appealing along this corridor of restaurants and shops, since it consists of entire building mockups instead of mere façades, each with a different theme. Begin with the Southwest adobe of Mark Miller's Coyote Café and Grill Room, then stroll immediately past the Art of Entertainment Gallery with an art deco look, continue on to the California mission style architecture of the Brown Derby and finally the weathered brick and colonial French wrought iron of Emeril's New Orleans Fish House.

9 *THE HI HO SILVER EXPERIENCE?: East end of the Fremont pedestrian mall* • *Fremont Street at Las Vegas Boulevard.*

No, that isn't the Lone Ranger on the rearing palomino sign at the east end of the Fremont Street Experience; it's a *vaquero,* complete with sombrero. Why is an old fashioned lightbulb-infested sign standing in the middle of Las Vegas Boulevard, near the space-age electronic canopy of the Fremont Street Experience? Because Las Vegans, despite their rush into the future, like to preserve bits of their past. That sign is all that remains of the old Hacienda Hotel, which was demolished recently to make way for a new resort. It's one of several historic Las Vegas neon signs installed on the first block of the Fremont Street Experience. Others in this "neon garden of nostalgia" include the Flame restaurant, a large "magic lamp" from Aladdin's Casino, a sign from the Chief Hotel Court and the smiling Anderson Dairy milkman.

10 *WHEN IN ROME, BUILD A GEODESIC DOME? Caesars Palace* • *3570 S. Las Vegas Blvd. (at Flamingo Road); (702) 731-7110.*

Caesars Palace is a splendid study in Roman columns and statuary, marble fountains and grand reflection pools. But what's that round brown thing rising above the main casino entrance? In contrast to the refined Roman architecture, it looks like something left over from a world's fair. That's the geodesic dome housing the huge, six-story curved screen and seating area of the Omnimax Theater. And if you think that's an odd attachment to this Roman architectural facsimile, check out the revolving blue globe with red twinkle lettering sitting atop a fluted column, advertising Caesars' Planet Hollywood café.

THE TEN DUMBEST THINGS YOU CAN DO IN GLITTER CITY

Most of the dumb things that people do in Las Vegas involve excessive gambling, and that leads our list.

1 *GAMBLING MORE THAN YOU CAN AFFORD TO LOSE* • The first rule of gambling, and the last rule of gambling, is to commit only what you can afford to lose. The odds are that you *will* lose, for it is losing that helps build and support Glitter City's multi-zillion dollar resorts. Think of your gambling money as entertainment money; an amount you plan to spend each day for amusement. And if you win, great! You've had fun *and* made a few dollars.

2 *PLAYING KENO* • "Are you kidding? Nearly every casino has a keno operation and *thousands* of people play it!" No, we aren't kidding. Keno has the worst odds of any game in town, with the house keeping 20 to 40 percent of the proceeds. Most of the thousands of people who play keno will lose. Why do you think nearly every casino has a keno game?

3 *SOLICITING A CALL GIRL* • Sex for hire is one of the few human urges that's illegal in Las Vegas and elsewhere in Clark County. It's legal in Nye County just over the line, and a town called Crystal is devoted entirely to commercial copulation. Sleek limos and even private jets take horny high rollers over there for a roll in the hay. Back in Las Vegas, you'll find Yellow Page adds and street flyers offering the services of sexy young ladies, who'll get naked in your room for a fee. It's legal to sit on the edge of the bed and twitch while they perform, but you're breaking the law if you join them in a romp. Your lady in waiting just might be a vice squad member, and it's illegal for either a man or a woman to solicit sex for hire.

4 *DRIVING THE STRIP ON A FRIDAY OR SATURDAY NIGHT* • Sixty percent of Glitter City's visitors come from southern California, and guess when most of them hit town? Since Las Vegas is just a few hours' drive or a cheap jet flight from the metroblob of Los

Angeles, thousands of Californians spend their weekends here. They hit town on Friday night, party through Saturday night and drive home Sunday.

5 DRIVING ANYWHERE DURING THE EVENING COMMUTE HOUR • From 3:30 until about 6:30 p.m. on weekdays, you should be at poolside or inside a casino feeding the local economy, not driving around the streets. This is particularly true of Las Vegas Boulevard, its major cross streets and the urban section of I-15. With its population topping a million, greater Las Vegas is suffering one of joys of urban growth, although its commute-hour traffic isn't as bad as most other major cities. Curiously, the rush hour traffic isn't generally as severe in the morning. Perhaps most Las Vegans sleep in, and of course many tourists are recovering from the previous night of partying.

6 DRIVING WHILE UNDER THE INFLUENCE • Metro Police, who cover the greater Las Vegas area, set up periodic sobriety checkpoints to keep drunk drivers off the streets, so don't even think about it. That's what cabs are for. Since there's a lot of partying and a lot of traffic in Las Vegas, Metro is tough on DWI enforcement. The legal blood-alcohol limit in Nevada is .10 and there is talk of joining several other states that have lowered it to .08.

7 CATCHING THE 301 STRIP BUS IF YOU'RE IN A HURRY • Citizens Area Transit operates a fine public bus system, and the 301 line runs for 24 hours along Las Vegas Boulevard, between downtown and Vacation Village, the southernmost Strip casino. Although it's transit, it isn't rapid. During morning and evening rush hours, the Strip often is choked with traffic; it can take an hour or more for a bus to make the seven-mile run. If you're in a hurry, grab a cab. Taxis must compete with the same traffic, of course. However, they don't stop every block to take on new passengers while the driver pleads futilely with those on board to move to the rear. For reasons we don't understand, most bus standees refuse to do so. The 301 Strip Express is a better bet since it makes fewer stops, although it runs only from 6 p.m. until midnight.

8 TRYING TO HAIL A CAB ON THE BOULEVARD • Most of the cabs dashing up and down the Strip already have a fare or they're going to get one or they can't get to you because you're on the sidewalk (hopefully) and they're on an inside lane. To catch a cab in this town, go to the motor entrance of any resort hotel. You'll usually find a row of them there, waiting obediently for the next fare. You should tip the hotel doorman a couple of dollars as he helps you aboard, but that's better than standing out on a hot sidewalk, wildly flailing your arms. (Only in the movies do cabs come on cue.)

9 *WALKING IN FRONT OF TREASURE ISLAND DURING THE PIRATE SHIP BATTLE* • It's fun, it's colorful and it's one of the best free shows in town. Which is why hundreds of folks jam the sidewalk in front of Treasure Island to watch Her Majesty's ship *Brittania* do battle with the pirate sloop *Hispañola.* A narrow sidewalk corridor is supposed to be reserved for through traffic, but during busy periods the crowd tends to spill into it. The sidewalk jam is even worse just after a show, when the mob disperses with the speed of cold molasses on a flat table. Shows are scheduled daily at 4, 5:30, 8:30 and 10, with 11:30 shows Friday and Saturday. Crowds begin gathering about half an hour before each performance. (Hours may change with the seasons; they're posted at the lagoon.)

10 *MAKING LAST-MINUTE WEEKEND RESERVATIONS* • If you try to get late reservations for a popular show or for a hotel room on Friday and Saturday, lotsa luck, particularly if there's a big convention in town. These are always the busiest nights of the week, and the reason for Glitter City's two-tiered room rates—one for Friday-Saturday, and a cheaper one for Sunday-Thursday. Year-around occupancy rate runs close to ninety percent, and on popular weekends, make that one hundred percent.

The solution for your procrastination? If you're in town, try one of the smaller motels or one of the outlying casino hotels. Several in next-door Henderson are within an easy commute of downtown and the Strip. Also, you might try one of those so-called tourist bureaus along the Strip, which basically are reservation services. If you're out of town? Find a good travel agent, do a lot of dialing or plan on arriving Sunday afternoon. As for Friday or Saturday night shows, get a copy of *What's On* or one of the other local entertainment guides, turn to the "Show Guide" section and just start punching phone numbers.

You'll have better luck getting late room reservations or last-minute show tickets during the slower periods of the year. These are early December before the holiday break, early January (but *not* Superbowl weekend) through February, and midsummer. However, with ample air conditioning and more all-family lures at the casino resorts, the summer school vacation period isn't as slow as it once was.

EASY LISTENING:
THE TEN BEST RADIO STATIONS

Our choices of radio stations reveal two things—that we don't like rap or hard rock, and that we've selected stations geared toward visitors. We begin, not necessarily with the best, but with the first stations that Las Vegas-bound travelers encounter if they're coming from California. Not surprisingly, the Golden State provides more visitors to Glitter City than any other.

1 *"THE HIGHWAY STATION"—KHYZ FM 98.1 and FM 99.5* • This powerful station beams is way across the Mojave Desert, playing "adult contemporary" music, offering Las Vegas tips and running lots of casino hotel commercials.

2 *"HIGHWAY COUNTRY"—FM 101.5* • If your taste tilts to country music, this station has a similar Las Vegas informational format, also beamed at Mojave Desert travelers.

3 *KJUL—FM 104.3* • This station plays popular oldies dating back to the 1940s, including the songs of those who have performed here, such as Sinatra, Newton and Presley.

4 *KUNV—FM 91.5* • Cool jazz sounds issue from this publicly supported station.

5 *KNPR—FM 89.5* • This is a blend of National Public Radio and Nevada Public Radio, playing mostly classical music.

6 *KMZQ—FM 100.5* • "Adult contemporary variety" might be a good description for this station's music; selections range from Top Forty vocals to light rock; no rap or hard rock.

7 *KWNR—FM 95.5* • This is one of Glitter City's stronger country and Western music stations.

8 *KKLZ—FM 96.3* • For fans of rock before rap, KKLZ plays rock 'n' roll oldies.

9 *KENO—AM 1460* • If you're a sports fanatic, that's all you'll get on "KENO Sports Radio."

10 *KNEW—AM 970* • News and talk fill this Las Vegas station's format.

The world is a book, and those who do not travel, read only a page.
— **Saint Augustine**

Chapter sixteen

LEAVING LAS VEGAS

REASONS FOR GETTING OUT OF TOWN

If you look at a map of Nevada, you'll see that the state comes to a point at the bottom. Most of its population has flowed into that point, like ink to a quill tip. All of this southern triangle is occupied by Clark County, which contains more than 65 percent of the state's population, even though it's one of Nevada's smaller counties. In fact, the Las Vegas-North Las Vegas-Henderson sprawl is the only true metropolitan area in the state.

Despite its small size, this urban pen point contains great topographic variety and many visitor attractions. It features fine desert wilderness, awesome geological shapes and a mountain range capped by often snow-dusted Mount Charleston. A short drive from Glitter City will take you to an assortment of interesting areas, and most of them are tucked into Clark County. Some of the region's largest casino resorts occupy these outlying areas as well.

THE TEN BEST NEARBY ATTRACTIONS

Our favorite excuse for leaving Las Vegas is to hike among the fantastic redrock formations of Valley of Fire State Park to the northeast. We've listed our next nine choices in a more or less logical order, as day trips out of Las Vegas. Some of them take us across the border into Arizona and California.

1 *VALLEY OF FIRE STATE PARK* ● *Fifty miles northeast of Las Vegas on I-15 to exit 75 and then east on State Route 168 into the park. For information: Valley of Fire State Park, P.O. Box 515, Overton, NV 89040; (702) 397-2088. Day use $4 for cars and $1 for hikers and bikers. Camping $11. Visitor Center open daily 8:30 to 4:30.*

This awesome collection of twisted and contorted sandstone is one of the most imposing geological areas in the Southwest, rivaling in beauty—if not in size—neighboring Zion, Bryce and Cedar Breaks in Utah. It's Nevada's oldest state preserve, originally set aside as part of the federal land for the Boulder Dam project. It was donated to the state in 1931 and became the first element of its park system.

After you enter the park, head for the visitor center, tucked into the base of a weather-sculpted escarpment. Study its exhibits, learn about its geology and hiking trails and then begin exploring. Follow Rainbow Drive from the visitor center five miles toward the White Domes area. En route, pause at a trailhead and take a short walk through a serpentine canyon to Mouse's Tank, a natural water hole. At Rainbow Vista, follow a 1.5-mile trail along the edge of Fire Canyon to Silica Domes. When you finally reach the end of the road at the White Domes area, you can check out these unusual off-white sandstone shapes, and then explore the area at will. Off-trail hiking is permitted in Valley of Fire, since wind and occasional rain erase any footprints. Dry washes make good trails, but make sure you note landmarks as you hike. It's easy to get lost in this wilderness of stone.

After you've finished with the White Domes area, retrace your route to the main road and continue east through the park. Watch on your left—as you approach the eastern exit—for the formation called Elephant Rock. It's the most photographed object in the park and everyone's favorite stone pachyderm.

2 *OVERTON TO MESQUITE & VIRGIN RIVER GORGE* ● *North from Valley of Fire. For information: Lost City Museum, P.O. Box 807, Overton, NV 89040, (702) 397-2193.*

Overton is a small farming community on the northern tip of Lake Mead. There would be little reason to pause here except for the excellent Lost City Museum on its southern edge. The pueblo style museum was erected during the Depression as a Civilian Conservation Corps project over the site of an abandoned Anasazi settlement. The interior contains fine displays of the social lives, agriculture, weapons, arts and crafts of the Anasazi and native groups that followed them. Outside, you can explore an above-ground pueblo and peer into a pit house; both were constructed by the CCC boys. The museum is open daily 8:30 to 4:30; $2 for anyone over 18.

Continue north a dozen miles from Overton, hang a right onto I-15 and follow it thirty-four miles to Mesquite. It's another ordinary farming town irrigated by the Virgin River. However, it's considerably more lively than Overton, for it's home to four mid-size casino hotels, giving Utah Mormons and others westbound on I-15 their first opportunity to gamble. (Mesquite is actually on the Nevada-Arizona border, although I-15 only nips a tip of Arizona and soon enters Utah.)

Take the first exit from the freeway and drag Mesquite Boulevard. You will encounter—in order of appearance—CasaBlanca on the western edge (formerly Players Island), the Oasis, which takes up most of downtown Mesquite and, at the eastern end and across the freeway, Virgin River Hotel-Casino and the new Holiday Inn Rancho Mesquite. Worthy of a brief pause, near the center of town, is the small Desert Valley Museum at 35 W. Mesquite Boulevard. It's open Monday-Saturday from 8 to 5; (702) 346-5705.

If you continue east from Mesquite on I-15, you'll soon enter the imposing Virgin River Gorge. This sheer walled canyon is worth the brief drive into Arizona. The river in this hot desert canyon is enticing but difficult to reach, since the freeway was carved high above. In fact, freeway builders cut into some of the walls to create a path, although most of them were carved by the river, leaving exposed slices of twisted and tilted strata. Unless you want to continue into Utah, take the Virgin River Recreation Area exit, cross over the freeway and return to Nevada. The next interchange is fourteen miles away and you've already seen the best of the canyon. A campground here operated by the Bureau of Land Management has several sites that overlook the canyon. A couple of tough, rocky trails lead down into it from the campground.

3 *HISTORIC BOULDER CITY* • *Twenty-five miles southeast of Las Vegas. For information: Boulder City Visitors Bureau, 1305 Arizona St. (in the Boulder Dam Hotel), Boulder City, NV 89005; 294-1330.*

Boulder City was born as a construction town for Hoover Dam because federal officials felt that neighboring Las Vegas was too sinful for their workers. Drinking, gambling and whoring were banned and it is still the only town in Nevada where gambling is specifically forbidden. (So is prostitution, of course, because it's part of Clark County.) No longer a government town, it's a small community with a nicely preserved historic district and handsome park on a crest between the town and the dam site. Stroll past the 1930s style art deco buildings along Arizona Street and step into the beautifully restored Boulder Dam Hotel. The town's visitor center resides in the lobby.

While you're in the neighborhood, stop by the Boulder City/Hoover Dam Museum, which contains exhibits concerning the dam's construction, and a gift shop. It's open daily 10 to 4, with a modest admission charge; (702) 294-1988.

Those of us who live in southern Nevada are aware that some residents of Boulder City are rather uppity about their community. This seems a bit ironic since it began as a blue-collar construction camp. What pleases the residents is their location on the far side of Railroad Pass, out of the greater Las Vegas basin and thus free of its congestion, general commotion and occasional smoggy skies. Growth is restricted by city fathers, so property values have been forced upward. Although most of the houses in older Boulder City are modest and nothing to shout about, some new homes and townhouses—particularly on the downslope between Boulder City and the dam—are rather pricey.

4 *LAKE MEAD AND HOOVER DAM* ● *For information: Lake Mead National Recreation Area, 601 Nevada Highway, Boulder City, NV 89005-2426; (702) 293-8907. Hoover Dam Visitor Services, P.O. Box 60400, Boulder City, NV 89005; (702) 293-8321. Guided tours daily 8:30 to 6:30; $5 for adults, $2.50 for kids. Alan Bible Visitor Center, Lake Mead NRA, North Lakeshore Drive and U.S. 93; open daily 8:30 to 5; free.*

Other than Las Vegas, Hoover Dam is the most visited attraction in southern Nevada. Without the dam, in fact, Glitter City wouldn't have much glitter, for it provides water and power to the desert metropolis. The idea for a dam to tame the free-flowing Colorado River was conceived early in this century, although construction didn't begin until 1931. The delay proved fortuitous. The stock market had crashed two years earlier, the Depression gripped the country and the government had a steady flow of workers willing to sweat in the burning depths of Black Canyon for fifty cents an hour.

When the dam was completed in 1935, it was the world's highest at 726 feet, holding back the world's largest reservoir, Lake Mead. This boaters' playground has more miles of shoreline than the state of California. To preserve it as a playground, along with Lake Mohave below the dam, America's first federal recreation area was established in 1935. Covering 1.3 million acres, Lake Mead National Recreation Area is the third largest element of the national park system outside of Alaska, and the fourth most-visited federal preserve, drawing nine million people a year. As you can see, Las Vegas isn't the only southern Nevada entity that overflows with superlatives.

U.S. Highway 93 winds down from Boulder City into the dramatic steep-walled Black Canyon, where this giant plug of concrete rests.

WHAT'S IN A DAM NAME?

Why is Hoover Dam, the nucleus of the Boulder Dam Project, in Black Canyon? Why isn't it in Boulder Canyon? And didn't it used to be called Boulder Dam?

When planning for a dam began early in this century, it was called the Boulder Canyon Project Act because the initial site of the dam was farther upstream, in Boulder Canyon. However, that site was laced with faults so Black Canyon was chosen several miles downstream. This site also permitted more water storage for Lake Mead.

As construction began, the dam was named for Herbert Hoover, not to honor him as President, but as the former secretary of commerce. In that post, he had overseen complicated water rights negotiations between Nevada, California and Arizona, which had to be settled before the dam could be built. Shortly after its completion, Secretary of the Interior Harold Ickes changed the name to Boulder Dam. It is no coincidence that Ickes was a Democrat and Hoover was a Republican.

It changed back and forth several times until 1947, when Democratic President Harry S Truman ordered Congress to settle the dam name issue once and for all. His Republican-dominated legislature did so, but not to Harry's liking; the name was changed permanently to Hoover Dam.

You'll shortly encounter a handsome new visitor center, wedged between the canyon and the dam and tinted russet to match the surrounding rock. From here, tours take you deep into the dam's innards, where guides will regale you with even more superlatives. You can watch videos of dam construction and adjourn to an observation deck for a splendid view of this massive wedge in Black Canyon.

5 LAUGHLIN ● *About ninety miles south of Las Vegas on U.S. 95, then east briefly on State Route 163. For information: Laughlin Visitors Bureau, P.O. Box 29849, Laughlin, NV 89029; (800) 4-LAUGHLIN or (702) 298-3321.*

In this unlikely corner of this unlikely state, a once nameless riverside hamlet with only a bankrupt bait shop soon may become the second largest gambling center in Nevada. Laughlin may pass Reno in both visitor traffic and gaming revenue. It's already in third place, ahead of Lake Tahoe, drawing more than two million visitors a year.

All of this is happening because an entrepreneur decided to build a gaming center on the Colorado River. He immodestly named the town for himself. Michigan-born Don Laughlin came to Las Vegas in 1954, tended bar, dealt cards, saved his money and bought a small casino. In 1966, at age 33, he sold the place, pocketed a nice profit and used it to buy a broken down bait shop and motel on the banks of the Colorado River. He moved his family into the motel and began building Laughlin. Slowly at first and then in growing numbers, folks began coming over from Bullhead City, Arizona, just across the river. Laughlin provided free shuttle service to lure them across and, as his gaming empire grew, he practically built the area's infrastructure. He spent $1 million on Laughlin streets, $3 million on a bridge to Bullhead and $6 to expand Bullhead's airport so it could handle scheduled service.

The town of Laughlin now has nine casino hotels, most of them relatively modern and spacious. Although most Nevada casinos are closed to the world outside, many Laughlin gaming areas have pleasing views of the river. The stream, whose flow is slowed by downriver Parker Dam, adds a nice dimension to a Laughlin visit. Shuttle boats cruise from one casino to the next and they still bring folks over from a large Don Laughlin-owned parking lot in Bullhead. Some of the casinos rent water play gear and Harrah's Laughlin has a sandy riverside beach. A river walk links several of the resorts, running from Laughlin's Riverside to the Golden Nugget.

Affordable Laughlin

Another Laughlin lure is price. Most of its hotel rooms are less expensive than comparable ones in Las Vegas. The town's main drawback is that it's hotter than the hinges of hades in summer, being 2,000 feet lower than Las Vegas. It's more popular as a fall-through-spring resort and it's particularly popular with Snowbirds who like to spend their winters in the warm sun. Bullhead is one of Arizona's most popular Snowbird roosts and its shores are lined with RV parks.

Touring Laughlin is a simple matter. Cruise along Casino Drive and you'll see the entirety of the town. The casinos are lined up along a two-mile front, like inviting sitting ducks. You first encounter Don Laughlin's Riverside Hotel and Casino, then the Flamingo Hilton Laughlin, the Edgewater Hotel & Casino, Ramada Express Hotel-Casino on the west side of the street (the only resort off the river), the Colorado Belle, the small Pioneer Hotel & Gambling Hall, Golden Nugget-Laughlin, Gold River Gambling Hall & Resort and, in a little cove off by itself, Harrah's Laughlin Hotel and Casino.

Before leaving Laughlin, drive a short distance north to Davis Dam, which forms craggy, steep-walled Lake Mohave, the lower pond of Lake Mead National Recreation Area. Self guiding tours will take you into the concrete and earthfill structure. You can look down a row of huge humming turbines and step onto the dam's lower deck, where you can watch water boiling up from the turbine outlets, or penstocks. The dam is open for touring daily 7:30 to 3:30, Arizona time. (Arizona doesn't go on daylight saving time.)

6 *OATMAN AND HISTORIC ROUTE 66* • *About twenty miles south and then east of Laughlin.*

This side trip will take you into Arizona, through the funky old mining town of Oatman and over a steep rocky pass on Historic Route 66. "Get your kicks on Route 66," invites the old song. During the Depression, hundreds of thousands followed it from Chicago to L.A., not for kicks, but for the promise of a better life in the Golden State. Most of that legendary highway is buried under Interstate 40, although some links survive. This particular section switchbacks over the Black Mountains, and it was one of the most intimidating climbs in the entire Route 66. It's still twisting, although it's easily navigable.

To begin your trip, cross the pond to Bullhead City and head south on Arizona Highway 95. After about ten miles, turn east (left) at a stop light onto Boundary Cone Road and begin climbing. Fourteen miles later, you'll hit funky old Oatman. This hamlet was established in 1909 and boomed as a lively mining area until the last mine was shut down in 1942. It struggled along as a way station on Route 66, then it appeared to be doomed after that highway was re-routed south to avoid the high pass over the Black Mountains. However, its citizens have managed to keep the town alive by turning it into a Western style tourist trap.

Gift shops and cowboy saloons thrive in false-front stores; some are originals, others are newly built to look old. Some of the trinket shops are in doublewides and tent shelters. Oatman ain't lovely, although it's kinda cute in a tacky sort of way. A favorite pastime for visitors, other than kicking up their heels in cowboy saloons, is to feed feral burros that wander the streets. (Watch where you step.) They're descendants of miners' pack animals abandoned when the mines closed. Shop owners encourage this activity by selling carrots and other burro food.

Gable and Lombard slept here

Worthy of a peek is the rickety Oatman Hotel, one of the town's original structures. Inside, you'll find a collection of early 20th century memorabilia such as old mining equipment, theater costumes and movie posters. Room 15 has an interesting claim to fame. Clark Gable and Carol Lombard spent their wedding night here after being married in Kingman on March 18, 1939. The hotel was closed for refurbishing and gentrification when we last visited, although it may have reopened by the time you arrive. The downstairs restaurant and saloon were alive and kicking, and presumably still are.

In Oatman, you pick up Historic Route 66, which twists and winds steeply up to 3,350-foot Sitgreaves Pass over the Black Mountains. Turnouts on either side provide vistas of this wildly rugged country of terraced buttes, conical spires and wave upon wave of ridges. During the Depression, this pass was so intimidating that some California-bound hopefuls hired locals to drive or tow their wheezing Model-T's and Model-A's over the top. A few miles down the other side, look to your left for a Bureau of Land Management display concerning old Highway 66. This is a logical turnabout point unless you want to continue downhill to Kingman.

7 RED ROCK CANYON NATIONAL CONSERVATION *AREA* ● *Twenty-five miles west of Las Vegas, out Charleston Boulevard. For information: Bureau of Land Management, HCR 33, Box 5500, Las Vegas, NV 89124; (702) 363-1921. Visitor center open daily 9 to 4; scenic drive open 8 a.m. to dusk; primitive camping at Oak Creek Road Campground.*

Red Rock Canyon is our second favorite regional retreat, after Valley of Fire. Actually more of an eroded cliff face than a canyon, it's a thirteen-mile multicolored fault extending along the base of the Spring Mountains. There is a Red Rock Canyon within this complex, although the overall region is defined geologically as the Keystone Fault, which exposed this dramatically rugged face. Much of it is a marbled blend of iron oxide sandstone and gray carbonate. Faulting action pushed the carbonate rocks of a primordial ocean over the sandstone of an ancient windblown desert to create this fascinating blend. Hiking trails lead into several side canyons along the cliff face, and we highlighted one of these in Chapter fourteen.

For your exploration, start at the Red Rock Canyon visitor center, where exhibits describe the action of the upthrusting Keystone Fault. Then follow the thirteen-mile scenic drive to the beautifully marbled Calico Hills and past several other points of interest and trailheads. This is a favorite route for bikers, so watch out for them as you drive.

8 SPRING MOUNTAIN RANCH STATE PARK AND OLD *NEVADA* ● *Spring Mountain Ranch State Park grounds open daily 8 to sunset; ranch house open Friday through Monday 10 to 4, closed Tuesday through Thursday; $3 entry fee. For information: Spring Mountain Ranch State Park, P.O. Box 124, Blue Diamond, NV 89004; (702) 875-4141. Old Nevada Western town open daily at 10; closing hours vary with the seasons. Adults $6.30, seniors $5.50 and kids 4 to 11, $4. For information: Old Nevada, NV 89004; (702) 875-4191.*

If you continue south from Red Rock Canyon on State Route 159, you'll encounter two attractions tucked against this rough-hewn escarpment. One is a nicely preserved ranch that had several famous owners; the other is a rather tacky Western style town.

Spring Mountain Ranch State Park shelters an oasis once owned—but never visited by—the reclusive Howard Hughes, who at the time was installed in the high roller suites of the Desert Inn. Views of the cliff face from here are awesome. The ranch began as a homestead in 1876, then it became a retreat for notables, including Chester Lauck, the "Lum" of *Lum and Abner*, and later German actress Vera Krupp. Hughes purchased it in 1967 as a retreat for his Summa Corporation executives and it was sold to the state in 1972. The ranch house is handsomely furnished to the rustic style of its wealthy former owners.

Bonnie Springs is another historic ranch and a former way station on the Spanish Trail, although little survives of the original. It has been gimmicked with a pretend Western town called Old Nevada, offering cowboy curio shops, a kids' petting zoo, shootouts and hangin's. The place could use a tad of paint here and a few nails there. Its best attractions are a pleasingly rustic restaurant filled with Western regalia, and a bar festooned with neckties surrendered by dudes foolish enough to arrive in city duds. An adjacent motel has attractive rooms with simple Western decor.

9 PAHRUMP VALLEY TO DEATH VALLEY JUNCTION •
The complete loop to Death Valley Junction and back to Las Vegas covers around 200 miles.

We begin by pointing out that there's nothing pretty about the Pahrump Valley; this unplanned sprawl of housing tracts and strip malls is as unattractive as its name. However the drive over Mountain Springs Summit into the valley is appealing. Further, you can visit Nevada's only winery and its very charming restaurant. And if you wish to push on to Death Valley Junction in California, you can visit Amargosa Opera House, kept alive by the determination of a former Broadway dancer. If your timing's right, you can watch her perform. You also can visit some legal brothels since the Pahrump Valley is in Nye County, if that sort of thing appeals to you.

To do all or part of this, continue south from Bonnie Springs on State Route 159, pick up Highway 160 and follow it into Pahrump Valley. If you're starting from Las Vegas, head south on I-15 nine miles to exit 33 and take 160 west. Either approach will take you a mile into the sky on a scenic, curving climb over Mountain Springs Summit. You'll pass the scalloped face of Potosi Mountain, which figures into Glitter City's early history. Shortly after Mormons built a fort there in 1855, lead was discovered in Potosi's cliff faces, and the settlers began a mining venture. It never was profitable and the mines soon were abandoned.

From 5,490-foot Mountain Springs Summit, you'll begin a quick spiral down into the Pahrump Valley, a former alfalfa and cotton growing area that now sprouts doublewides and budget-priced subdivisions. The name is Paiute for "plenty of water" or "water on a flat rock," referring to springs in the area.

If Pahrump is drab, its recent history isn't. In 1976, citizens of this still-innocent little farming town threw a fifteen dollar fit when Walter Plankinton opened the Chicken Ranch brothel. The original Chicken Ranch, so-named because its patrons were so poor that they traded poultry for copulation, thrived in Texas for 140 years. It was the basis for the musical, *The Best Little Whorehouse in Texas.* When it became the first little whorehouse in the Pahrump Valley, citizens fought mightily and unsuccessfully to get rid of it. The resulting mayhem and political intrigue was chronicled in *The Nye County Brothel Wars,* a briefly popular book by Jeannie Kasindorf.

As you cruise through the haphazard scatter that is Pahrump's suburbs, watch on your right for a sign to Pahrump Valley Winery, up Winery Road. It's open daily 10 to 4:30 with tasting, sales, a gift shop and a fine restaurant serving American and continental fare. Overall, the food is better than the wine, since the Pahrump Valley isn't exactly a vintner's eden. However, through careful viticulture and the use of some grapes trucked in from California, the winery has won a few medals in tasting competitions.

Pressing on through town, you'll pass the small business district and the cowboy-style Saddle West Casino. You can shorten this loop tour by staying on Highway 160, which continues north to U.S. Highway 95, passing the turnoff to Crystal, a town comprised of a quartet of cathouses. This is the destination of many horny high rollers from Las Vegas, who come by limo and even by private plane, since Crystal has a landing field.

If you want to take the longer route home and check out the Amargosa Opera House, turn left from the north end of Pahrump at a sign indicating "Ash Meadows Wildlife Area" and "Death Valley Junction." This unnamed route climbs quickly into desert hills and enters California seven miles from the tiny town of Death Valley Junction.

From borax to ballet

Here, at the cute little Amargosa Opera House, former Broadway dancer Marta Becket has been performing ballet pantomimes since 1967. Her shows are Saturday and Monday at 7:45 p.m. in November, February, March and April; and Saturdays only the rest of the year. For information: P.O. Box 8, Death Valley Junction, CA 92328; (619) 852-4441. The "opera house" originally was a community hall, part of an attractive Spanish style plaza in this company town built by the Pacific Coast Borax Company. Becket and her former husband, passing through here in 1967, liked the old hall, refurbished it and started doing the shows. Should you want to stay and catch her act, a motel with inexpensive rooms is adjacent. Call the opera house number for reservations, and to confirm performance times.

Head north from Death Valley Junction on Highway 127, which becomes Route 373 in Nevada. As you cross back into the Silver State, you'll encounter the attractive new Victorian style Longstreet Inn and Casino, sitting right on the border and offering rooms, an RV park and the usual casino games.

From the Longstreet, you have choices. The smoother, longer Highway 373 will take you sixteen miles to the junction of U.S. 95 at Amargosa Valley. A gravel, slightly bumpy but easily passable route is more direct, taking you through the alkaline wetlands of the Ash Meadows Wildlife Management Area. The turnoff is two miles above the Longstreet Inn. The area is interesting if not pretty, with willows growing along seeping springs. Stay to the north as you drive through the wildlife area and you'll encounter a small enclave of Death Valley National Park. There isn't much to it—a small puddle in a hole among desert rocks that contains the entire population of *sytrinodon diabolis* or desert pupfish. It's fenced off and the fish are hard to see, but you can say you've been there.

The dirt road becomes smoother above the pupfish enclave and eventually delivers you through the back door of Crystal and its cathouses, and thence to State Route 160, which shortly connects to Highway 95.

10 MOUNT CHARLESTON RECREATION AREA • *Sixteen miles northwest of Las Vegas on U.S. 95 and then eighteen miles west on State Route 157. For information: Las Vegas Ranger District, Toiyabe National Forest, 550 E. Charleston Blvd., Las Vegas, NV 89014; (702) 388-6255. There's also a seasonal ranger office on the mountain.*

The crowning glory of the Spring Mountain range, Mount Charleston is the favorite retreat of Las Vegans, perhaps even more than the Valley of Fire and Red Rock Canyon. In summer, they can escape the desert heat and hike in cool pines; in winter they can ski at the small Lee Canyon Ski Area.

If you're returning from the Pahrump-Death Valley Junction loop, you can head west to the mountain on either State Route 156 or 157. A third number, 158, links the two and forms a loop through these alpine heights. The climb up the mountain is quite dramatic, taking you quickly from the dusty desert floor to ponderosa forests. Botanists dig this route, since it carries them within minutes from yucca and creosote bush through Joshua trees to a piñon-juniper woodland and finally into the pines.

Once into those pines, you can prowl the woodsy Mount Charleston Village, check out the ski area or do a bit of hiking. Maps are available at a ranger station on Highway 157 just below the village. The truly ambitious can hike all the way to the top of Mount Charleston after the winter snows melt; see Chapter fourteen. Views of the desert floor are awesome, particularly from the twelve-mile strip of Highway 158. Pause at a turnout and walk the short Desert View Trail for a grand panorama. Signs at the overlook discuss the geology, flora and fauna of the area. You'll also learn about the above-ground atomic tests that were conducted in 1957 at the Nevada Test Site, sixty-five miles away and visible from here. Folks would come up the mountain to picnic and admire the mushroom clouds. (*"There she goes, Martha! Cover the potato salad!"*)

THE TEN BEST FAR OUT CASINOS

When we say "far out," we mean farther out than next-door Henderson, since we have included this community with Las Vegas listings. What we really mean is the rest of southern Nevada, which has four casino clusters. You'll find them at Primm where northbound I-15 enters the state from California (also known as Stateline, which irritates the folks at the real Stateline, Nevada, at South Lake Tahoe); twelve miles northeast of Primm on I-15 at Jean; in Mesquite, where southbound I-15 enters the state from Arizona and Utah; and in Laughlin, at Nevada's southern tip on the Colorado River.

1 *HARRAH'S LAUGHLIN HOTEL AND CASINO* ● *2900 S. Casino Dr. (P.O. Box 33000), Laughlin, NV 89028; (800) 447-8700 or (702) 298-4600.*

Our number one selection is one of the largest, most complete and certainly most attractive casino resorts outside of Las Vegas. Originally called Harrah's Del Rio, it has a handsome Spanish colonial look inside and out, with tile roofs, pink stucco, and painted tile and wrought iron accents. Of the several riverside resorts in Laughlin, it's the only one with a sandy swimming beach, plus a pool deck just above the water. Harrah's occupies its own little cove apart from the other casinos. It isn't isolated from the rest, however; both river and street shuttles connect one casino to the other.

Harrah's features a full range of restaurants, from the elegant riverview William Fisk's Steakhouse to the attractive Spanish-style Fresh Market Square Buffet, with American, Chinese, Italian and Mexican fare at separate serving stations. Other facilities include a showroom, large video arcade and shopping arcade.

2 *BUFFALO BILL'S* ● *Primm, off I-15. Mailing address: P.O. Box 19139, Las Vegas, NV 89193; (800) FUN-STOP or (702) 382-1212.*

It's hard to miss Buffalo Bill's as you enter Nevada from California on I-15. Just look to your right for a gigantic red barn with a rollercoaster wrapped around it. Not the sort of thing you see every day. That thrill ride twists in, around and through one of the largest casino structures outside of Las Vegas. A lofty interior shelters a Western village façade, a couple of choo-choos, old mining scenes and several amusement rides, including a log ride that passes through the casino.

This is a full-scale destination resort with a large casino, inexpensive hotel rooms, major showroom that books stars such as the Moody Blues and Alabama, five restaurants and a buffet, a movie theater, shopping arcade, video arcade, swimming area and spa.

3 COLORADO BELLE • 2100 S. Casino Dr. (P.O. Box 77000), Laughlin, NV 89028; (800) 47-RIVER or (702) 298-4000.

With a little imagination, one could picture the Colorado Belle chugging up the Colorado River, and indeed, riverboats did cruise these waters before dams blocked navigation. The main casino building is a faithful if oversized replica of a turn-of-the-century side-wheeler. The riverboat theme continues inside, with Gay Nineties decor, flocked rose-colored wallpaper, polished brass and woods, beaded chandeliers and a sweeping grand staircase. Restaurants continue the theme, from the Orleans gourmet room and Mark Twain Restaurant to the Mississippi Lounge Seafood Bar and Captain's Food Fare buffet. The strolling "Riverboat Ramblers" entertain patrons on the casino floor. A microbrewery, the Boiler Room, was added to the Belle in late 1997, featuring "beer, food and entertainment."

4 DON LAUGHLIN'S RIVERSIDE HOTEL & CASINO • P.O. Box 500, Laughlin, NV 89028; (800) 227-3849 or (702) 298-2535.

Low coffered ceilings, touches of Gay Nineties decor, globe chandeliers and mirror tiles mark the oldest of the Laughlin Casinos. It was here, in a much smaller version, that Don Laughlin launched the gaming resort that became a town. It offers all of the destination resort trimmings—swimming pools, a dance hall, movie theaters, restaurants and a buffet. Laughlin's only commercial RV park is across the street, also operated by the hotel. (However, most of the town's casinos permit free overnight RV parking.)

Several antique slot machine exhibits are on display in the Riverside's casino, and a free exhibit of seventy classic cars occupies an upper floor in the large resort. Most are on loan from the Imperial Palace auto collection. They range from early 20th century horseless carriages to contemporary classics such as first-year Thunderbirds, Mustangs and a Delorean.

5 FLAMINGO HILTON LAUGHLIN • 1900 S. Casino Dr. (P.O. Box 30630), Laughlin, NV 89028; (800) 292-3711 or (702) 298-5111.

One of the largest of southern Nevada's outlying casinos, the 1,974-room Flamingo Hilton has full resort facilities, including several restaurants, tennis courts, gift shops and a large video arcade. The exterior, with its requisite Flamingo pink-tinted windows and Florida-modern design, is one of the more attractive in Laughlin. The casino is bright and spacious with high, pink coffered ceilings, beaded lighting and windows on the river. It's the only casino resort in Laughlin with a river-view buffet, the Fruit Basket.

A recent addition to the resort is the Nevada Gold Museum, with exhibits tracing the history of gaming in the state, particularly in Las Vegas and Reno. You'll find no nuggets here; the "Gold" refers to wealth brought to Nevada through legalized gaming. Displays include historic photos of Las Vegas and Reno resorts, gaming chips and antique slot machines.

6 GOLD RIVER GAMBLING HALL & RESORT • 2700 S. Casino Dr. (P.O. Box 77700), Laughlin, NV 89028; (800) 835-7904 or (702) 298-2242.

The look of Gold River is "mine shaft modern," with a towering hotel structure resembling an ore stamp mill and industrial strength decor in the gaming area. Neon signs with the names of famous Nevada mines hang from the high exposed-truss ceilings. All of this is described by the resort owners as "Gold rush era Victorian." The look carries into the attractive Opera House Buffet and several other dining venues. Particularly handsome is the Hunting Lodge Restaurant and Lounge, a log and fieldstone structure decorated with hunting trophies (a polite expression for dead wild animals). Other facilities include a bingo parlor, pool, shops and video arcade.

This complex originally was built by the Boyd Group of Las Vegas as Sam's Town Gold River. It was later sold, and the new owners have expanded and enlarged it.

7 CASABLANCA RESORT CASINO • 950 W. Mesquite Blvd., Mesquite, NV 89024; (800) 896-4567 or (702) 346-7529.

This was Merv Griffin's Players Island until mid-1997, when it was purchased by the owners of Mesquite's Virgin River Casino. The interior look is bright and cheerfully tropical, although that may change to more of a Casablanca theme, based on the classic Humphry Bogart film. Some of the gimmicks were already in place when we last checked; the main restaurants are Katherine's of CasaBlanca and the Purple Fez. The focal point of the attractive casino is a curved central bar and cabaret theater surrounded by lush foliage (mostly *faux*), with a sky canopy overhead. Out front is a large, elaborately landscaped tropical lagoon, which hopefully will be retained by the new owners.

CasaBlanca offers full resort amenities—hotel tower, several restaurants and a buffet, a showroom, gift shop, elaborate swimming complex (see page 229), full service spa, wedding chapel, eighteen-hole golf course and tennis and volleyball courts, plus an RV park.

8 RAMADA EXPRESS HOTEL-CASINO • 2121 S. Casino Dr. (Box 658), Laughlin, NV 89028; (800) AGENT-46 or (702) 298-4200.

Express, indeed. This large complex across Casino Drive from the river features a pleasing yesterday railroad look. A cute pretend steam train (diesel engine, recorded chuff-chuff) takes visitors on a one-mile loop around the complex. Inside, the main casino has the look of a railway station waiting room with a curved iron truss ceiling. Employees wear striped shirts with gartered sleeves, and railroading memorabilia abounds. Guests, who are referred to as "passengers," can eat in the Roundhouse Buffet or several railway theme restaurants, and have a libation in the Caboose Lounge. Although Ramada Express isn't on the river, its passengers can still keep cool; it has a large, shaded swimming pool and spa complex.

A recent addition to the resort—with quite a different theme—is "Back to the 1940s," a combined museum and entertainment center. It features World War II memorabilia, classic 1940s movies, jitterbug and swing dance contests and big band-style "USO shows."

9 *THE OASIS* • *1137 Mesquite Blvd. (P.O. Box 360), Mesquite, NV 89024; (800) 621-0187 or (702) 346-5232.*

This large complex, which seems to be spreading over most of downtown Mesquite, is owned by Si Redd, who made a fortune with the invention of the video gaming machine. He built the Oasis as Mesquite's first casino resort, sold it to the Peppermill corporation and then regained control of it in 1993. Redd added more rooms and a parking facility across the street, linked to the main resort by a pedestrian bridge.

The large two-level casino retains the distinctive Peppermill look—sexy blue, red and magenta lighting, accented by reflective ceilings. This large complex includes a hotel structure, gift shop, cabaret, tennis courts, two nearby golf courses, putting green, swimming pools, spas, a mini-mart and shopping arcade, kids video parlor, miniature golf and three restaurants. Its Paradise Buffet is one of the most attractive in all of Nevada, with lush tropical decor, cozy tables and booths with drop lamps. The adjacent Oasis RV Park has full hookups.

10 *WHISKEY PETE'S CASINO HOTEL* • *Primm, off I-15. Mailing address: P.O. Box 93718, Las Vegas, NV 89193; (800) 367-PETE or (702) 382-4388.*

Pete seems to have something of an identity problem, with a medieval castle façade, an old West theme inside and two 1920s gangster cars on display. Of course, this curious mix only adds to the appeal of this complex sitting on the Nevada-California border. This is the oldest of the Primm casinos, dating back to the 1950s when it was a two-pump gas station and bar. Primm's history roughly parallels that of Laughlin's; it was named for Primadonna Resorts CEO Gary Primm, who built Whiskey Pete's. Joined by the Primadonna and Buffalo Bill's, the area has grown from—we love this expression from the press kit—"a traffic capture property to a final destination resort complex."

Indeed, Pete's has all the properties of a resort—a large hotel, three restaurants and a buffet, a major showroom that has drawn the likes of Crystal Gayle and Mickey Gilley, a swimming complex and those two gangster cars. The "Bonnie and Clyde Death Car" and "Dutch Schultz/Al Capone" armored Lincoln are on display near the entrance to a monorail that links Pete's to the Primadonna across the freeway.

THE TEN BEST FAR OUT CASINO FEATURES

Many of the far out casinos have special themes or other characteristics, which provides us with an excuse to create just one more list. These appear in no particular order.

1 BEST EXTERIOR LOOK: Nevada Landing Hotel & Casino • *P.O. Box 19278, Jean, NV 89019; (800) 628-6682 or (702) 387-5000.*

At night, this steamboat-theme resort is the brightest thing between Barstow and Las Vegas, all aglitter with neon piping. Two Mississippi-style paddlewheelers ran aground a long way from water, bringing the dock with them, and thus the name: "Nevada Landing." The two riverboats flank a mock-up dock and tower. The interior of this mid-size casino has a pleasing turn-of-the-century Mississippi-Victorian theme, with five large beaded chandeliers, plush red wallpaper, brass trim and knurled ceiling beams. Nameplates and other replica regalia from famous steamboats decorate the walls.

2 BEST INTERIOR LOOK: Golden Nugget Laughlin • *2300 S. Casino Dr., Laughlin, NV 89028-7111; (800) 950-7700 or (702) 298-7111.*

Although the Golden Nugget's main gaming area is rather ordinary, with low ceilings and conventional décor, its entry is the most striking of the outlying casinos, bearing the tropical signature of owner Steve Wynn (Mirage, Treasure Island). Patrons approaching by car or by foot will pass beneath an arched *porte cochere* trimmed with 11,000 lights. Then they step into a smaller version of the famous Mirage rainforest. The Golden Nugget rendition is housed under a thirty-foot-high atrium with waterfalls and palms wrapped in orchids, creepers and other tropical flora.

The jungle theme continues with Tarzan's Bar to the right just inside the main entrance, and Jane's Grill on the left side. You'll find the third member of the famous Edgar Rice Burroughs family on the far side of the casino, at Cheetah's Pub, where patrons have a view of the river.

3 *THE BEST OVERALL THEME: Buffalo Bill's • Primm, off I-15. Mailing address: P.O. Box 19139, Las Vegas, NV 89193; (702) 382-1212; (800) FUN-STOP.*

Barnlike from the outside, Buffalo Bill's is cavernous within, fashioned as a Western frontier town, with storefront façades, early-day mining scenes and a pair of steam locomotives nestled into giant niches above the gaming area. Several large pretend trees reach into the darkness of the lofty ceiling. A log chute ride passes through the casino on an elevated stream bed. These indoor heights offer an advantage to non-smokers; fumes from puffing gamblers are dissipated into the vast inner atmosphere.

4 *THE MOST ATTRACTIVE GAMING AREA: Harrah's Laughlin Hotel & Casino • 2900 S. Casino Dr. (P.O. Box 33000), Laughlin, NV 89028; (800) 447-8700 or (702) 298-4600.*

The look of Harrah's large gambling area is Spanish California colonial, with pink stucco walls, wrought iron and painted tile accents and tiled false ceilings over the slot and table game areas. Slot and video poker players have a view of the Colorado River—a refreshing change from the normally enclosed gaming areas. Another major plus for Harrah's Laughlin—one entire casino area is smoke free.

5 *THE BEST SWIMMING OASIS: CasaBlanca Resort Casino • 950 W. Mesquite Blvd., Mesquite, NV 89024; (800) 896-4567 or (702) 346-7529.*

The CasaBlanca (formerly Players Island) swimming and recreation complex rivals most of those along the Las Vegas Strip. A large freeform pool and spa are rimmed by sundecks, contoured lawns and a pretend-rock peninsula with a water slide. Palms and bright patches of flowers accent this pleasing desert oasis. Other facilities include a pool bar, sandy volleyball court, night-lighted tennis courts and a complete health and fitness center.

6 *THE BEST SPECIAL ATTRACTION: Bonnie and Clyde Death Car at Whiskey Pete's • Primm, off I-15. Mailing address: P.O. Box 93718, Las Vegas, NV 89193; (800) 367-PETE or (702) 383-4388.*

Two gangster cars are on display at Whiskey Pete's, near the entrance to the tram that links the casino to Primadonna across the freeway. The bullet-riddled "Bonnie and Clyde death car" is the stolen Ford V-8 in which outlaws Bonnie Parker and Clyde Barrow were shot to death by lawmen near Gibsland, Louisiana, on May 23, 1934. A hundred and sixty-seven holes were counted in the car and the two fugitives were hit more than fifty times each—a classic case of overkill. A video tells the story of this notorious gangster couple. Clyde's bloody, bullet-riddled shirt, which resort officials recently purchased at auction for a sizable sum, may be on display by the time you get there. Among other exhibits are a copy of this letter written by Barrow to Henry Ford, a month before the outlaw died:

While I still have got breath in my lungs, I will tell you what a dandy car you make. I have drove Fords exclusively when I could get away with one. For sustained speed and freedom from trouble the Ford has got ever' other car skinned, and even if my business hasn't been strickly legal, it don't hurt eny thing to tell you what a fine car you got in a V-8.

Yours truly,

Clyde Champion Barrow

An adjacent 1931 armored Lincoln was used by Dutch Schultz and Al Capone during their gangster days in Chicago. The car is bullet-proof, but Schultz was gunned down by FBI agents as he fled from the vehicle. He shoulda stayed inside. Capone, who was not at that particular shootout, died in prison.

7 THE BEST FAMILY CASINO: *Harrah's Laughlin* ● *2900 S. Casino Dr. (P.O. Box 33000), Laughlin, NV 89028; (800) 447-8700 or (702) 298-4600.*

Decisions, decisions! We agonized between Buffalo Bill's with its rides and attractions and Harrah's Laughlin with its extensive facilities and riverfront setting. In the end, we decided: How many times can a family on vacation ride a rollercoaster and a log flume? Harrah's is the only casino resort in southern Nevada—in fact in all of Nevada—with a sandy beach. Kids aren't likely to get bored at the beach, playing in the sand and swimming in the river or the adjacent pool. Both Laughlin and Primm are beastly hot during the summer school vacation season—all the more reason to favor Harrah's with its extensive water sports facilities. It also has a large amusement arcade with lots of video machines and a few carnival midway games.

8 THE BEST AMUSEMENT RIDE: *Desperado roller-coaster at Buffalo Bill's* ● *Primm, off I-15. Mailing address: P.O. Box 19139, Las Vegas, NV 89193; (702) 382-1212; (800) FUN-STOP. Operates 10 a.m. to 9 p.m.; $5 per ride; combination tickets available with other attractions, including a log chute, 200-foot "Turbo Drop" and simulated motion machine.*

Hold onto your toupee, Teddy. The Desperado is billed as America's tallest and fastest rollercoaster, climbing to 209 feet and attaining speeds of ninety miles an hour. The lift takes about a minute and the initial drop takes only 3.5 seconds. After you climb to these dizzying heights, roar downward at speeds that appear to approach mach one, and then hurl into a black hole, you will believe those statistics.

9 *THE BEST BUFFET: Harrah's Laughlin* ● *2900 S. Casino Dr. (P.O. Box 33000), Laughlin, NV 89028; (800) 447-8700 or (702) 298-4600. Breakfast 7 to 11, $5.49; lunch 11 to 2, $6.49; dinner 5 to 10 Sunday-Thursday and 5 to 11 Friday-Saturday, $6.49.*

Harrah's Spanish-style Fresh Market Square is one the largest and most versatile buffets outside the Las Vegas area. It features American, Chinese, Italian and Mexican serving stations, plus a salad and fruit bar, carving station and a bakery that offers various breads and pastries. While some of the dishes suffer steam table trauma and many could use more spicing, Market Square has the best variety of the outlying buffets.

The large salad bar has the usual range of fresh veggies, plus prepared salads such as bean medley, tuna pasta, Hawaiian, Caesar and Greek. Diners can build their own fajitas and tacos at the Mexican station, while the Chinese and Italian stations offer stir fries and hot pasta dishes. Typical meat 'n' potatoes dishes, plus carved beef, turkey and ham are issued from the American section.

10 *THE BEST NEST OF INEXPENSIVE CASINO RE-SORTS: Primm* ● *For information: **Buffalo Bill's**, Mailing address: P.O. Box 19139, Las Vegas, NV 89193; (800) FUN-STOP or (702) 382-1212; **Primadonna Resort & Casino**, P.O. Box 95997, Las Vegas, NV 89193-5997, (800) 367-7383 or (702) 382-1212; **Whiskey Pete's**, P.O. Box 93718, Las Vegas, NV 89193; (800) 367-PETE or (702) 382-4388.*

We noted before that sixty percent of the visitors to Las Vegas and southern Nevada come from southern California. Some of these folks don't get much beyond the border on Interstate 15. If all they desire is a bit of inexpensive Nevada action and entertainment, that's as far as they need to go. Three casino resorts sitting right on the border, built by Gary Prim of Primadonna Resorts (for which this wide, glittery spot in the freeway is named), offer full gaming facilities, amusement rides, swimming lagoons, hotel rooms, RV parks, restaurants, buffets and other lures—some of which we've cited earlier in this chapter They are among the most inexpensive resorts in the state, with rooms for as little as $25 per couple, cheap buffets and deep discounts on restaurant food. They may be inexpensive, although these aren't cut-rate operations. Their showrooms attract top talent, usually country stars, and their hotel rooms are quite nice and comfortable.

We aren't recommending that you limit your southern Nevada visit to Primm, of course. Otherwise, why buy this book?

DOROTHY: Toto, I have a feeling we're not in Kansas anymore.
TOTO: Sweetheart, I don't think we're even on the same planet!
— **With apologies to** *The Wizard of Oz*

Chapter seventeen

QUICKLISTS
WHICH HOTELS OFFER WHAT

Obviously, not every hotel in Glitter City was mentioned in our various lists. For your convenience, we present here a complete listing of nearly every casino hotel in the area, except for a few small sawdust joints. The list includes those mentioned elsewhere in this book. These are all casino hotels, large and small, with full gaming facilities, restaurants and rooms. The resorts' other lures appear after each listing. In the second part of this chapter, we list hotel facilities by subject.

Aladdin Hotel & Casino, *3667 S. Las Vegas Blvd., Las Vegas, NV 89109; (800) 634-3424 or (702) 736-0111* ● Beauty salon, bingo parlor, buffet, convention facilities and meeting rooms, lounge entertainment, shops, showroom, swimming pool, tennis/racquetball, video arcade.

Arizona Charlie's, *740 S. Decatur Blvd., Las Vegas, NV 89107; (800) 342-2695 or (702) 258-5200* ● Bingo parlor, buffet, convention facilities and meeting rooms, lounge entertainment, showroom, swimming pool.

Bally's Las Vegas, 3645 S. Las Vegas Blvd., Las Vegas, NV 89109; (800) 634-3434 or (702) 739-4111 ● Monorail to MGM Grand, beauty salon, buffet, convention facilities and meeting rooms, health club/spa, lounge entertainment, shops, showroom, swimming pool, tennis/racquetball, video arcade, wedding chapel.

Barbary Coast, 3695 S. Las Vegas Blvd., Las Vegas, NV 89109; (888) BARBARY or (702) 737-7111 ● Lounge shows, video arcade.

Binion's Horseshoe, 128 E. Fremont St., Las Vegas, NV 89101; (800) 237-6537 or (702) 382-1600 ● Currency display, bingo, buffet.

Boomtown Hotel, Casino & RV Resort, 333 Blue Diamond Rd., Las Vegas, NV 89139; (800) 588-7711 or (702) 263-7777 ● Buffet, dance hall, lounge entertainment, meeting rooms, RV park, shops, showroom, swimming pool, video arcade.

Boulder Station Hotel & Casino, 4111 Boulder Highway, Las Vegas, NV 89121; (800) 683-7777 or (702) 432-7777 ● Bingo parlor, buffet, lounge entertainment, movie theater, shops, showroom, swimming pool, video arcade.

Bourbon Street Hotel & Casino, 120 E. Flamingo Rd., Las Vegas, NV 89109; (800) 634-6956, (702) 737-7200 ● Lounge entertainment.

Caesars Palace, 3570 S. Las Vegas Blvd., Las Vegas, NV 89109; (800) 634-6661 or (702) 731-7110 ● Caesars World, Caesars Magical Empire, motion simulator rides, Festival Fountain Show, beauty salon, buffet, convention facilities and meeting rooms, dance floor (Cleopatra's Barge), health club/spa, lounge entertainment, Omnimax movie theater, shopping arcades, showroom, swimming complex, video arcades, wedding chapel.

California Hotel & Casino, 12 Ogden Ave., Las Vegas, NV 89101; (800) 632-6255 or (702) 385-1222 ● Lounge entertainment, shops, video arcade.

Casino Royale, 3411 S. Las Vegas Blvd., Las Vegas, NV 89109; (800) 854-7666 or (702) 737-3500 ● Lounge entertainment.

Circus Circus, 2880 S. Las Vegas Blvd., Las Vegas, NV 89109; (800) 634-3450 or (702) 734-0410 ● Grand Slam Canyon amusement park, carnival midway, circus acts, beauty salon, buffet, lounge entertainment, RV park, swimming pools, video arcades, wedding chapel.

Debbie Reynolds Hollywood Hotel, 305 Convention Center Dr., Las Vegas, NV 89109; (800) 633-1777 or (702) 734-0711 ● Movie museum, Sunday brunch, lounge shows, meeting rooms, showroom.

Desert Inn, 3145 S. Las Vegas Blvd., Las Vegas, NV 89109; (800) 634-6906 or (702) 733-4444 ● Beauty salon, convention facilities and meeting rooms, health club/spa, golf course, lounge entertainment, shops, showroom, swimming complex, tennis/racquetball.

El Cortez Hotel & Casino, *600 E. Fremont St., Las Vegas, NV 89101; (800) 634-6703 or (702) 385-5200* ● Beauty salon, meeting rooms, video arcade.

Excalibur, *3850 S. Las Vegas Blvd., Las Vegas, NV 89109; (800) 937-7777 or (702) 597-7777* ● Carnival midway, King Arthur tournament, Lipizzaner stallions, beauty salon, buffet, lounge entertainment, shopping arcade, showroom, swimming pool, video arcade.

Fiesta Hotel Casino, *2400 N. Rancho Dr., Las Vegas, NV 89130; (800) 731-7333 or (702) 631-7000* ● Bingo parlor, buffet, dance floor, lounge entertainment, meeting rooms, showroom, swimming pool, video arcade.

Fitzgerald's Casino Hotel, *301 E. Fremont St., Las Vegas, NV 89101; (800) 274-LUCK or (702) 388-2400* ● Buffet, lounge entertainment, meeting rooms.

Flamingo Hilton, *3555 S. Las Vegas Blvd., Las Vegas, NV 89109; (800) 732-2111 or (702) 733-3111* ● Beauty salon, buffet, convention facilities and meeting rooms, health club/spa, lounge entertainment, shopping arcade, showroom, swimming complex, tennis/racquetball, video arcade, wedding chapel.

Four Queens Hotel & Casino, *202 E. Fremont St., Las Vegas, NV 89101; (800) 634-6045 or (702) 385-4011* ● Convention facilities and meeting rooms, lounge entertainment, video arcade.

Fremont Hotel & Casino, *200 E. Fremont St., Las Vegas, NV 89101; (800) 634-6182 or (702) 385-3232* ● Buffet, meeting rooms.

Frontier Hotel & Gambling Hall, *3120 S. Las Vegas Blvd., Las Vegas, NV 89109; (800) 421-7806 or (702) 794-8200* ● Beauty salon, buffet, lounge entertainment, shops, swimming complex, tennis/racquetball, video arcade.

Gold Coast Hotel & Casino, *4000 W. Flamingo Rd., Las Vegas, NV 89103; (800) 402-6278 or (702) 367-7111* ● Beauty salon, bingo parlor, buffet, convention facilities and meeting rooms, dance floor, lounge entertainment, movie theater, swimming pool, video arcade.

Gold Spike Casino, *400 E. Ogden Ave., Las Vegas, NV 89101; (800) 634-6703 or (702) 384-8444* ● Bingo parlor.

Golden Gate Casino Hotel, *One E. Fremont St., Las Vegas, NV 89101; (800) 426-1906 or (702) 382-6300* ● Piano bar

Golden Nugget, *129 E. Fremont St., Las Vegas, NV 89101; (800) 634-3454 or (702) 385-7111* ● Gold nugget display, beauty salon, buffet, health club/spa, lounge entertainment, meeting rooms, shops, showroom, swimming pool, video arcade.

Hard Rock Hotel & Casino, *4455 Paradise Rd., Las Vegas, NV 89109; (800) HRD-ROCK or (702) 693-5000* ● Rock star memorabilia, beauty salon, health club/spa, lounge entertainment, meeting rooms, shops, showroom, swimming complex, video arcade.

Harrah's Las Vegas, 3475 S. Las Vegas Blvd., Las Vegas, NV 89109; (800) HARRAHS or (702) 369-5000 ● Beauty salon, buffet, convention facilities and meeting rooms, health club/spa, lounge entertainment, shopping arcade, showroom, pool, video arcade.

Holiday Inn Boardwalk, 3750 S. Las Vegas Blvd., Las Vegas, NV 89109; (800) HOLIDAY or (702) 735-2400 ● Buffet, lounge entertainment, meeting rooms, shops, showroom, pool, video arcade.

Imperial Palace, 3535 S. Las Vegas Blvd., Las Vegas, NV 89109; (800) 634-6441 or (702) 731-3311 ● Classic car collection, beauty salon, buffet, convention facilities and meeting rooms, health club/spa, lounge entertainment, shops, showroom, swimming pool, video arcade, wedding chapel.

Jackie Gaughan's Plaza, One Main St., Las Vegas, NV 89101; (800) 634-6575 or (702) 386-2110 ● Greyhound station, beauty salon, convention facilities and meeting rooms, health club/spa, lounge entertainment, showroom, swimming pool, tennis/racquetball, video arcade, wedding chapel.

Lady Luck Casino Hotel, 206 N. Third St., Las Vegas, NV 89101; (800) 523-9582 or (702) 477-3000 ● Buffet, lounge entertainment, showroom, swimming pool.

Las Vegas Club, 18 E. Fremont St., Las Vegas, NV 89101; (800) 634-6532 or (702) 385-1664 ● Sports memorabilia collection, lounge entertainment, meeting rooms.

Las Vegas Hilton, 3000 Paradise Rd., Las Vegas, NV 89109; (800) 732-7117 or (702) 732-5111 ● "Star Trek" adventure, Elvis Presley exhibit, beauty salon, buffet, convention facilities/meeting rooms, dancing (The NightClub), golf course, health spa, lounge shows, shopping arcade, showrooms, pools, tennis/racquetball, video arcade.

Luxor Hotel & Casino, 3900 S. Las Vegas Blvd., Las Vegas, NV 89109; (800) 288-1000 or (702) 262-4000 ● Motion simulator ride, King Tut Museum, beauty salon, buffet, convention facilities and meeting rooms, health club/spa, lounge entertainment, IMAX theater, shopping arcade, showroom, swimming pools, video arcades.

Main Street station, 200 Main Street (between Ogden and Stewart); (800) 713-8933 or (702) 387-1896 ● Buffet, lounge entertainment, micro-brewery/restaurant.

Maxim Casino Hotel, 160 E. Flamingo Rd., Las Vegas, NV 89109; (800) 634-6987 or (702) 731 4300 ● Beauty salon, buffet, lounge entertainment, shops, showroom, swimming pool, video arcade.

MGM Grand, 3799 S. Las Vegas Blvd., Las Vegas, NV 89109; (800) 929-1111 or (702) 891-1111 ● MGM Grand Adventure theme park, monorail to Bally's, Emerald City Walk, beauty salon, buffet, convention facilities and meeting rooms, health club/spa, lounge shows, shopping arcades, showroom, pool, tennis/racquetball, video arcades.

The Mirage, 3400 S. Las Vegas Blvd., Las Vegas, NV 89109; (800) 627-6667 or (702) 791-7111 • Tram ride to Treasure Island, dolphins and animal habitat, white tiger exhibit, volcano, indoor rainforest, beauty salon, buffet, convention facilities and meeting rooms, dance floor (Lagoon Saloon), health club/spa, lounge entertainment, shopping arcade, showroom, swimming complex, video arcade.

Monte Carlo, 3770 S. Las Vegas Blvd., Las Vegas, NV 89109; (800) 311-8999 or (702) 730-7777 • Beauty salon, bingo parlor, buffet, convention facilities and meeting rooms, health club/spa, lounge entertainment, shopping arcade, showroom, swimming complex, tennis/racquetball, video arcade, wedding chapel.

Nevada Palace, 5255 Boulder Hwy., Las Vegas, NV 89122; (800) 634-6283 or (702) 458-8810 • Buffet, meeting rooms, RV park, swimming pool, video arcade.

New York New York, 3790 S. Las Vegas Blvd., Las Vegas, NV 89109; (800) NY-FORME or (702) 740-6969 • Rollercoaster, carnival midway, beauty salon, convention facilities and meeting rooms, health club/spa, lounge entertainment, shops, showroom, swimming complex, video arcade, wedding chapel.

Orleans Hotel & Casino, 4500 W. Tropicana Ave., Las Vegas, NV 89103, (800) ORLEANS or (702) 365-7111 • Beauty salon, bowling alley, buffet, convention facilities and meeting rooms, lounge entertainment, shops, showroom, swimming pool, video arcade, wedding chapel.

Palace Station Hotel & Casino, 2411 W. Sahara Ave., Las Vegas, NV 89102; (800) 634-3101 or (702) 367-2411 • Beauty salon, bingo parlor, buffet, convention facilities and meeting rooms, lounge entertainment, swimming pool, video arcade.

Rio Suite Hotel & Casino, 3700 W. Flamingo Rd., Las Vegas, NV 89103; (800) PLAYRIO or (702) 252-7777 • Mardi Gras-style "Show in the Sky," beauty salon, buffet, convention facilities and meeting rooms, health club/spa, lounge entertainment, shopping arcade, showroom, swimming pools, video arcade.

Riviera Hotel, 2901 S. Las Vegas Blvd., Las Vegas, NV 89109; (800) 634-6753 or (702) 734-5110 • Beauty salon, buffet, convention facilities and meeting rooms, health club/spa, lounge entertainment, shopping arcade, showroom, swimming complex, tennis/racquetball, video arcade, wedding chapel.

Sahara Hotel & Casino, 2535 S. Las Vegas Blvd., Las Vegas, NV 89109; (800) 634-6666 or (702) 737-2111 • Beauty salon, buffet, convention facilities and meeting rooms, lounge entertainment, shops, showroom, swimming complex, video arcade, wedding chapel.

Sam's Town Hotel, 5111 Boulder Hwy., Las Vegas, NV 89122; (800) 634-6371 or (702) 456-7777 • Mystic Falls Park show, bingo, bowling alley, buffet, convention facilities and meeting rooms, dancing, lounge shows, RV park, shops, showroom, pool, video arcade.

San Remo Hotel, *115 E. Tropicana Ave., Las Vegas, NV 89109; (800) 522-7366 or (702) 739-9000* ● Buffet, convention facilities and meeting rooms, lounge entertainment, showroom, pool, video arcade.

Santa Fe Hotel & Casino, *4949 N. Rancho Dr., Las Vegas, NV 89130; (800) 872-6823 or (702) 658-4900* ● Ice skating rink, bingo parlor, bowling alley, buffet, convention facilities and meeting rooms, lounge entertainment, shops, video arcade.

Showboat Hotel, *2800 E. Fremont St., Las Vegas, NV 89104; (800) 826-2800 or (702) 385-9123* ● Beauty salon, bowling alley, buffet, convention facilities and meeting rooms, lounge entertainment, RV park, swimming pool, video arcade.

Stardust Hotel, *3000 S. Las Vegas Blvd., Las Vegas, NV 89109; (800) 824-6033 or (702) 732-6111* ● Beauty salon, buffet, convention facilities and meeting rooms, health club/spa, lounge entertainment, shops, showroom, swimming complex, video arcade.

The Stratosphere, *2000 S. Las Vegas Blvd., Las Vegas, NV 89104; (800) 99-TOWER or (702) 380-7777* ● Rollercoaster, free-fall ride, observation tower, revolving restaurant and bar, buffet, lounge entertainment, meeting rooms, shopping arcade, showroom, swimming pool, video arcade, wedding chapel.

Sunset Station Hotel-Casino, *1301 W. Sunset Rd., Henderson, NV 89014; (888) SUNSET-9 or (702) 547-7777* ● Buffet, lounge entertainment, meeting rooms, movie theater, shops, showroom, swimming pool, video arcade.

Texas Station Gambling Hall, *3140 N. Rancho Dr., Las Vegas, NV 89015; (800) 654-8888 or (702) 631-1000* ● Bingo parlor, buffet, lounge entertainment, movie theater, swimming pool, video arcade.

Treasure Island at the Mirage, *3300 S. Las Vegas Blvd., Las Vegas, NV 89109; (800) 944-7444 or (702) 894-7111* ● Carnival midway, tram ride to the mirage, pirate ship battle, beauty salon, buffet, convention facilities and meeting rooms, health spa, lounge shows, shopping arcade, showroom, pool, video arcade, wedding chapel.

Tropicana Resort & Casino, *3801 S. Las Vegas Blvd., Las Vegas, NV 89109; (800) 634-4000 or (702) 739-2222* ● Wildlife Walk animal exhibit, beauty salon, buffet, convention facilities and meeting rooms, health club/spa, lounge entertainment, shops, showroom, swimming complex, video arcade, wedding chapel.

Vacation Village, *6711 S. Las Vegas Blvd., Las Vegas, NV 89119; (800) 338-0608 or (702) 897-1700* ● Beauty salon, buffet, lounge entertainment, meeting rooms, showroom, swimming pool, video arcade.

Westward Ho, *2900 S. Las Vegas Blvd., Las Vegas, NV 89109; (800) 634-6803 or (702) 731-2900* ● Buffet, lounge entertainment, meeting rooms, showroom, swimming pool.

Resort facilities by type

Amusement parks, rides, carnival midways

Bally's Las Vegas (monorail to MGM Grand)

Caesars Palace (motion simulator)

Circus Circus (Grand Slam Canyon; carnival midway)

Excalibur (motion simulator ride; midway)

Luxor Hotel & Casino (motion simulator ride)

MGM Grand (MGM Grand Adventure Park; monorail to Bally's)

Mirage (tram to Treasure Island)

New York New York (rollercoaster; carnival midway)

The Stratosphere (rollercoaster, free-fall ride)

Treasure Island (carnival midway; tram ride to the Mirage)

Attractions or exhibits

Binion's Horseshoe (million dollar currency display)

Caesars Palace (Caesars World, Festival Fountain Show)

Circus Circus (circus acts, carnival midway)

Debbie Reynolds Hollywood Hotel (movie museum & show)

Excalibur (King Arthur Tournament, Royal Lipizzaner stallions)

Golden Nugget (world's largest nugget display)

Hard Rock Hotel & Casino (rock star memorabilia displays)

Imperial Palace (car collection)

Las Vegas Club (sports memorabilia collection)

Las Vegas Hilton ("Star Trek" adventure, Elvis Presley exhibit)

Luxor Hotel & Casino (King Tut Museum, IMAX 3-D theater)

MGM Grand (Emerald City walk)

The Mirage (dolphins and animal habitat, white tiger exhibit, volcano, indoor rainforest)

Rio Suite Hotel & Casino (Mardi Gras "Show in the Sky")

Sam's Town Hotel (Mystic Falls park with water & laser show)

Santa Fe Hotel & Casino (ice skating rink)

Stratosphere (observation tower with rollercoaster, free-fall ride and revolving restaurant)

Treasure Island (pirate battle)

Tropicana Resort & Casino (Wildlife Walk animal exhibits)

Beauty salons

Aladdin Hotel & Casino
Bally's Las Vegas
Caesars Palace
Circus Circus Hotel Casino
Desert Inn
El Cortez Hotel & Casino
Excalibur Hotel & Casino
Flamingo Hilton
Frontier Hotel & Gambling Hall
Gold Coast Hotel & Casino
Golden Nugget Hotel & Casino
Hard Rock Hotel & Casino
Harrah's Las Vegas
Imperial Palace
Jackie Gaughan's Plaza
Las Vegas Hilton
Luxor Hotel & Casino
Maxim Casino Hotel
MGM Grand
The Mirage
Monte Carlo
New York New York
Orleans Hotel & Casino
Palace Station Hotel & Casino
Rio Suite Hotel & Casino
Riviera Hotel

Sahara Hotel & Casino
Showboat Hotel
Stardust Hotel
Treasure Island at the Mirage
Tropicana Resort & Casino
Vacation Village

Bingo parlors

Aladdin Hotel & Casino
Arizona Charlie's
Binion's Horseshoe
Boulder Station Hotel & Casino
Fiesta Hotel Casino
Gold Coast Hotel & Casino
Gold Spike Casino
Monte Carlo
Palace Station Hotel & Casino
Sam's Town Hotel
Santa Fe Hotel & Casino
Texas Station Gambling Hall

Bowling alleys

Gold Coast Hotel & Casino
Orleans Hotel & Casino
Sam's Town Hotel
Santa Fe Hotel & Casino
Showboat Hotel

Buffets/brunches

Aladdin Hotel & Casino
Arizona Charlie's
Bally's Las Vegas
Binion's Horseshoe
Boomtown Hotel
Boulder Station Hotel & Casino
  (buffet & midnight buffet)
Caesars Palace
Circus Circus Hotel Casino
Debbie Reynolds Hollywood Hotel
  (Sunday brunch)
Excalibur Hotel & Casino
Fiesta Hotel Casino
Fitzgeralds Casino Hotel
Flamingo Hilton
Fremont Hotel & Casino
Frontier Hotel & Gambling Hall
Gold Coast Hotel & Casino
Golden Nugget Hotel & Casino
Harrah's Las Vegas

Holiday Inn Boardwalk
Imperial Palace
Lady Luck Casino Hotel
Las Vegas Hilton
Luxor Hotel & Casino
Main Street Station
Maxim Casino Hotel
MGM Grand
The Mirage
Monte Carlo
Nevada Palace
Orleans Hotel & Casino
Palace Station Hotel & Casino
Rio Suite Hotel & Casino
Riviera Hotel
Sahara Hotel & Casino
Sam's Town Hotel
San Remo Hotel
Santa Fe Hotel & Casino
Showboat Hotel
Stardust Hotel
The Stratosphere
Sunset Station
Texas Station Gambling Hall
Treasure Island at the Mirage
Tropicana Resort & Casino
Vacation Village
Westward Ho

Convention facilities

Aladdin Hotel & Casino
Arizona Charlie's
Bally's Las Vegas
Caesars Palace
Desert Inn
Flamingo Hilton
Four Queens Hotel & Casino
Gold Coast Hotel & Casino
Harrah's Las Vegas
Howard Johnson Hotel & Casino
Imperial Palace
Jackie Gaughan's Plaza
Las Vegas Hilton
Luxor Hotel & Casino
MGM Grand
The Mirage
Monte Carlo
New York New York
Orleans Hotel & Casino

Palace Station Hotel & Casino
Rio Suite Hotel & Casino
Riviera Hotel
Sahara Hotel & Casino
Sam's Town Hotel
San Remo Hotel
Santa Fe Hotel & Casino
Showboat Hotel
Stardust Hotel
Treasure Island at the Mirage
Tropicana Resort & Casino

Dancing

Boomtown Hotel, Casino & RV
  Resort (Rattlesnake Saloon)
Caesars Palace (Cleopatra Barge)
Fiesta Hotel (Western dance hall)
Gold Coast Hotel (dance floor)
Las Vegas Hilton (The NightClub)
The Mirage (Lagoon Saloon)
Sam's Town (Western dance hall)

Golf courses

Desert Inn
Las Vegas Hilton

Health clubs or spas

Bally's Las Vegas
Caesars Palace
Desert Inn
Flamingo Hilton
Golden Nugget Hotel & Casino
Hard Rock Hotel & Casino
Harrah's Las Vegas
Imperial Palace
Jackie Gaughan's Plaza
Las Vegas Hilton
Luxor Hotel & Casino
MGM Grand
The Mirage
Monte Carlo
New York New York
Rio Suite Hotel & Casino
Riviera Hotel
Stardust Hotel
Treasure Island at the Mirage
Tropicana Resort & Casino

Lounge entertainment

Aladdin Hotel & Casino
Arizona Charlie's
Bally's Las Vegas
Barbary Coast
Boomtown Hotel
Boulder Station Hotel & Casino
Bourbon Street Hotel & Casino
Caesars Palace
California Hotel & Casino
Circus Circus Hotel Casino
Debbie Reynolds Hollywood Hotel
Desert Inn
Excalibur Hotel & Casino
Fiesta Hotel Casino
Fitzgeralds Casino Hotel
Frontier Hotel & Gambling Hall
Flamingo Hilton
Four Queens Hotel & Casino
Gold Coast Hotel & Casino
Golden Gate Casino hotel
Golden Nugget Hotel & Casino
Hard Rock Hotel & Casino
Harrah's Las Vegas
Holiday Inn Boardwalk
Howard Johnson Hotel & Casino
Imperial Palace
Jackie Gaughan's Plaza
Lady Luck Casino Hotel
Las Vegas Club
Las Vegas Hilton
Luxor Hotel & Casino
Main Street Station
Maxim Casino Hotel
MGM Grand
The Mirage
Monte Carlo
New York New York
Orleans Hotel & Casino
Palace Station Hotel & Casino
Rio Suite Hotel & Casino
Riviera Hotel
Sahara Hotel & Casino
Sam's Town Hotel
San Remo Hotel
Santa Fe Hotel & Casino
Showboat Hotel
Stardust Hotel
The Stratosphere

The Stratosphere
Sunset Station
Texas Station Gambling Hall
Treasure Island at the Mirage
Tropicana Resort & Casino
Vacation Village
Westward Ho

Meeting rooms

Aladdin Hotel & Casino
Arizona Charlie's
Bally's Las Vegas
Boomtown Hotel
Caesars Palace
Debbie Reynolds Hollywood Hotel
Desert Inn
Fiesta Hotel Casino
Fitzgeralds Casino Hotel
Flamingo Hilton
Four Queens Hotel & Casino
Fremont Hotel & Casino
Gold Coast Hotel & Casino
Golden Nugget Hotel & Casino
Hard Rock Hotel & Casino
Harrah's Las Vegas
Holiday Inn Boardwalk
Howard Johnson Hotel & Casino
Imperial Palace
Jackie Gaughan's Plaza
Luxor Hotel & Casino
MGM Grand
The Mirage
Monte Carlo
Nevada Palace
New York New York
Orleans Hotel & Casino
Palace Station Hotel & Casino
Rio Suite Hotel & Casino
Riviera Hotel
Sahara Hotel & Casino
Sam's Town Hotel
San Remo Hotel
Santa Fe Hotel & Casino
Stardust Hotel
Showboat Hotel
The Stratosphere
Sunset Station
Treasure Island at the Mirage
Tropicana Resort & Casino

Movie theaters

Boulder Station Hotel & Casino
Caesars Palace (Omnimax)
Gold Coast Hotel & Casino
Luxor Hotel & Casino (IMAX 3-D)
Sunset Station
Texas Station Gambling Hall

Rec vehicle parks

Boomtown Hotel
Circus Circus Hotel Casino
Nevada Palace
Sam's Town Hotel
Showboat Hotel

Shops or shopping arcades

Aladdin Hotel & Casino
Bally's Las Vegas
Boomtown Hotel
Boulder Station Hotel & Casino
Caesars Palace
California Hotel & Casino
Circus Circus Hotel Casino
Desert Inn
Excalibur Hotel & Casino
Flamingo Hilton
Frontier Hotel & Gambling Hall
Golden Nugget Hotel & Casino
Hard Rock Hotel & Casino
Harrah's Las Vegas
Holiday Inn Boardwalk
Imperial Palace
Las Vegas Hilton
Luxor Hotel & Casino
Maxim Casino Hotel
MGM Grand
The Mirage
Monte Carlo
New York New York
Orleans Hotel & Casino
Rio Suite Hotel & Casino
Riviera Hotel
Sahara Hotel & Casino
Sam's Town Hotel
Santa Fe Hotel & Casino
Stardust Hotel
The Stratosphere
Sunset Station

Treasure Island at the Mirage
Tropicana Resort & Casino

Showrooms

Aladdin Hotel & Casino
Arizona Charlie's
Bally's Las Vegas
Boomtown Hotel
Boulder Station Hotel & Casino
Caesars Palace
Debbie Reynolds Hollywood Hotel
Desert Inn
Excalibur Hotel & Casino
Fiesta Hotel Casino
Flamingo Hilton
Golden Nugget Hotel & Casino
Hard Rock Hotel & Casino
Harrah's Las Vegas
Holiday Inn Boardwalk
Howard Johnson Hotel & Casino
Imperial Palace
Jackie Gaughan's Plaza
Lady Luck Casino Hotel
Las Vegas Hilton
Luxor Hotel & Casino
Maxim Casino Hotel
MGM Grand
The Mirage
Monte Carlo
New York New York
Orleans Hotel & Casino
Rio Suite Hotel & Casino
Riviera Hotel
Sahara Hotel & Casino
Sam's Town
San Remo Hotel
Stardust Hotel
The Stratosphere
Sunset Station
Treasure Island at the Mirage
Tropicana Resort & Casino
Vacation Village

Swimming pools

Aladdin Hotel & Casino
Arizona Charlie's
Bally's Las Vegas
Boomtown Hotel
Boulder Station Hotel & Casino
Caesars Palace

Circus Circus Hotel Casino
Desert Inn
Excalibur Hotel & Casino
Fiesta Hotel Casino
Flamingo Hilton
Frontier Hotel & Gambling Hall
Gold Coast Hotel & Casino
Golden Nugget Hotel & Casino
Hard Rock Hotel & Casino
Harrah's Las Vegas
Holiday Inn Boardwalk
Howard Johnson Hotel & Casino
Imperial Palace
Jackie Gaughan's Plaza
Lady Luck Casino Hotel
Las Vegas Hilton
Luxor Hotel & Casino
Maxim Casino Hotel
MGM Grand
The Mirage
Monte Carlo
Nevada Palace
New York New York
Orleans Hotel & Casino
Palace Station Hotel Casino
Rio Suite Hotel & Casino
Riviera Hotel
Sahara Hotel & Casino
Sam's Town Hotel
San Remo Hotel
Showboat Hotel
Stardust Hotel
The Stratosphere
Sunset Station
Texas Station Gambling
Treasure Island at the Mirage
Tropicana Resort & Casino
Vacation Village
Westward Ho

Tennis or racquetball

Aladdin Hotel & Casino
Desert Inn
Bally's Las Vegas
Flamingo Hilton
Frontier Hotel & Gambling Hall
Jackie Gaughan's Plaza
Las Vegas Hilton
MGM Grand

Monte Carlo
Riviera Hotel

Video arcades

Aladdin Hotel & Casino
Bally's Las Vegas
Barbary Coast
Boomtown Hotel
Boulder Station Hotel & Casino
Caesars Palace
California Hotel & Casino
Circus Circus Hotel Casino
El Cortez Hotel & Casino
Excalibur Hotel & Casino
Fiesta Hotel Casino
Flamingo Hilton
Four Queens Hotel & Casino
Frontier Hotel & Gambling Hall
Gold Coast Hotel & Casino
Golden Nugget Hotel & Casino
Hard Rock Hotel & Casino
Harrah's Las Vegas
Holiday Inn Boardwalk
Howard Johnson Hotel & Casino
Imperial Palace
Jackie Gaughan's Plaza
Las Vegas Hilton
Luxor Hotel & Casino
Maxim Casino Hotel
MGM Grand
The Mirage
Monte Carlo
Nevada Palace

New York New York
Orleans Hotel & Casino
Palace Station Hotel & Casino
Rio Suite Hotel & Casino
Riviera Hotel
Sahara Hotel & Casino
Sam's Town Hotel
San Remo Hotel
Santa Fe Hotel & Casino
Stardust Hotel
Showboat Hotel
The Stratosphere
Sunset Station
Texas Station Gambling Hall
Treasure Island at the Mirage
Tropicana Resort & Casino
Vacation Village

Wedding chapels

Bally's Las Vegas
Caesars Palace
Circus Circus
Flamingo Hilton
Imperial Palace
Jackie Gaughan's Plaza
Monte Carlo
New York New York
Orleans Hotel & Casino
Riviera Hotel
Sahara Hotel & Casino
The Stratosphere
Treasure Island at the Mirage
Tropicana Resort & Casino

The public is the only critic whose opinion is worth anything at all.

— Mark Twain

Chapter eighteen

READERS' FORUM

AND NOW, IT'S YOUR TURN

Now that you've learned all about Glitter City and its attractions, we'd like your input. We invite you to submit your own list of what's best in Las Vegas, using the form that follows. (You can photocopy these pages or write your selections on a piece of paper, if you don't want to dismember the book.) Of course, we don't expect you to come up a nomination in each category. Any and all entries will be welcomed. You can choose some of the same selections that we have, or you can dare to disagree.

All who send us a reasonable number of nominations will earn the right to buy one or more of our other books at a thirty percent discount, and we'll pay the shipping. What's a reasonable number of nominations? We'd like at least ten. Then make your book selection from the list in the back of this book and send the order form (or a facsimile of it), along with a check.

NOTE: There's absolutely no obligation to buy a book to in order to participate in our readers' poll. We welcome your nominations anyway, and you don't have to make fifteen or more choices. All selections will be compiled and presented in a special "Readers' Choice" chapter in the next edition of this book.

READERS' SURVEY FORM

THE BEST CASINO RESORT _____

THE BEST GAMING AREA _____

THE BEST OUTLYING CASINO _____

THE BEST CASINO SWIMMING AREA _____

THE BEST CASINO RESTAURANT_____

THE BEST NON-CASINO RESTAURANT _____

THE BEST THEME RESTAURANT _____

THE BEST ALL-AROUND BUFFET _____

THE BEST CHEAP BUFFET _____

THE BEST SHRIMP COCKTAIL _____

THE BEST CHEAP PLACE TO GAMBLE _____

THE BEST FREE ATTRACTION _____

THE BEST CHEAP CASINO FOOD (Casino with good food specials)

_____

BEST CASINO FOOD COURT _____

THE BEST CHEAP CASINO ROOM _____

THE BEST "BIG ROOM" SHOW _____

THE BEST SMALL SHOW _____

THE BEST COMEDY CLUB_____

THE BEST PLACE TO DANCE _____

THE BEST LATE NIGHT BAR _____

THE BEST ROCK CLUB _____

THE BEST CASINO BAR _____

THE BEST NON-CASINO BAR _____

THE BEST DRINKING BAR _____

THE BEST PARTY BAR _____

THE MOST ROMANTIC BAR _____

THE BEST THEME BAR _____

THE BEST NOSTALGIA BAR_____

THE BEST BEER PUB _____

THE MOST ROMANTIC BAR _____

THE BEST CASINO COZY CORNER _____

_____

THE MOST ROMANTIC RESTAURANT _____

THE CUTEST WEDDING CHAPEL _____

PRETTIEST CASINO COCKTAIL WAITRESSES (Name of casino)

_____

SEXIEST COCKTAIL WAITRESS OUTFITS _____

CUTEST COCKTAIL WAITRESS OUTFITS _____

PRETTIEST CHANGE GIRLS _____

PRETTIEST CIGARETTE GIRLS _____

PRETTIEST SHOWGIRLS _____

SEXIEST MAJOR REVUE _____

SEXIEST CABARET SHOW _____

BEST TOPLESS BAR _____

BEST CASINO ATTRACTION (Rides, games, exhibits, etc.)

_____

BEST NON-CASINO ATTRACTION (Rides, video parlors, exhibits, etc.)

_____

BEST MUSEUM _____

BEST KIDS ATTRACTION _____

BEST FAMILY CASINO RESORT _____

BEST VIDEO ARCADE _____

BEST LAS VEGAS VIEW _____

BEST LAS VEGAS PHOTO ANGLE _____

BEST SHOPPING MALL _____

BEST CASINO SHOPPING ARCADE _____

BEST SPECIALTY STORE (in or outside of a casino)

_____

BEST WALKING AREA (in or outside of Las Vegas)

_____

BEST HIKING AREA (in southern Nevada)

_____

BEST PLACE TO PEOPLE-WATCH _____

BEST LAS VEGAS RADIO STATION _____

WHAT'S THE DUMBEST THING YOU'VE DONE IN LAS VEGAS?

_____

_____

BEST ATTRACTION OUTSIDE OF LAS VEGAS (in southern Nevada)

_____

MOST INTERESTING NEARBY AREA _____

BEST CASINO OUTSIDE OF LAS VEGAS _____

- -

THANKS FOR CONTRIBUTING TO OUR SURVEY!

Please give us your name and address and, if you wish to order any books, list them below and enclose a check. There is absolutely no obligation to buy books to take part in the survey.

___ **Yes,** I want to buy one or more Pine Cone Press books at a thirty percent discount. (See list on the pages after the index)
I have enclosed my check/money order in the amount of :

$ _____

BOOK OR BOOKS SELECTED:

_____

_____

_____

___ **No,** I don't want any books; who has time to read?

Name _____

Address _____

City/state/ZIP _____

Phone number (in case there's a question about your order):

Area code (_____) _____

Please send this form or a facsimile to:
**Pine Cone Press, Inc.**
**631 N. Stephanie St., #138**
**Henderson, NV 89014**

INDEX: Primary listings indicated by *bold face italics*

A BIT ABOUT THE AUTHORS

The Martins have written more than a dozen guidebooks, mostly under their Pine Cone Press banner. When not tending to their publishing company in Henderson, Nevada, they explore America and the world beyond, seeking new places and new experiences for their readers. Both are members of the Society of American Travel Writers.

Don, who provides most of the adjectives, has been a journalist since he was 16, when classmates elected him editor of his high school newspaper. (No one else wanted the job.) After school, he left his small family farm in Idaho, wandered about the country a bit, and then joined the Marine Corps. He was assigned as a military correspondent in the Orient and at bases in California. Back in civvies, he worked as a reporter, sports writer and editor for several West Coast newspapers, then he became associate editor of a San Francisco-based travel magazine. He now devotes his time to writing, travel, sipping fine Zinfandel and—for some odd reason—collecting squirrel and chipmunk artifacts.

Betty, a Chinese-American who's varied credentials have included a doctorate in pharmacy and a real estate broker's license, does much of the research, editing and photography for their books. She also has sold articles and photos to assorted newspapers and magazines, and she's a member of the Society of American Travel Writers' Publications Committee. When she isn't helping Don run Pine Cone Press, Inc., she wanders the globe—with or without him. Her travels have taken her from Cuba to Antarctica. She also can play a mean game of blackjack.

REMARKABLY USEFUL GUIDEBOOKS
from *PINE CONE PRESS*

Critics praise the "jaunty prose" and "beautiful editing" of Pine Cone Press guidebooks by Don and Betty Martin. In addition to being comprehensive and "remarkably useful," their books are frank, witty and opinionated.

ADVENTURE CRUISING
This book focuses on small ship cruises, listing over a hundred cruise lines and hundreds of worldwide itineraries. "Cruise closeups" provide an intimate look at more than a dozen different voyages.　*— 352 pages; $15.95*

ARIZONA DISCOVERY GUIDE
This detailed guide covers attractions, scenic drives, hikes and walks, dining, lodgings, RV parks and campgrounds. A "Snowbird" section helps retirees plan their winters under the Arizona sun.　*— 408 pages; $15.95*

ARIZONA IN YOUR FUTURE
This is an all-purpose relocation guide for job-seekers, retirees and winter "Snowbirds" planning a move to Arizona. It provides essential data on dozens of cities, from recreation to medical facilities. *— 272 pages; $15.95*

THE BEST OF THE WINE COUNTRY
Where to taste wine in California? Nearly 300 wineries are featured, along with nearby restaurants, lodging and attractions. Special sections offer tips on selecting, tasting, serving and storing wine.　*— 336 pages; $13.95*

LAS VEGAS: THE BEST OF GLITTER CITY
This is a delightfully impertinent insiders' guide to the world's greatest party town, with detailed descriptions of the Ten Best casinos, restaurants, shows, attractions, bars, bargains, buffets and more! *— 256 pages; $14.95*

NEVADA DISCOVERY GUIDE
This guide covers all of Nevada, with a special focus on gaming centers of Las Vegas, Reno-Tahoe and Laughlin. A special section advises readers how to "Beat the odds," with casino gambling tips.　*— 416 pages; $15.95*

More books and ordering information on the next page

NORTHERN CALIFORNIA DISCOVERY GUIDE

This detailed guide to the Golden State's upper half takes you from San Francisco Bay and the scenic north coast to the Wine Country, Gold Country, the "Big Valley" and the lofty Sierra Nevada. **—356 pages; $12.95**

OREGON DISCOVERY GUIDE

From the wilderness coast to the Cascades to urban Portland, this book takes motorists and RVers over Oregon's byways and through its cities. It's another in the Martins' new Discovery Guide series. **— 352 pages; $12.95**

THE TOLL-FREE TRAVELER

This handy pocket or purse sized companion lists hundreds of toll-free phone numbers for airlines, hotel and motel chains, rental car agencies and more. It's also packed with useful travelers' tips. **—162 pages; $8.95**

THE ULTIMATE WINE BOOK

It's the complete wine guide, covering the subject in three major areas: wine and health, wine appreciation and wine with food. It's loaded with useful information for both casual and serious wine lovers. **— 176 pages; $8.95**

UTAH DISCOVERY GUIDE

This remarkably useful driving guide covers every area of interest in the Beehive State, from its splendid canyonlands to Salt Lake City to the "Jurassic Parkway" of dinosaur country. **— 360 pages; $13.95**

WASHINGTON DISCOVERY GUIDE

This handy book takes motorists and RVers from one corner of the Evergreen State to the other, from the Olympic Peninsula and Seattle to Eastern Washington's wine country and great rivers. **— 372 pages; $13.95**

MARTIN GUIDES ARE AVAILABLE AT MOST BOOK STORES, OR YOU CAN ORDER DIRECTLY FROM THE PUBLISHER

Order from us and we'll charge you only a nickel shipping! Add five cents to the prices listed above and send us your check or money order.

Send your order to: *Pine Cone Press, Inc.*
631 N. Stephanie St., #138, Henderson, NV 89014
Got a question? Call (702) 558-8242